Poetic Interplay

MARTIN CLASSICAL LECTURES

■ ■

The Martin Classical Lectures are delivered annually at Oberlin College through a foundation established by his many friends in honor of Charles Beebe Martin, for forty-five years a teacher of classical literature and classical art at Oberlin.

John Peradotto, *Man in the Middle Voice: Name and Narration in the Odyssey*

Martha C. Nussbaum, *The Therapy of Desire: Theory and Practice in Hellenistic Ethics*

Josiah Ober, *Political Dissent in Democratic Athens: Intellectual Critics of Popular Rule*

Anne Carson, *Economy of the Unlost (Reading Simonides of Keos with Paul Celan)*

Helene P. Foley, *Female Acts in Greek Tragedy*

Mark W. Edwards, *Sound, Sense, and Rhythm: Listening to Greek and Latin Poetry*

Michael C. J. Putnam, *Poetic Interplay: Catullus and Horace*

Poetic Interplay

CATULLUS AND HORACE

Michael C. J. Putnam

PRINCETON UNIVERSITY PRESS

PRINCETON AND OXFORD

Requests for permission to reproduce material from this work should be sent to
Permissions, Princeton University Press

Published by Princeton University Press, 41 William Street, Princeton, New Jersey 08540
In the United Kingdom: Princeton University Press, 3 Market Place, Woodstock,
Oxfordshire OX20 1SY

LIBRARY OF CONGRESS CATALOGING-IN-PUBLICATION DATA

Putnam, Michael C. J.
    Poetic interplay : Catullus and Horace / Michael C. J. Putnam.
        p.   cm.—(The Martin classical lectures)
    "Expanded version of the Charles Beebe Martin Classical Lectures, delivered at
    Oberlin College in March 2004"—Pref.
    Includes bibliographical references (p.) and indexes.
    ISBN-13: 978-0-691-12537-4 (acid-free paper)
    ISBN-10: 0-691-12537-6 (acid-free paper)
    1. Horace—Knowledge—Literature.   2. Helen of Troy (Greek mythology) in
    literature.   3. Catullus, Gaius Valerius—Influence.   4. Influence (Literary, artistic,
    etc.)   5. Odes—History and criticism.   6. Virgil—In literature.   7. Rome—In
    literature.   I. Title.   II. Martin classical lectures (Unnumbered). New series.
    PA6411.P84 2006
    874'.01—dc22   2005054516

British Library Cataloging-in-Publication Data is available

This book has been composed in Sabon

Printed on acid-free paper. ∞

pup.princeton.edu

Printed in the United States of America

10   9   8   7   6   5   4   3   2   1

for Kenneth Gaulin

Contents

Preface

This is the first book-length study of the influence of the poetry of Catullus, whose lifespan extended from approximately 95 to 54 BCE, on the work of Horace, who was born eleven years before his predecessor's death and who lived until 8 BCE. It is only a beginning. For one thing, the book's primary focus is on the *Carmina*. There is scant mention of the *Epodes* or of Horace's hexameter poetry, though here, too, the presence of Catullus is as strongly, if not as universally, felt as upon his lyric output. For another, the project itself by its nature can never be considered complete. More allusions will continue to be noted and their richness explained. Many of the suggestions presented in the subsequent chapters will no doubt be deepened or rethought. At best, as with any work of practical criticism, what follows can serve only as one example out of many ways to approach a subject, scrutiny of which must be ever ongoing. It will achieve its goal if it stimulates further research into, and enhances our appreciation of, the extraordinary dialogue between two of Rome's greatest poets—a dialogue that has as much to tell us about the earlier poet as it does about his emulator.

Though this is the first detailed survey of the complementarity between Catullus and Horace, there have been many individual studies devoted to particular examples of verbal interaction between the two poets. These stretch from analyses of individual words to critiques of whole poems and groups of poems. I have endeavored to acknowledge, in the notes and in the bibliography, the many debts that my work owes to previous investigations of the topic. I can only appeal to the extensive nature of the scholarship involved as excuse for the omissions that will have occurred.

The book is an expanded version of the Charles Beebe Martin Classical Lectures, delivered at Oberlin College in March 2004. I am honored to have been chosen as the sixty-seventh presenter in a series initiated in 1931, and I am grateful to Thomas Van Nortwick and to the other members of the Martin Committee for their invitation. The warm, attentive hospitality of the faculty of the college's Classics Department and its associates in other fields left nothing to be desired, and would have been applauded by the two authors who form the subject of the pages that follow.

The fifth chapter is an expanded version of a paper, entitled "Catullus and Horace: Some Questions of Genre," delivered at the University of Chicago in February 2004.

The book is the product of many years of teaching, and writing about, these extraordinary poets. I am grateful to my students and colleagues during those years, at Brown and elsewhere, for their affectionate stimulus. I must also thank my two readers, Ronnie Ancona, for Oberlin College, and Ortwin Knorr, for Princeton University Press. Their criticisms, both collectively and individually, helped improve the manuscript, in general presentation and in detail. Friends and family, especially Polly Chatfield, have been ever helpful. My discussions of Latin poetry with Kenneth Reckford go back farther than perhaps he and I would now prefer to remember. I must also extend my gratitude, in particular, to Alessandro Barchiesi, Jenny Clay, Jonathan Culler, Denis Feeney, William Fitzgerald, Michèle Lowrie, Ellen Oliensis, Pietro Pucci, Matthew Santirocco, the late Charles Segal, and David Wray, superlative readers of these poets, whose work touches many of the pages that follow. I am also most grateful to Sherry Wert of Princeton University Press for the care of her editing. The blemishes that remain are my responsibility.

Michael C. J. Putnam
Providence, Rhode Island

Poetic Interplay

Introduction

Horace's only mention of Catullus occurs in the final poem of his first collection, the initial book of *Satires*, published probably in 35 BCE. We come in on the narrator arguing that, for a great poet, particularly one writing in a genre like satire, whatever brings a smile (*ridiculum*) can often put across "mighty matters" better than what is bitter or sardonic (*acri*) (16–19):

> illi scripta quibus comoedia prisca viris est
> hoc stabant, hoc sunt imitandi; quos neque pulcher
> Hermogenes umquam legit neque simius iste
> nil praeter Calvum et doctus cantare Catullum.

> By this means those who wrote Old Comedy gained success, in this
> they are worthy of imitation—men whom pretty Hermogenes never
> reads nor that ape of yours whose skill lies in declaiming nothing
> except Calvus and Catullus.[1]

What is meant as a rebuke to the *simius*, who has no imagination and can only imitate others, serves equally as a compliment—as the saying has it, the sincerest form of flattery—to Calvus and Catullus, friends who are on occasion linked by later authors. Both were key figures in the group of neoteric poets, the so-called *poetae novi*, active in the middle decades of the first century BCE and writing fresh verse in a variety of meters, often after the manner of Callimachus. Their work set a standard for originality that challenged poets to come, whatever genre they embraced. Put another way, to Horace, publishing his first book of poetry some twenty years after Catullus's death, the earlier master has already become a paragon, worthy of emulation but, for the very reason of his excellence, easily showing up the mediocrity of imitators lacking individual talent.

When we survey the four books of odes that form Horace's lyric masterpiece, we find no immediate mention of Catullus, nor in fact of any earlier, non-epic Roman forebear (at C. 4.8.15–20 Horace pays vicarious attention to Ennius for the immortalizing power of his verse). By contrast, on several occasions Horace refers to the poets of archaic Greece as creative ancestors of obvious importance (he names Sappho and Alcaeus at C. 2.13.25–27, and the latter again at C. 4.9.7). This public bow is reinforced in two ways. First, the meters that bear their names are the ones that Horace most favors (thirty-seven poems are written in alcaics, two-thirds that number in sapphics). Second, there are frequent instances where Horace begins an ode with a clear gesture toward a poem of Alcaeus via close rendering of the Greek original.[2] We presume that his contemporary readership would have had the privilege, as well as the enjoyment, of testing Horace's genius against the background of the model poems that we now lack nearly completely.

Perhaps the most surprising is the later poet's failure to mention Catullus in poems like *C.* 3.30, where "Horace" takes pride in his achievement, in the initial gathering of three books of odes, published in 23 BCE. In the opening poem of Book 1 he had concluded by mention of the Lesbian lyre (*Lesboum barbiton, C.* 1.1.34) as the instrument that Polyhymnia must tune for him, and of his own hoped-for position as one situated among "lyric bards" (*lyricis vatibus,* 35). In *C.* 3.30, the concluding *sphragis,* or "seal" poem, that stamps the poet's "I" on what had gone before, it is Aeolian song (*Aeolium carmen,* 13) that is his boast to have led in triumph to Italian beats. In *Epi.* 1.19, moreover, where he discusses his heritage and accomplishment in more detail, it is to Alcaeus that he specifically turns (*Epi.* 1.19.32–33):

hunc ego, non alio dictum prius ore, Latinus
volgavi fidicen.

He is the one, not sung before by other lips, that I, the Latin
lyre-player, have made known.

In the ode, Horace sidesteps the issue by using "chief" (*princeps, C.* 3.30.13) rather than "first" (*primus*) to describe his accomplishment, and in *Epi.* 1.19 he reserves the latter adjective to qualify his performance in the *Epodes,* not the *Carmina.*[3] Nevertheless, in neither instance does he take note of Catullus, whether directly or indirectly.

One reason for this lack of public obeisance to Catullus on Horace's part, a reason that may seem superficial to the modern reader but was of importance to the literary world of classical antiquity, is purely technical. It is the question of meter. Because of the prominence of iambic meters among Catullus's so-called polymetric poems, numbers 1–60, Quintilian, the late-first-century CE writer on rhetoric, ranks him among writers of iambic verse. This literary type he distinguishes for its sharpness (*acerbitas*), an abstraction, also bestowed by him upon the satirist Lucilius, that has about it notions of vitriol and anger combined with acuity of wit. Horace alone among Roman authors, according to Quintilian, deserves to be singled out as a lyricist worthy of mention:

at lyricorum idem Horatius fere solus legi dignus; nam et
insurgit aliquando et plenus est iucunditatis et gratiae et varius
figuris et verbis felicissime audax.[4]

> But of the writers of lyric, this same Horace [who also wrote iambic
> verse in his *Epodes*] is nearly alone worthy to be read. For he both
> reaches the sublime, at times, and is full of delight and charm,
> variegated in his figuration and most happily daring in his word
> choice.

It is as lyricist that we have seen Horace single himself out: he is the
"Latin lyre-player" (*Latinus fidicen*) and, according to his later definition at *C.* 4.3.23, "player on the Roman lyre" (*Romanae fidicen lyrae*).
In *C.* 1.32, a poem I will be looking at in detail, a speaker, whose self-
presentation verges on what we would expect from Horace himself, can
call on the Greek *barbitos* to sing a Latin song (*Latinum, barbite, carmen*, 3–4).

Therefore, in terms of antiquity's regular complementarity between
meter and genre, Horace is justified in proclaiming his primacy as Latin
lyricist, and Quintilian is equally correct not only in singling out Horace as unique among Roman writers of lyric verse, but also in labeling
Catullus primarily a writer of iambic poetry. If we look again at Catullus's polymetric poems, by a large margin the majority of them are
written in iambic verse forms. Chief among these are phalaecean (also
known as hendecasyllabics), which he employs in some forty poems,
followed numerically by choliambic (which also bears the title scazon),
the meter of eight poems. There are also scattered compositions (poems
4, 25, 29, and 52) written in variations of straight iambs. Poems couched
in meters technically associated with lyric verse make up only a handful
of the corpus: two are written in sapphics (11 and 51), one in the so-
called greater (or fifth) asclepiadean (30), and three (17 and 34, plus
the long first epithalamium, 61) in varying combinations of pherecratean and glyconic lines, a mixture that the poets of archaic Greece also
utilized.

If, however, we allow ourselves a broader, more comprehensive definition of lyric that transcends meter—which is to say, at least in part, if we
extend our consideration beyond the particularities of a poem's con-
struction or manner of presentation so as to combine them, to whatever
degree, with the matter and content of the poem itself—then the relationship between our two poets takes a different, more universal form.
From the start of Greek literature, lyric poetry is indelibly associated
with music, as an individual or chorus gives utterance to a combination

of words and sounds. Such a generality is useful in seeking a definition that leaves consideration of topics such as meter in a place of ancillary importance and looks to some combination of emotion and song, of personal sensitivity (often, but by no means always, the product of a speaking "I") and what the poet makes it into during performance, with a melodic line that can vary from the highly structured, as in the case of classical lyric, to the far freer arrangements of *vers libre*. This is the poetic universe that Horace so brilliantly imagines in C. 1.22, his hymn to Lalage, the songstress of la-la, which is to say, to the origins and dynamism of lyric song itself.

Horace himself in the *Ars poetica* sets out the bounds of lyric not in terms of modes of exposition, but of content (83–85):

> musa dedit fidibus divos puerosque deorum
> et pugilem victorem et equum certamine primum
> et iuvenum curas et libera vina referre.

> The muse granted to the lyre to tell of gods and children of gods, of
> the victorious boxer and horse, first in his contest, and of the trials of
> youth and wine's freedom.

If Horace is thinking of his own work and not just of Greek lyric from its beginnings to Pindar, then, unless we extend the range of the final two categories to an inordinate degree, he has unduly, perhaps deliberately, limited the breadth and depth of his own accomplishment.

In itself, a survey of the contents of the two lyric collections, which is to say *Carmina* 1–3, published in 23 BCE, and *Carmina* 4, issued most likely in 13, gives Horace's summary the lie, if we apply it to his work. But we can also look at its intellectual expanse by another means germane to our topic, namely the ubiquity of Catullus as a presence in his work. We would expect that the lyric Horace, in the adjective's restricted sense, would be deeply cognizant, and therefore show extensive reflection in his poetry, of the (technically) lyric Catullus. This is indeed the case. Not only the two poems in sapphics (11 and 51) but also the hymn to Diana (34) and the plaint addressed to Alfenus Varus (30) all appear as prominent influences in the *Carmina*. Poem 51, for instance, makes appearances in three of the following chapters.

Nevertheless, his lyric output forms only one segment of Catullus's poems that Horace allows us to see as among the inspirations for his odes. To put the situation in terms of statistics, in the subsequent pages we will be looking at some thirty-five poems of Catullus and nearly forty-five works of Horace, only a few of which will be outside the lyric corpus. And in spite of what one might be led to conclude from such numbers, it must be emphasized that neither this study, nor any parallel examination of the interaction between poets, can, or could, make any claims to comprehensiveness. Like the imaginations of the authors themselves, the detailing of what one poet absorbs from another, or of what form or forms this acceptance takes, is an inexhaustible topic.

In the light of what was said above about meter, we must look at these statistics in a more expansive way. As far as his larger influence on Horace is concerned, we will find ourselves tracing the presence of Catullus in all four books of Horace's *carmina*. Though his prominence has a slight edge in Book 1, nevertheless the force of the earlier poet is found exerted as strongly, proportionately, in the fourth book—a point to which I will return in a moment—as it is in any of the three that make up the earlier grouping of odes. Equally important, the types of poem to which Horace makes his references are as varied as the oeuvre itself. We will be watching the appearance of the long, central works of Catullus as well as that of the shorter pieces in diverse meters and of the poems in elegiac couplets that flank them in the larger gathering. Within the polymetric group, though, as we have seen, the poems in strictly lyric meters appropriately made considerable impact on the *Carmina*. Nevertheless, their sway over Horace's imagination in no way predominates over that of the iambic poetry in its several forms. And even within this group, the range is extensive, embracing long-cherished and imitated poems, such as 5 and 7, the addresses to Lesbia on her kisses; 46, on the coming of spring; or 31, on the speaker's return to his beloved Sirmio; as well as many others that have been less influential on later poetry or less subject to critical evaluation.[5]

In sum, whether we are dealing with matter or manner, with mode of presentation or with content, Horace seems to have set no limits on the aspects of Catullus to which he was drawn. Even if he makes no direct mention of him in his lyric work as he does of the poets of archaic Greece, nevertheless he pays him the enormous compliment of accepting into his own the work of his predecessor in its manifold aspects. Though time and again Horace exerts his magic, especially when turning what he has gleaned from Catullus's iambic and elegiac verse into lyric form, and claims for himself what would have seemed indelibly Catullan, it is to the Republican poet across the spectrum of his work, as much as to the singers of Lesbos, that he turned for inspiration.

Meter and genre will also play their part in the essays that follow, especially the final chapter, which opens with segments devoted to the hymn and to its subdivision, the epithalamium. Mostly, however, I have grouped poems within more spacious categories where they seemed naturally to fall. The first chapter, entitled "Time and Place," begins with a look at a poem of Catullus where one word, *angiportum* ("alleyway"), which the poet uses to locate Lesbia's vulgarity, leads Horace to a meditation on the future effects of the passage of time upon the life of the courtesan Lydia. Catullus's most gripping précis of human life's passing, vis-à-vis external nature's steadiness, occurs in poem 5 and serves as background for several of Horace's masterly meditations on modes of appreciating time. The poems where Catullus most strikingly combines time and place, for example 46, on the arrival of spring in Bithynia, and its effects, as seen in poems 4 and 31, are absorbed by Horace into several odes that center on the idea of journey, whether literal or figurative, experiential or allegorical.

We also follow Catullus in the later poet's contemplation of Virgil's poetic itinerary, of the hazards that confront a youth embarked on love's treacherous seas, or of the ship of state. Likewise we watch how Catullus permeates C. 1.22, a poem ostensibly addressed to the girl Lalage, but in fact concerned with the lyric poet's creative course, embracing his Greco-Roman past and marking the outlines of his own imagination's enterprise. Finally, we turn to Catullus's moving elegy on his brother's death and examine how Horace's remembrances of it are absorbed into an assurance of poetry's power to immortalize.

The imagination and its varied potential is also a central theme of the second chapter, on "Speech and Silence." We begin with a look at *otium* ("leisure") and its variants as forceful presences in the work of both poets. C. 1.32 figures prominently here as a catalyst for a Horatian glimpse at his Alcaic past that also encloses strong allusions to several poems of Catullus. Common use of the greater asclepiadean, as well as another direct acknowledgment on Horace's part of Alcaeus, link Catullus 30 with C. 1.18. Their joint but idiosyncratic reflections on *Fides* form a transition to two poems, Catullus 6 and C. 1.27 respectively, where the need to speak out on one poet's part is answered by the other's witty narrative on the suppression of voice. Finally, we will look closely at a series of interconnected works that deal with wine-bibbing, inspiration, and the particular revelations that come from poems signaling the introductions and conclusions of books.

Chapter 3 concentrates on the figure of Helen, as she takes on various guises in three central odes of Book 1. The Catullan background leads us through a variety of poems, both lyric and invective, extensive and concise, and we return to Horace via a prime example of his own sally into iambic verse, epode 17. The abstraction *otium* is again a unifying presence, and we end once more on the common themes of poetry-making and of the interdependence of bards.

For the fourth chapter we return to Virgil for an examination of the poems specifically addressed to Horace's friend and fellow poet. Though C. 1.3, 1.24, and 4.12 are my primary focus, I also look at other odes where Horace pursues kindred themes. Once again, Catullus's influence is regularly felt, and here, too, the types of poem on which Horace draws are manifold, and the transformations that he effects are as diverse as the poems themselves. The later poet again moves easily between long poems (61, 68, and especially 64 here make notable appearances), polymetrics, and elegiac verse.

The last chapter looks first at genres that we have not hitherto closely examined. We begin with Catullus's unique hymn, 34, and watch how it and other Catullan poems find presence in six odes of Horace, whether hymns in and of themselves or poems dealing with the performance of hymn, whether parodic of the hymnic form or, in the case of C. 3.13, acting to ennoble its subject through the use of the genre. We examine here more closely Catullus's two epithalamia and how Horace both absorbs and spoofs his predecessor's material. In conclusion, we look at two poems that are without parallel in the Catullan corpus and the collections of Horace. The comparison of Catullus 45 with C. 3.9 will lead us in turn to some general propositions about the relationship between the two masters, in particular about how Horace read Catullus, and therefore about how reading him through Horace's eyes helps us all the more be certain of his own originality.

We noted earlier the catholicity of Horace's borrowings. Our study will also confirm certain familiar themes in the criticism of each author and in the comparison of them. The persona that Catullus tends to present is one for whom intensity, projected by immediate reaction to the present, is paramount. He works often by a form of physical and spiritual metonymy whereby the self seeks to share in, or gain a share of, some other. The first seven poems of the corpus deal with the speaker's book and its dedicatee, with a sparrow and the complex relationship that it suggests with his girl, with a yacht that bore him from Bithynia to his clear lake, and with the arousal and quiescence of the emotion this journey represents. In poems 5 and 7 we watch an enormity of kisses shared between lover and beloved, put into the larger, more universal circumstances of time and space, and, in poem 6, the poet's voice serves as an emanation that unites Flavius and his scandalous girl, just as the sharing of the *libellus*, in the initial poem, wittily reveals both intimacy with, and distance from, the intellectual world of the historian Cornelius Nepos.

We cannot imagine Horace indulging in the interior conversation that is so frequent in Catullus and seems so strong a part of the same intellectual pattern we have been discussing: Catullus addresses his alter ego who is deeply, but more often than not ingenuously, involved in a situation whose portentousness the aloof narrator appears to comprehend and to attempt to explicate. His persona is ever reaching out, proving its dependency, craving mutuality. However compressed the presentation, dialogue comes naturally to him. His is a world built on analogy, on definition by distinctions from or similarities with others, including a part of himself.

If Catullus works by metonymy, Horace, by contrast, is a poet of metaphor and allegory, in its comprehensive sense. Catullus lives by the actual and the concrete, Horace more in terms of the abstract and symbolic. If we view our two poets broadly by means of some traditional categories, Catullus would appear more the naïve, romantic poet, Horace more classic and sentimental.

The persona projected by Horace is of someone ever in the process of mastering feelings through art, as if writing were a means of gaining distance from emotionality rather than of presenting it and weighing its potential. This sublimation of sexuality, and again I paint with a wide brush, is an aspect of the Horatian impulse to control, in this case to ameliorate Catullus's emotional energy, to smooth over his graphic immediacy. The restraining especially of the destructive among human passions may have its artistic counterpart in the suppression of any direct mention of Catullus in Horace's lyric corpus. And, as if to underscore this propensity, failure to mention Catullus occurs in poems where Horace not only names his Greek predecessors, but also appropriates the earlier Latin poet, sometimes sedulously, for his own purposes.[6]

But none of these differences would be apparent unless Horace's constant references to Catullus helped engage his readers as they shaped their critical responses to his special genius. Indeed, if poetic creativity is a major theme in Horace's work, lyric or otherwise, poetic rivalry is a constant motif beneath its surface. Allusivity asks us to coopt one poetic context into another, so as, in part at least, to foster comparisons between their creators, in whatever direction this complementarity may lead us. The intellectual itineraries on which this act urges us to embark, in contemplating the poetry of Horace with Catullus at our side, are multifarious. Sometimes, as in the case of C. 1.22, we find many Catulluses in a single ode; on other occasions, notices of one Catullus poem— I think, for example, of his hymn to Diana (34)—are spread out over a series of adjacent poems in Horace. Catullus is a regular "third party" in a variety of Horatian situations. The later poet, for example, seems to enjoy poking fun at Catullus's apparent high seriousness. This sometimes is a question of genre (the hymn and the epithalamium), sometimes a question only of subject matter, such as the actions of gods and heroic mortals as related in a poem like C. 3.27.

Still, it is best to let the poems speak for themselves. But first I would like to point out one further phenomenon, namely the deepening influence of Catullus on the fourth book of odes. With this new invigoration comes a richer personalizing on Horace's part, a more direct expression of response to emotional situations that draws him closer than ever to his predecessor. Horace offers a very gentle signpost of this heightened Catullan presence in the first poem of the book, as he describes the symptoms he feels in the presence of Ligurinus (C. 4.1.33–36):

> sed cur, heu, Ligurine, cur
>   manat rara meas lacrima per genas?
> cur facunda parum decoro
>   inter verba cadit lingua silentio?

> But, alas, why, Ligurinus, why does an occasional tear trickle across my cheeks? Why does my eloquent tongue amid its words fall into a less-than-graceful silence?

Horace is thinking back to "Catullus's" sensations, which he absorbs and varies from his original in Sappho, upon watching Lesbia (51.9–12):

> lingua sed torpet, tenuis sub artus
> flamma demanat, sonitu suopte
> tintinant aures, gemina teguntur
>   lumina nocte.

> But my tongue grows numb and a slender flame drips under my limbs, my ears ring with their own sound, my eyes are covered with twin night.[7]

And Catullus's mention of "twin night" is picked up by Horace in the phrase *nocturnis . . . somniis* in his immediately subsequent line.

It is fitting that Horace make reference to a poem of Catullus in the programmatic first poem of his final book. For it is in the course of the fourth book, with its extraordinary meditations on the pressures of temporality and the diminution of desire, that Catullus's presence is felt with particular urgency. It is now "we" who are "setting" with a finality that does not pertain to celestial bodies with their rejuvenating powers (C. 4.7.14), just as, for Catullus, it is "we" who only have a brief existence, for life and love, until our light "sets" (5.5).

There would therefore seem to be a more pronounced circling back to his Catullan inheritance on the part of the older Horace, and a more ready willingness to admit his indebtedness to a poet so deeply committed to the moment and to responding to its importunities. Catullus says: seize the day, with its joys and sorrows, and, if you happen to be a poet, ask of your imagination to pose for itself as its primary task the framing of the hour's essence. Aging Horace now says: since time is passing, live life to the full before it's too late, and capture that sensation, as a reminder of what is to come or as a weapon, enduring for a poem's brief moment, to keep death's inexorability at bay.

We as readers are following our own several forms of chronology. We survey the Catullan corpus (whether or not it was arranged by its author is a problem to which we may never know the answer) just as we follow the carefully constructed sequence of Horace's odes, in each case learning, comparing, and rethinking as we progress. We also move forward in historical time, from the world of Caesar and the late Republic to the Rome of Augustus's early years as *princeps* (*Carmina* 1–3 were published eight years after the decisive battle off Actium in 31 BCE). But, along with our reading forward from Catullus into Horace, as we duly acknowledge how one master surmounts the anxiety of influence his predecessor has provoked, we also work backward with new eyes, and with a deepened sense of admiration for Catullus and his accomplishment. It is this many-layered interaction that is the subject of the pages that follow.

CHAPTER ONE

Time and Place

There are occasions where the repetition of one word, especially if it is a unique usage by each poet, will connect a work of Catullus with one of Horace. A case in point is the word *angiportum* (*-us*). We find it in poem 58 of the earlier poet and in C. 1.25 of his successor. Both compositions are in large measure meditations on aspects of time and time's passage. Discussion of them will serve to introduce a series of poems where Horace is clearly pondering, and reacting to, Catullus's versions, and visions, of temporality as well as of topography. The juxtapositions, as always, have something to tell us of each writer.

First, Catullus 58:

> Caeli, Lesbia nostra, Lesbia illa,
> illa Lesbia, quam Catullus unam
> plus quam se atque suos amavit omnes,
> nunc in quadriviis et angiportis
> glubit magnanimi Remi nepotes.   5

> Caelius, our Lesbia, that Lesbia, that Lesbia whom Catullus loved
> alone more than himself and all his own, now on the street corners
> and in the alleyways shucks the descendants of high-souled Remus. (5)

Catullus takes us from then to now, in the narrative of his and Caelius's relationship with Lesbia, and in the history of Rome from Remus to the doings of the founder's offspring. The poet may wish us to sense a bitter side to *magnanimus*, aiming to contrast a heroic Remus with his contemptible progeny, a group given to sexual profligacy.[1] He may also have us see the story of Lesbia as parallel to that of Rome in moving from an ideal, heroic past to a realistic present. Whatever the case, the repetition of *illa* sends us back into a time when a third-person Catullus viewed a former Lesbia as more than the equivalent of himself and his kinfolk.[2] The speaker at that time viewed the bond between their distant selves as based on *pietas*, on a mutual respect founded on duty. She stood unique by comparison to all of Catullus's familial world.

The pointed use of *nunc* takes us from a dream of the past into a present reality that use of the obscenity *glubit* carefully qualifies. As we move from ideal to real, we pass into a practical realm: the farmer's peeling the bark off of his trees finds its sexual equivalent in Lesbia's gratification of Rome's citizenry.[3] This degeneration from the spiritual into the mundane is complemented by the change from implicit interior, private space to the exterior, public sphere of crossroads and alleys. The unstated, symbolic realm of home and domestic piety based on reciprocal devotion, a piety surpassed in Catullus's feelings for the Lesbia of once-upon-a-time, yields to a tactile, explicit universe where the plurality of trysting places for the Lesbia of the present, which the reader is asked to visualize, is matched in the countless Roman lovers to whom she is available. (The poem slides with easy, bitter rhythm from *omnes* to the immediate physicality of *angiportis* and *nepotes*, where the places for assignations, and pool of potential amours, find ready correspondence.)

For Horace's parallel meditation, C. 1.25, we move from hendecasyllabics to the meter that bears Sappho's name, from Lesbia to Lydia:[4]

Parcius iunctas quatiunt fenestras
iactibus crebris iuvenes protervi
nec tibi somnos adimunt amatque
    ianua limen,

quae prius multum facilis movebat   5
cardines. audis minus et minus iam:
"me tuo longas pereunte noctes,
    Lydia, dormis?"

in vicem moechos anus arrogantis
flebis in solo levis angiportu   10
Thracio bacchante magis sub inter-
    lunia vento,

cum tibi flagrans amor et libido,
quae solet matres furiare equorum
saeviet circa iecur ulcerosum,   15
    non sine questu,

laeta quod pubes hedera virenti
gaudeat pulla magis atque myrto,
aridas frondes hiemis sodali
    dedicet Hebro.   20

Forward youths less persistently shake your closed shutters with frequent blows, nor do they deprive you of sleep, and the door, which earlier used to move its readily compliant hinges, loves its threshold.

(5) Now you hear less and less: "Are you sleeping, Lydia, while I, who am yours, perish night after long night?" In your turn, aged and inconstant, in a lonely alleyway you will weep at your lovers' disdain, (10) as the Thracian wind grows more wild at moonless times, when the burning passion and lust, which is wont to drive mares mad, will rage around your festering liver, (15) while you complain that happy youth takes more delight in green ivy and dark myrtle, committing dry leaves to the Hebrus, companion of winter (20).[5]

Whereas Catullus makes a clear, abrupt distinction between time past and time present, Horace brilliantly poises us at a moment of transition in the life of his protagonist, giving us a sense of time actually passing. Her present—where reciprocated love, ironically, exists only between closed door and threshold—looks back on a time when her young suitors, now less and less demanding of her affection, had regularly frequented her house. Her future anticipates the further advances of age and the graphic changes it brings, as attractiveness yields to the repellant, and calm to wild, and as the luxuriant becomes dry and life's amatory summer gives way to winter's chill lovelessness.

If Catullus shows us a promiscuous Lesbia in the present, with no hint that the passage of time diminishes her physical charm, we find Horace's Lydia at a liminal moment in an ongoing temporal narrative where the effects of time's ravages became more and more apparent in her life as a courtesan—a new role for Lesbia in her poem's present. But the commonality of *angiportum* (*-us*) between the two poems, and the fact that these are the only uses of the word by each poet, suggest that Horace looked closely at Catullus and varied one of the latter's major themes to suit his own purposes. For Horace, too, builds his poem around the difference between inner and outer worlds, between an interior existence, implicit for Catullus and Lesbia, explicit for Lydia, that is in contrast with an exterior life in which each protagonist shares. Lesbia's comes to her presumably of her own volition, Lydia's because—such is the speaker's wish—time's passage forces it upon her.

In Catullus elsewhere, the house (*domus*) is at once literal and figurative, for it serves as symbol for the continuity of family as well as for the many bonds that hold it together.[6] In poem 58 its presence is merely suggested in the mention of self and all other relatives. Catullus's love for them is surpassed by his devotion to Lesbia, with its non-sexual as well as erotic sides. Lydia's dwelling, by contrast, is brought before us in detail, with windows, door, threshold, and hinges. While time is on Lydia's side, her house is also both real and symbolic. It is an actual home, presided over by a woman who is likewise the lover of one or many paramours and who is pictured so often by the Roman elegists with a swain languishing before her unresponsive door. It is also an emblem of her beauty and of the power that she has over her lovers.

Lydia was once the perfect elegiac mistress (Horace avoids the usual word *domina*), as haughty as she was alluring, just as Lesbia was, for Catullus, the ideal lover, adored by him, as poem 72 puts it, "as a father loves his sons and sons-in-law" (*pater ut gnatos diligit et generos*, 72.4). While inside, Lydia is in control, true "mistress" of her dwelling, lording it over her shut-out lovers (*exclusi amatores*, to borrow the designation of Lucretius[7]). Once her beauty begins to leave her and the journey of her life heads toward winter, she is forced from within to without. She will become "fickle" (Horace applies to her the same adjective, *levis*, that Catullus does to the inconstant Lesbia later in poem 72, at line 6), but with the irony that, unlike the licentious Lesbia, Lydia will find herself alone in an alleyway, searching in her turn for her now-disdainful lovers and, again unlike Lesbia, finding no one there but her infatuate, arid, ironically nimble self.[8]

For Lesbia, the abrupt change from past to present, and from private to public, betokens the alteration from being the subject of an idealized love to playing the whore to the city of Rome. Hendecasyllabics are an appropriate vehicle for making such a vitriolic exposé. For Horace, by contrast, Lydia has the future prospect of modulating from the potent, seductive lover celebrated by the elegists, to an aging whore who soon will futilely ply her trade outdoors to an unresponsive clientele. But Catullus plays a major role in suggesting this sequence of alterations to Horace, who works his own generic magic on them, combining lyric's immediacy and elegy's sense of loss with a touch of vituperation still lingering from his Catullan inheritance.[9]

Another of Catullus's most influential poems, both for Horace and for many other later authors, also makes a suggestive appearance in C. 1.25. When Horace puts into words the lover's lament that Lydia now hears less and less—"*me tuo longas pereunte noctes, / Lydia, dormis?*"—he is plausibly thinking back to Catullus's vivid distinction between daily and human time in lines 4–6 of poem 5:

> Vivamus, mea Lesbia, atque amemus,
> rumoresque senum severiorum
> omnes unius aestimemus assis!
> soles occidere et redire possunt:
> nobis cum semel occidit brevis lux, 5
> nox est perpetua una dormienda.
> da mi basia mille, deinde centum,
> dein mille altera, dein secunda centum,
> deinde usque altera mille, deinde centum.

dein, cum milia multa fecerimus,   10
conturbabimus illa, ne sciamus,
aut ne quis malus invidere possit
cum tantum sciat esse basiorum.

Let us live, my Lesbia, and let us love, and let us value all the
chatterings of gruff old men as worth one penny! Suns can set and
return. When once our brief light has set, (5) it is one continuous night
of sleeping. Give me a thousand kisses, then a hundred, then another
thousand, then a second hundred, then another continuous thousand,
then a hundred. Then, when we will have made many thousands,
(10) we will throw the count into confusion so that we won't know,
and so that no evil creature may stare with envy when he knows that
there are so many kisses.

Horace's querulous lover turns Catullus's lucid apothegm into an elegiac
paradigm. For the earlier poet, our brief light leads to a night of ongoing
sleep. The lyric suitor, by contrast, divides what the Catullan speaker fo-
cuses pointedly: easy sleep is available to Lydia, whereas an elegiac love-
death is her lover's continuous lot. Catullus's *brevis lux* merged into *nox
una* yields to the *longas noctes*—long night after long night—that his
mistress forces on her unrequited paramour. Catullus addresses Lesbia in
warning that brief life and death's enduring sleep are their common future (lines 5–6 splendidly blend *nobis* with the demarcating monosyllables *lux* and *nox*), so that they should both take full advantage of the
present. Horace separates Catullus's "we" (*nobis*) into *me* and *tuo*, giving a species of "death" and its continuity (*perpetua* become *pereunte*)
to the lover, while sleep, cousin of death but here with sensual overtones,
belongs to Lydia. Catullan immediacy pits life against death. Horace absorbs us into the non-mortal world of elegiac tristesse, where sleep's long
nights, and the lover's ongoing "perishing," form a standard complex.

I spoke earlier of differentiation between the two poems based on the
fact that Catullus makes a brisk distinction between then and now,
whereas Horace has us look at a Janus-like present in the life of Lydia
that glances at once forward and backward in time. But perhaps the dual
allusions in Horace to poems 5 and 58 of Catullus suggest that we posit
a continuum in Horace's thinking between Catullus's poems, and therefore that we form our own imagined narrative from the sequence of one
to the other. This would mean a progress from a "now" of continuous
kissing with Lesbia, when carping elders are kept at bay, to a "now" of
her imagined wantonness on the streets of Rome. Horace may be giving
us a unity inspired by a possible sequence that Catullus leaves to our
imaginations.

The influence of Catullus 5 can often be felt elsewhere in Horace's lyric corpus, in a variety of ways, but always in contexts concerned with temporality. One way is simply through uses of the gerundive that parallel Catullus's powerful *dormienda* in contexts where the inevitability of death and its consequences are a matter of primary concern. In C. 1.28.15–16, for instance, the dead speaker, addressing Archytas of Tarentum, offers a variation on the Catullan theme:

> . . . sed omnis una manet nox
> et calcanda semel via leti.

> But one night awaits us all, and the road to death must be trodden but once.

The repetitions of *una . . . nox* and *semel* assure the close connection with Catullus, but, whereas Catullus allots the gerundive's importunate necessity to a verb of sleeping, with all its suggestiveness in a poem dealing so directly with eroticism, Horace makes the finality of the journey toward death a prominent feature of a poem concerned with the hazards of travel and the burial of those lost from shipwreck. And, though there are no direct lexical parallels, we think also of the succession of gerundives that dot C. 2.14, where Postumus is repeatedly reminded of what must be done before and after death. We have to approach the Styx, whose wave must be crossed (*enaviganda*, 11) by us all, who likewise must view the black waters of Cocytus (*visendus*, 17) after we have been forced to leave land (*linquenda*, 21) and house and a wife who gives pleasure.[10]

The initial appearance of Catullus 5 in the *Carmina*, however, is in the first of his poems that uses the coming of spring as the impetus for a meditation on the difference between seasonal and human time, and on the singular periodicity of our mortal existence. The poem of Catullus speaks prominently at the moment when Horace apostrophizes his addressee (C. 1.4.14–16):

> . . . o beate Sesti,
> vitae summa brevis spem nos vetat inchoare longam;
> iam te premet nox fabulaeque Manes.

> O blessed Sestius, the brief span of life forbids us to enter on lengthy hope. Now night and the storied shades will weigh upon you.

What unites Sestius and the poem's speaker (*nos*), just as it does Catullus and Lesbia (*nobis*), is not only the brevity of life's light, as the earlier poet puts it (which is to say its short extent, in the words of Horace), but also the proximity of death's night that soon follows. Catullus would have him and his beloved imagine the equivalence of life and love as elaborated in the physical immediacy of innumerable kisses, to count which would be to effect a curse and therefore to bring an end to the dream that eroticism, at least momentarily, renders the lovers atemporal. Horace begins with the rebirth of nature in the spring and its consequences for men and gods, and with the necessary sacrifice that must be offered to Faunus, the Cherisher of life and living creatures, in his shady groves.[11]

Into this world of Venus dancing and of her husband Vulcan aflame and renewing the fires of his workshops, death makes a sudden, contrasting entrance.[12] But the poem ends with a reminder to Sestius of what he will lose in death, a reminder that skillfully ties the poem together as it returns us to the passage of human time, but only in the context of an equally human spring (17–20):

> . . . quo simul mearis
>   nec regna vini sortiere talis
> nec tenerum Lycidan mirabere, quo calet iuventus
>   nunc omnis et mox virgines tepebunt.

> As soon as you arrive there, you will no longer be chosen by the dice
> as lord of the wine, nor will you marvel at tender Lycidas, for whom
> now all the youths are warm and soon the girls will glow.

The commanding "now" of death gives place momentarily to the immediacy of Lycidas's spring and to a reminder of the idea of warmth, here associated with erotic coming of age, as affection for him is transferred from boys to girls. But death lurks even here. By placing the monosyllable *mox* in exactly the same metrical position in the poem's final line as he had *nox* in the last verse of the preceding quatrain, the poet offers us a subtle reminder that the controlled moment of time's passage within the life of the young is also part of the larger movement of human temporality. This takes us beyond our spring and its emphatic present into a realm of dark and unchanging sameness.[13]

Horace's focused reminder of the two presents, of life and of death, inherent in our mortal existence has its roots in another Catullus poem, 46, which deeply influenced the later poet.[14] It, too, is a study of the coming of spring:

> Iam ver egelidos refert tepores,
> iam caeli furor aequinoctialis
> iucundis Zephyri silescit aureis.

> linquantur Phrygii, Catulle, campi
> Nicaeaeque ager uber aestuosae: 5
> ad claras Asiae volemus urbes.
> iam mens praetrepidans avet vagari,
> iam laeti studio pedes vigescunt.
> o dulces comitum valete coetus,
> longe quos simul a domo profectos   10
> diversae varie viae reportant.

Now spring brings back warmth without chill, now the rage of the heavens at the equinox grows silent in the gentle breezes of Zephyrus. Let the Phrygian plains be abandoned, Catullus, and the fertile field of sultry Nicaea. (5) Let us fly to the luminous cities of Asia. Now my mind, aquiver, yearns to wander; now my joyous feet grow strong with eagerness. Farewell, o sweet bands of comrades, whom, having set out together from home afar, (10) sundry routes bring back in different ways.

The poem's intricate structure depends on both balance and cyclicity. The double anaphora of *iam*, whose repetitions also helped effect the formal shaping of Horace's ode, links the poem's two halves, which revolve around the central line 6. This parallelism links the two monosyllables *ver* and *mens* whose complementarity advances the poem's main theme: the calming presence of nature in the spring, and how it energizes the speaker to hasten from Bithynia toward the Asia Minor coast and on to Italy. Cyclicity also abets this same goal as the sound of the first line resonates in the last, with *ver* and *-fert* picked up in *diversae varie viae*, and with the phrase *refert tepores* compressed and rearranged in *reportant*. Spring not only empowers the poet's mind, the recurrence of its warmths also initiates the movement that sends him and his friends homeward by their various ways. The completion of the work's unity, as nature and man conspire, thus complements a cycle in the speaker's life, away from and back to his fatherland.

By one word prominently placed, Horace lets his readers know that he would have us read the two poems in conjunction. *Tepebunt*, the last word of his poem's final line, and his only use of the verb *tepeo* in the *Carmina*, echoes *tepores*, the final word of Catullus's first verse, and his only use of *tepor*. The carefully balanced reflection, as the notion of seasonal warmth is absorbed, and varied, by one author from the other, points to further connections that lead from the repetition of *ver* in the opening line of each poem, to the complementarity of the spring winds Zephyrus and Favonius,[15] to the emphasis on "now," which both works bring to prominence. Also conspicuous is the image of feet, which serves as a forceful synecdoche in Catullus (*pedes*, 8) and as a critical element in Horace's distinction between the lightness of a spring dance (*alterno pede*, 7) and death's persistence (*aequo pede*, 13).

Both poems, therefore, have as their main concern the passage of time and take as their starting point the arrival of spring. Both poems also find their structure in a series of distinctions. In Catullus, they build cumulatively into each other, as the parallel uses of anaphora suggest. Passive turns to active, mental to physical when spring's effectiveness works its magic first on mind and then on body. Horace, by contrast, takes Catullan direct experience and expands its spiritual horizons to embrace a sequence of alternatives, centered on the grand antinomy of life and death, that play off each other, such as variability and the inexorable, the warmth of external and human nature in the springtime of each, and death's nocturnal pressure. Catullus looks at one person's limited journey home (*domo*), with its special excitement. Horace exchanges particularity for the more generalized, final march toward the insubstantial dwelling of Pluto (*domus exilis Plutonia*, 17).

Both of the Catullan poems that we have been looking at, 5 and 46, stayed with Horace's imagination as he wrote his second magnificent reflection on the coming of spring, C. 4.7:

> Diffugere nives, redeunt iam gramina campis
>   arboribusque comae;
> mutat terra vices, et descrescentia ripas
>   flumina praetereunt.
>
> Gratia cum Nymphis geminisque sororibus audet   5
>   ducere nuda choros.
> inmortalia ne speres, monet annus et almum
>   quae rapit hora diem.
>
> frigora mitescunt Zephyris, ver proterit aestas,
>   interitura, simul   10
> pomifer autumnus fruges effuderit, et mox
>   bruma recurrit iners.
>
> damna tamen celeres reparant caelestia lunae:
>   nos ubi decidimus
> quo pius Aeneas, quo dives Tullus et Ancus,   15
>   pulvis et umbra sumus.
>
> quis scit an adiciant hodiernae crastina summae
>   tempora di superi?
> cuncta manus avidas fugient heredis, amico
>   quae dederis animo.   20

cum semel occideris et de te splendida Minos
    fecerit arbitria,
non, Torquate, genus, non te facundia, non te
    restituet pietas.

infernis neque enim tenebris Diana pudicum   25
    liberat Hippolytum
nec Lethaea valet Theseus abrumpere caro
    vincula Pirithoo.

The snows have fled, now grass returns to the fields and leaves to the trees; earth alters its circumstances, and the waning streams pass within their banks. The naked Grace, with the Nymphs and her twin sisters, (5) dares to lead her dancers. The year and the hour that snatches the nourishing day warn not to expect the deathless. Chill grows mild with the Zephyrs, summer treads on spring, about to die (10) once fruitful autumn has poured forth her crops, and soon torpid winter comes back.

Still swift moons restore heaven's losses. We, when we have gone down to join pious Aeneas, to join rich Tullus and Ancus, (15) we are dust and shade. Who knows whether the gods on high might add tomorrow's time to the sum of today? Everything that you have given to your friendly spirit will escape the greedy clutches of your heir. (20) When once you have died and Minos has pronounced his gleaming judgments about you, neither your ancestry, Torquatus, nor your eloquence, nor your piety will restore you. For Diana does not free chaste Hippolytus from the darkness below, (25) nor does Theseus have the strength to rend the Lethaean bonds from his dear Pirithous.

Let us begin with poem 5, the pivotal lines of which, once again, are 4–6:

soles occidere et redire possunt:
nobis cum semel occidit brevis lux,
nox est perpetua una dormienda.

There is a hint that the difference between seasonal or annual repetition and the uniqueness of our human passage through time will again be a central theme already with the word *redeunt* in Horace's first line, and this notion of renewing iterations in nature is brought up again with *recurrit* (12)—what happens repeatedly in nature—and *restituet* (24)— what cannot come about in the life of Torquatus.[16] The presence of Catullus gains fuller prominence with the phrase *nos ubi decidimus* (14).

Just as Catullus's speaker had equated the lives of himself and Lesbia metaphorically with the light of day only to point up the difference between the two entities, so Horace urges the commonality between himself, the as-yet-unnamed addressee Torquatus, and the *lunae* whose restorative characteristic he has just mentioned, only to illustrate that any parallel between human and celestial time immediately breaks down.

We meet another, still closer, variation on the same Catullan phraseology shortly later at the beginning of line 21, *cum semel occideris*. This time the lecturer turns away from mutual union with his addressee to look squarely at Torquatus metaphorized as a heavenly body (the specificity of Catullus would have us think of the sun) that sets only once, and whose brightness is replaced by the brilliance of Minos's judgments in the afterlife. Torquatus's unavailing *pietas* (24) links him with *pius* Aeneas, and the connection prepares for the analogies from myth that round out the poem.

In both the fourth and the final stanzas, Horace powerfully varies the notion that Catullus treats so essentially in line 6 of his poem. There is one continuity that we must anticipate in our future, the uninterrupted present of death. The demands of this "is" (*est*), which await us after we have passed through the single cycle allotted humankind, are taken up by Horace, first, with the word *sumus* (16)—we are, not will be, dust and shade—and in the final quatrain with *liberat* (26) and *valet* (27). Horace would have us sense ongoing emotional connection, whether erotic or otherwise, between god, demigod, and mortal (perhaps a hint that resonances of Catullus's *dormienda* have not been completely forgotten). This perpetuity is reflected in the constancy of the present tenses. Immortal Diana, now and forever, fails to free Hippolytus, and Theseus for eternity lacks the strength to rend the fetters that bind Pirithous.

Both Catullus and Horace build the finales of their poems on repetition. In Catullus we have *deinde* or *dein* repeated six times, along with four uses of *mille*, three of *centum*, and two each of *altera* and of forms of *basium*. Reiteration of words mimics reiteration of kisses, and both repetitions, of language and the eroticism of which it tells, obsessive though they be, abstract us from the time-ridden existence of old men and of suns that set forever. They demand that we look only at the immediate and actual. By contrast, Horace, in his final two stanzas, through the triple use of *non* followed by *neque* and *nec*, is bent on the negation of the particularities that give us self-definition while still alive.

Catullus the lover urges forgetfulness, as momentary displacement of temporality, and non-acceptance of man's incompatibility with nature's changing unchangeability, which is to say with the imperturbabilities of celestial time. Whereas Horace asks that we accept the truth of our differences with nature, Catullus urges that we attempt to obfuscate them by reveling in the moment's passion. For Horace, even love, love with the mythic dimensions of Diana's for Hippolytus or of Theseus's for Pirithous, cannot save the mortals among its devotees from an end to life. Whatever dreams a Torquatus, or we, might have of sharing in seasonal nature's constant, vigorous dance of flight and return, are nullified in the face of the realities of death.

The reciprocation here between the two poets typifies, in a more general way, their relationship. Catullus makes open mention of future death only to attempt the nullification of its omnipotence through heightening of the present's emotionality. Horace, the philosopher here in lyric guise, abides death's force, with its power to eliminate the erotic from the curricula of even god and demigod.

Catullus 46 also makes a brief but pointed appearance in C. 4.7. Horace's ninth line—*frigora mitescunt Zephyris, ver proterit aestas*—is a clear reminder of 46.1–3, which takes us from *iam ver* to the silence of the post-equinoctial spring (*iucundis Zephyri silescit aureis*). The double appearance of the Zephyr, with an adjacent inchoative verb in each instance, projects the allusion, which is abetted, again in both instances, by the iterations of verbs beginning with *re-* that we have traced in each poet.[17] In Catullus, they take us from *refert* to *reportant*; in Horace, from *redeunt* to *reparant* and *restituet*.

But once again in this notion of repetition lies both the reason for Horace's reminiscence and the distinction that he creates, and that we must draw, between himself and his predecessor. Catullus presents us with a splendidly controlled, closed cycle—his two verbs are in the bounding verses of his poem as Horace's three are not—devoted to spring alone and its invigorating effects on the Catullus within the poem, first on his mind, then on his feet. The end of the poem makes a distinction between the "comings together" (*comitum* and *coetus* both play on the preposition *cum* and forms derived from the verb *eo*) of Catullus and his friends and their ways of return (*diversae . . . viae*). But the poem is united by its very limitations. We are dealing with one particular appearance of one season, in the presumed biography of a poet, and with how the resulting emotion speeds him on his way on a specific journey from Bithynia homeward.

Horace takes the earlier poet's impassioned immediacy and expands on it in several ways. From spring alone, and one man's specific, symbiotic relation to it, we turn to all the seasons, and after the contemplation of a one-time, fulfillable itinerary, we ponder those grander schedules of nature's annual mutations and of humankind's progress from life to the land of death, where no motion is possible in a changeless present and

certainly no sharing in nature's cyclicity. Catullus first solipsistically addresses himself and then his friends, carefully delimiting the poem's initial readership. Horace at the start aims to reach a more universal audience, a "we" that embraces addressee, author, and all who, together
with them, face the finality of our mortal lot.

Typically, then, Catullus takes the specific moment and expands upon
his personal response to it. Horace turns particular to universal, urging
his addressee and us, his readers, to join him in more panoramic acts of
contemplation.

Journey in Horace takes many forms, as it does in Catullus. One of the
most extraordinary manifestations of how Horace regularly commingles
literal with figurative when dealing with the topic occurs in *C*. 3.29, the
penultimate in the first full collection of odes and the last in which Maecenas is apostrophized (*C*. 3.30 looks solely at the poet and his *monumentum*). It balances the dedicatory first poem in the gathering but is, in
some deep spiritual sense, a declaration of independence from patron by
poet. One of the honorific words, for instance, by which he apostrophizes
Maecenas in the second line of the initial ode, *praesidium—o et praesidium et dulce decus meum*—"O my bastion and my sweet honor"—
Horace takes to himself in the balancing, antepenultimate verse of *C*. 3.29
(*praesidio*, 62). Catullus 46 is again part of the intellectual background,
as are several other poems by the earlier author. But before we look at
them and at their relation to Horace, it is best to turn to 3.29 itself, which
moves seamlessly through several stages. The first segment, outlining the
initial itinerary of the ode, is an invitation to Maecenas, in a show of im-
patience, asking the great man to leave Rome, with all its complexity and
the political worries that come Maecenas's way, no doubt in his role as
confidant of the emperor (17–24):

iam clarus occultum Andromedae pater
ostendit ignem, iam Procyon furit
  et stella vesani Leonis
    sole dies referente siccos;   20

iam pastor umbras cum grege languido
rivomque fessus quaerit et horridi
  dumeta Silvani caretque
    ripa vagis taciturna ventis.

Now the bright father of Andromeda displays his hidden fire, now
Procyon rages and the mad Lion's star, as the sun brings back dry
days. (20) Now the weary shepherd with his lethargic flock seeks

shade and a stream and the thickets of bristly Silvanus, and the quiet riverbank lacks wandering winds.

The implication is that Maecenas, in conforming to the speaker's advice to seek proper change of circumstances in his own life, should follow the instinctive path of a shepherd who protects himself and his flock from the swelter of the midsummer heat, safeguarding himself by exchanging Roman worries for Horace's *convivium*.[18]

At this point the speaker turns from particular to general (29–52):

> prudens futuri temporis exitum
> caliginosa nocte premit deus   30
>   ridetque, si mortalis ultra
>   fas trepidat. quod adest memento
>
> conponere aequos: cetera fluminis
> ritu feruntur, nunc medio alveo
>   cum pace delabentis Etruscum   35
>   in mare, nunc lapides adesos
>
> stirpisque raptas et pecus et domos
> volventis una, non sine montium
>   clamore vicinaeque silvae,
>   cum fera diluvies quietos   40
>
> inritat amnis. ille potens sui
> laetusque deget, cui licet in diem
>   dixisse "vixi. cras vel atra
>   nube polum pater occupato
>
> vel sole puro; non tamen inritum   45
> quodcumque retro est efficiet neque
>   diffinget infectumque reddet
>   quod fugiens semel hora vexit."
>
> Fortuna saevo laeta negotio et
> ludum insolentem ludere pertinax   50
>   transmutat incertos honores,
>   nunc mihi nunc alii benigna.[19]

The perspicacious god hides the outcome of future time in the darkness of night (30) and laughs if a mortal is anxious beyond due measure. Remember to settle with equanimity whatever is at hand.

The rest is borne along like a river, now gliding peaceably in the middle of its channel toward the Etruscan sea, (35) now rolling all together rocks it has devoured, trees torn up, a flock and houses, not without reverberation from the mountains and the nearby forest when a fierce flood arouses calm streams. (40) That man will pass through life as lord of himself and happy who, day by day, can say: "I have lived. Tomorrow let the Father invade the sky either with black cloud or clear sun; (45) nevertheless, he will not make invalid what is past nor reshape and render undone what once the fleeing hour has carried with it." Fortuna, rejoicing in her harsh profession and committed to playing her wanton game, (50) alters unsure honors, now kindly toward me, now to someone else.

Only in the final three stanzas does the speaker focus directly upon himself (53–64):

> laudo manentem: si celeris quatit
> pinnas, resigno quae dedit et mea
>   virtute me involvo probamque   55
>   pauperiem sine dote quaero.
>
> non est meum, si mugiat Africis
> malus procellis, ad miseras preces
>   decurrere et votis pacisci,
>   ne Cypriae Tyriaeque merces   60
>
> addant avaro divitias mari:
> tunc me biremis praesidio scaphae
>   tutum per Aegaeos tumultus
>   aura feret geminusque Pollux.

I praise her while she stays. If she shakes her swift wings, I renounce what she has given me and I wrap myself in my virtue (55) and pursue poverty, chaste and dowerless. It is not my course to rush into pitiful prayer if my mast groans from gusts of the Southwestern, and to make contract with vows that my Cyprian and Tyrian wares (60) not add riches to the greedy sea. At that time the breeze and twin Pollux will carry me safely through the Aegean's turmoil, protected by my twin-oared skiff.

We are dealing essentially with three journeys here. The first is of Maecenas from Rome to the speaker's celebration, with wine, roses, and balsam, which is to say into the poet's mental world, with its wise distance on the great man's concerns. The second is a philosopher's examination of the passage of everyman through life, an examination that preaches equanimity in the face of the alternations with which fluctuating Fortune challenges her prey. The third is the speaker's allegorical life-odyssey. The cloak in which he wraps himself is an abstraction, *virtus* (55); the wife he woos is poverty (*pauperies*, 56). Spiritually he travels unencumbered. The bastion that he needs for shield against fate's foibles is not a solid merchantman, filled with the world's goods yet at the mercy of the Aegean's upheavals, but a tiny rowboat, manned by himself alone, as master of his inner destiny, and buoyant enough sturdily to withstand the buffets of life's vicissitudes.

Catullus 46 makes a brief appearance at lines 17–21, where the triple use of *iam*, in anaphora, and the resonance of *furor* in *furit* recalls the earlier poem's opening lines—*Iam ver egelidos refert tepores,* / *iam caeli furor aequinoctialis*—as well as the second repetitions of *iam* at 46.7–8. In Horace's importunate "now," Catullus's spring changes to summer, and a moment when nature's madness is past becomes the full frenzy of July heat. We have earlier watched how the onset of spring for Catullus makes itself felt tangibly, first in mind, then in body. Here Horace treats the season and its arrival as a metaphysical paradigm for Maecenas the politician to ponder: the provident shepherd knows enough to escape heat's menace, on behalf of himself and his charges. But the interpenetration of *ver* and *mens*, of season and processes of thought, of external nature and the journey man takes in response to its provocation, that Catullus outlines so sharply, helped Horace to develop his more expansive typology of humankind's itinerary through life.

An even more apparent stimulus is to be found in another Catullus poem, 4, that can be readily associated with 46. If 46 tells a tale of yearning to return home from Bithynia, 4 finds a speaker addressing guests who are gazing at a sloop that magically narrates its own story of traveling from east to west through the Mediterranean. It is an easy assumption, though one by no means essential for the interpretation of the poem, that the "master" (*erum*, 19) being transported is Catullus himself and that the *limpidum lacum* (24) that the boat reaches near the poem's conclusion is Lacus Benacus, modern Lago di Garda, from whose southern shore projects the peninsula of Sirmio (modern Sirmione), where, poem 31 tells us, Catullus had a home. If such is the case, then the boat's story follows on the emotional excitement of poem 46 and covers the narrative distance between its story of spring's potent effect on the speaker in Bithynia and his actual return to Sirmio. Whatever the case, the poem's animation is palpable:

Phaselus ille, quem videtis, hospites,
ait fuisse navium celerrimus,
neque ullius natantis impetum trabis
nequisse praeterire, sive palmulis
opus foret volare sive linteo.   5
et hoc negat minacis Hadriatici
negare litus insulasve Cycladas
Rhodumque nobilem horridamque Thraciam
Propontida trucemve Ponticum sinum,
ubi iste post phaselus antea fuit   10
comata silva; nam Cytorio in iugo
loquente saepe sibilum edidit coma.
Amastri Pontica et Cytore buxifer,
tibi haec fuisse et esse cognitissima
ait phaselus: ultima ex origine   15
tuo stetisse dicit in cacumine,
tuo imbuisse palmulas in aequore,
et inde tot per impotentia freta
erum tulisse, laeva sive dextera
vocaret aura, sive utrumque Iuppiter   20
simul secundus incidisset in pedem;
neque ulla vota litoralibus deis
sibi esse facta, cum veniret a mari
novissimo hunc ad usque limpidum lacum.
sed haec prius fuere: nunc recondita   25
senet quiete seque dedicat tibi,
gemelle Castor et gemelle Castoris.

Guests, the boat that you see says that it was the swiftest of ships and
that the thrust of any bark at sea could not pass it by, whether it was
necessary to speed with oars or with sail. (5) And it says that the shore
of the threatening Adriatic does not deny this, nor the isles of the
Cyclades and noble Rhodes and the dread Thracian Propontis and
fierce Pontic bay, where the future boat you watch used before to be a
leafy forest. (10)

For on the ridge of Cytorus it often rustled from its talkative
leafage. O Pontic Amastris and Cytorus, bearer of boxwood, the boat
says that this was and is most well known to you: it says that at its
very beginning (15) it stood on your crest, and dipped its oars in your
waters, and from there it bore its master through so many wild seas,
whether the breeze called on the left or on the right, or whether a
favorable Jupiter (20) fell on each sheet at once, and no vows were

made by it to gods of the shore, when it came from the sea most
recently all the way up to this clear lake. But these things were once
upon a time. Now it grows old in the peace of seclusion (25) and
offers itself to you, twin Castor and twin of Castor.

The poem is structured so as to take the reader, as he listens in on the
story of the chatty boat, backward in time and space, and then forward
again from the poem's center and its second apostrophe, now to the
town of Amastris and Mt. Cytorus. The initial backward journey carries
us from the Adriatic to a mountain ridge on the shore of the Black Sea,
and we pass some notable features on the way. This itinerary, as we learn
from the poem's point of climax at its center, as our eye sweeps up a
mountainside in Bithynia, serves also to detail the course of the boat's
life, from its *origo* out of woods that are already talkative.

But space and time here serve as complements, for the source of the
boat's begetting, its own lifeline, and the starting point for the course on
which it took its master are one and the same. From here the journey
picks up again, not at first to furnish us with more place names but to offer vignettes of the experience of sailing, and of the challenges that sea,
sky, and shore offer the sailor as the boat follows out its treacherous
path.[20] At lines 23–24, however, we return to topographical specifics,
picking up where we had begun—the "most recent sea" is the same as the
threatening Adriatic of line 6—and leading us still farther from the sea to
the clear lake at the route's end. But these final lines also have a double
role. They bring to an end the geographical and meteorological challenges and complexities that the boat has confronted. The *impotentia
freta* (18) give place to a *limpidum lacum* (24), a motionless, unthreaten-
ing inland water, as itinerary, and poem, gain their calm conclusions. We
also reach *quies* (26) in the life story of the boat whose course we have
followed from its birth on Mt. Cytorus to its present old age (*senet*), and
its dedication to the divinities who brought it safely through the marine
world's perils, with no need to pray to shore gods to avert shipwreck.[21]

There may be yet a third aspect to the poem's ultimate verses. We hy-
pothesized earlier on a connection between poem 46 and the story of
the *phaselus*; and poem 31, the speaker's apostrophe to his beloved
Sirmio upon his return from Bithynia, has also entered our discussion of
poem 4.[22] The three works are discrete entities in the Catullan corpus as
we now have it, and each clearly stands on its own. But the biographical
data shared by the trio—spring in Bithynia and the trip home that the
season initiates, arrival at Sirmio, with the province long left behind, and
a journey catalogued that begins on the Black Sea and concludes on a
clear lake reached from the Adriatic—also suggest that they be read as a
continuum that is both literal and tropical.[23] If so, we can grant a further

level of meaning to the *phaselus* as the object that helps fulfill the speaker's desire (poem 31 is essentially a love poem addressed to the poet's peninsular home) and therefore as an emblem of his emotion in progress, from arousal to consummation. The actual journey and the boat's *vita* serve as complements to, and facilitators of, the yearning voiced by the speakers of poems 46 and 31. This cycle, too, has a beginning, a middle, and a satisfying finale.[24]

That Horace was thinking of Catullus 4, and would have us read the two poems together, is shown, first, by the concatenation of *aura, vota,* and *mari* (4.20–23) echoed in *votis, mari,* and *aura* at C. 3.29.59–64, then by the concluding reflection of *gemelle Castor et gemelle Castoris* in *geminus Pollux*, with Horace capping his predecessor by spelling out the name of the twin that Catullus's meter will not admit. But the difference between these two sets of allusions points up the distinctions between the two poems. Catullus stays in the realm of the actual, of actual vows and an actual dedication. Horace takes us into the world of the symbolic. The presumably real *phaselus* that carries its master past the Cyclades, whatever its symbolic role as reflection of a desire, or a life, in progress, is replaced by an imagined, emblematic *scapha*, embarked on a voyage where the breeze bears the speaking "I" safely through the *Aegaeos tumultus* (63) that stand for life's tergiversations. Horace here personalizes what Catullus leaves implicit. We are dealing with the speaker's experiences. But his words document not a real itinerary but the inner voyaging of someone proud of his self-sufficiency and of his philosophical savoir-faire in facing and accepting life as it evolves.

The alternatives that the generalized subject of Horace's discourse, who becomes the speaker himself by the poem's end, must endure are not whether the ship presses on with oars or sail, or whether Jupiter falls on the left or right sheet or on both at once. Rather, we go through life with the challenges of our quotidian existence, finding their parallels in a river that is destructive or calm, in the day itself, which can be sunny or dark, or in fortune, kind to me or to someone else. For Horace, life is not a question of surmounting the *impotentia freta* (18), be they furious, powerless, or both, that a literal voyage presents, but of being spiritually *potens sui* (41), in true control of one's inner self, in which case mutations in the exterior world do not matter. His *curriculum vitae* embraces an ethos of equilibrium, in life and in art.

On the surface, then, Horace's reference to Catullus, and the comparison it asks, might seem to suggest a change from physical to metaphysical, from the experiential diary of a real journey, excitedly demarcated in space and time, to abstract *dicta* suggesting to us how we should react to the course of life's grander sweep. But the several other levels to Catullus's poem, which imply that the journey of which it tells is equivalent also to the temporal span of the boat's existence and to the extent and duration of the poet's emotion, suggest that it served as a synecdoche for Horace's more expansive vision, detailing one circumscribed event that helped produce the later poet's holistic reflections on how we confront the vicissitudes of the actual.

The influence of Catullus 4 is often to be felt elsewhere, when Horace turns to sea journey as allegory. Let me offer three brief examples, taken in order of their appearance in the Horatian corpus. I will deal later in detail with C. 1.3, in connection with the poems addressed to Virgil.[25] Here we should take note of the resonances of Catullus 4 that are scattered throughout the poem: *trucem Ponticum sinum* (4.9) becomes *truci pelago* (C. 1.3.10–11); *Hadriatici* ends line 6 and *freta* line 18 of Catullus, as *Hadriae* does C. 1.3.15 and *freta* 16; the use of *sive* to describe alternative experiences on the part of the *phaselus* at 4.4–5 and at 19–20 is taken up by Horace in the phrase *tollere seu ponere volt freta* (C. 1.3.16). The parallel suggests what many critics sense, that Horace is using Virgil's putative journey to Greece as a grand metaphor not only for the hazards and potential punishment in store for any human undertaking not natural to man, but more specifically for the perils of Virgil's present journey of the mind as he writes the saga of Aeneas.[26]

Turning to C. 1.5, we find a conjunction of words—*aurae, votiva,* and *mari*, with, in this case, the addition of *deo* (C. 1.5.16) reflecting *deis* (4.22)—parallel to what we saw at the end of C. 3.29. Instead of contemplating the challenges facing the writer of Roman epic, we now discover ourselves watching both an ill-fated youth and the luckier speaker set sail on the sea of fickle, potentially destructive love. Unlike Catullus's carefree *phaselus*, which had no need for vows to shore gods to avoid shipwreck, Horace's speaker has narrowly escaped drowning, as evidenced by his *tabula votiva*, offered in fulfillment of a vow uttered at a moment of jeopardy. Catullus's *dedicat* (26), confirming the boat's safe arrival at its lake where it can remain unchallenged into old age, becomes Horace's *indicat* (14), the sign not only that prayers were necessary for salvation from passion's treacherous waters, but also that they had saved "the speaker" from anything worse than a drenching.

Our third example of Horace's deepening of the allegorical implications of Catullus 4 occurs at C. 1.14:

> O navis, referent in mare te novi
> fluctus. o quid agis? fortiter occupa
>   portum. nonne vides, ut
>   nudum remigio latus

et malus celeri saucius Africo   5
antemnaeque gemant ac sine funibus
   vix durare carinae
      possint imperiosius

aequor? non tibi sunt integra lintea,
non di, quos iterum pressa voces malo.   10
   quamvis Pontica pinus,
      silvae filia nobilis,

iactes et genus et nomen inutile:
nil pictis timidus navita puppibus
   fidit. tu nisi ventis   15
      debes ludibrium, cave.

nuper sollicitum quae mihi taedium,
nunc desiderium curaque non levis,
   interfusa nitentis
      vites aequora Cycladas.   20

O ship, new floods will carry you back into the sea. What are you
about? Take courage and seize the port. Don't you see that your side
is bereft of oars and that your maimed mast and yard (5) are groaning
in the swift wind from Africa and that your keel can scarcely
withstand the sea's preemptive power? Your sails are not whole, nor
are there gods upon whom you can call when once again plagued
with trouble. (10) Daughter of a famous forest, although fashioned of
Pontic pine, you will probably boast of both your origin and your
name in vain: the fearful sailor puts no trust in painted poops.[27] Take
care lest you become the plaything of the winds. (15) You who were
until recently both wearisome and fretted over, now my desire and
my serious concern, shun the seas poured among the glistening
Cyclades. (20)

The parallels this time take a more specific turn. *Linteo* (4.5) is picked
up by *lintea* (C. 1.14.9), both at line endings, and we have common
mention of the *Cycladas* (4.7 and C. 1.14.20, again each ending a verse),
while *Ponticum sinum* and *Amastri Pontica* (4.13) reverberate lexically
and sonically in *Pontica pinus* (C. 1.14.11), Horace's only use of the adjective *Ponticus*.[28]

    From at least Quintilian on, Horace's ode has been taken as an alle-
gory in which the *navis* represents the ship of the Roman state, buffeted

by the storms of Roman civil war.²⁹ This interpretation is abetted by the ambiguity of the word στάσις, meaning both direction of wind and civil strife, in the first line of a fragment of Alcaeus that is perhaps also on Horace's mind.³⁰ The forceful personification, so immediate also in Catullus 4, further strengthens this reading. The speaker watches, with apparent helplessness, as the naïve ship, with its misplaced trust in the superficial, betrays its self-ignorance, unaware, it would seem, that, in its present condition, venturing again into the open seas would put it in mortal danger. The speaker, urging caution, announces that he, too, is entering a new phase in his relation to the boat, having exchanged deep dispassion for a lover's desire.

The verb that Horace uses to describe the Cyclades, which the speaker urges the ship to avoid, is *niteo*, the same that he had given in C. 1.5 to the seductress Pyrrha, who, as a gleaming Circe, lures unwary lovers to a watery doom on the sea of love. This self-reference, combined with the implicitly erotic language of the ode as it reaches its conclusion, suggests that we can also read the poem's protagonist allegorically as a ship of love or, at the least, as a ship of state that has metaphorically taken to itself the guise of a beloved.³¹

Here, as regularly in Horace, a second poem of Catullus enters the picture, to confirm this further level of intent with which the poet leaves his reader. The verb *niteo* looks back not only to earlier Horace but also to the second poem of Catullus, addressed to Lesbia's sparrow. In line 5 Lesbia is entitled, by metonymy, *desiderio meo nitenti* ("my shining desire"). Horace divides the phrase between two lines (1.14.18–19) where *desiderium* is metonymic for *navis*, now the speaker's desire, and *nitentis*, as we have seen, is attached to the alluring Aegean isles. The boat is a potential *ludibrium*, a toy for unloving winds, whereas twice over Catullus uses *ludere* (2, 9) for sporting with the sparrow. On the first occasion, the bird is Lesbia's plaything; on the second, it is the speaker who asks to "play" with the creature "to lighten the sad cares of his heart" (*tristis animi levare curas*, 2.10). Horace has also adapted the phrase's concluding words into his last metonymy for the ship he loves, his *cura . . . non levis* (18).³² In sum, by bringing the amatory Catullus directly before his readers, Horace suggests that some form of the erotic lies behind the relationship of his speaker and the endangered boat. If Horace isn't dealing with the ship of love, he is at least concerned with a much-loved ship, whatever else it may allegorize beyond the state and the state's upheavals.³³

As we continue to pursue his adaptations of how Catullus depicts time and place, let us turn to one of Horace's most famous odes, C. 1.22:

> Integer vitae scelerisque purus
> non eget Mauris iaculis neque arcu

nec venenatis gravida sagittis,
    Fusce, pharetra,

sive per Syrtis iter aestuosas   5
sive facturus per inhospitalem
Caucasum vel quae loca fabulosus
    lambit Hydaspes.

namque me silva lupus in Sabina,
dum meam canto Lalagen et ultra   10
terminum curis vagor expeditis,
    fugit inermem,

quale portentum neque militaris
Daunias latis alit aesculetis
nec Iubae tellus generat, leonum   15
    arida nutrix.

pone me pigris ubi nulla campis
arbor aestiva recreatur aura,
quod latus mundi nebulae malusque
    Iuppiter urget,   20

pone sub curru nimium propinqui
solis, in terra domibus negata:
dulce ridentem Lalagen amabo,
    dulce loquentem.

The man whose life is upright and who is guiltless of crime has no
need, Fuscus, of Moorish darts nor bow nor a quiver weighted with
poisoned arrows, whether he will make his way through the sweltering
Syrtes (5) or through the unwelcoming Caucasus or the places fabled
Hydaspes laps. For while I sing of my Lalage (10) and, carefree, wander
unarmed beyond the bounds, a wolf takes flight from me in the Sabine
woods, such a monster as neither martial Daunia fosters in its broad
forests of oak nor the land of Juba begets, dry nurse of lions. (15) Place
me in torpid plains where no tree is refreshed by the summer breeze, a
region of the earth oppressed by clouds and evil weather, (20) place me
beneath the chariot of a sun too near the earth, in a land denied to
houses: I will love my Lalage as she sweetly laughs, sweetly speaks.

Horace's love song to Lalage, the "prattler," is also a hymn to the sacrosanctity of the poet, and to the Orphic power of the singer and his song

to protect him from every form of external, physical menace, be it a Sabine wolf or the extremes of hot and cold that would threaten the life of any ordinary mortal.[34] The speaker's inner "purity," which feels no menace from the threatening realms of south or east, of sea, mountain, or river, is at one with the mesmeric quality of poetry, whose spiritual force surmounts any corporeal threat. Though addressed to the critic Aristius Fuscus, who would no doubt readily admire the poem's extraordinary richness, it is in fact a hymn to Lalage, which is to say, to inspiration that ever stays with its creator.[35] Horace may mean us to think of Lalage as real, but she is also a figure for lyric song.

Catullus is omnipresent in Horace's ode, as one poet absorbs his predecessor into work at once indebted and novel. With Catullus comes Sappho and the whole tradition of previous lyric, for it is Catullus's two poems in sapphic meter, 11 and 51, that critics have long recognized as exerting a particularly strong influence here. In one salient instance, Horace even restores words of Sappho suppressed by Catullus, but he does so with an individual turn that deepens its final originality. I will deal elsewhere with the concluding lines of poem 51.[36] Let me quote here its opening six verses:

> Ille mi par esse deo videtur,
> ille, si fas est, superare divos,
> qui sedens adversus identidem te
>   spectat et audit
>
> dulce ridentem, misero quod omnis   5
> eripit sensus mihi.

That man seems to me equal to a god, that man, if it may be said, seems to surpass the gods who, sitting across from you, again and again watches you and hears you laughing sweetly—(5) which snatches away all senses from lovesick me.

Catullus's *dulce ridentem* (5) translates γελαίσας ἰμέροεν, also in the fifth line of Sappho's original. What Catullus suppresses is the phrase ἆδυ φωνείσας ("speaking sweetly"), from the two preceding lines in the Greek original.[37] In C. 1.22 Sappho's phrase is restored by Horace, who translates it as *dulce loquentem* (24). Horace's language, therefore, is emphatic both for supplementing Catullus and for recalling the latter's source in its original wording.

Equally important is the stress the words gain by placement. Horace brilliantly modifies his duplex heritage by moving ἆδυ φωνείσας / *dulce loquentem* from near the start of the earlier poem to the end of his ode. In both Sappho and Catullus, we progress to verses dealing with a complex amalgam of attraction, jealousy, and potential hurt. In Horace, we end with laughter and, above all, with speech that is implicitly song as well. The eroticism we are schooled to expect ends before it begins. For substitute we have Lalage and her seductive world of lyrical words and music. Horace creates his symbol for song just as in C. 3.13, on the Bandusian spring, he brings into being a new fountain of inspiration for himself alone. This, too, ends on the sound of words, as its "talkative waters" (*loquaces lymphae*, 15–16) complement the poet who at once tells of them (*me dicente*, 14) and creates them as well. It is the seductive music of lyric words about words that rings beyond the conclusion of C. 1.22.

Catullus's first poem in sapphics, 11, was also much on Horace's mind as he wrote C. 1.22.[38] Each poem is exactly the same length, and each starts with a travelogue:

> Furi et Aureli, comites Catulli,
> sive in extremos penetrabit Indos,
> litus ut longe resonante Eoa
>   tunditur unda,
>
> sive in Hyrcanos Arabasve molles,   5
> seu Sagas sagittiferosve Parthos,
> sive quae septemgeminus colorat
>   aequora Nilus,
>
> sive trans altas gradietur Alpes,
> Caesaris visens monimenta magni,   10
> Gallicum Rhenum horribile aequor ulti-
>   mosque Britannos,
>
> omnia haec, quaecumque feret voluntas
> caelitum, temptare simul parati,
> pauca nuntiate meae puellae   15
>   non bona dicta.
>
> cum suis vivat valeatque moechis,
> quos simul complexa tenet trecentos,
> nullum amans vere, sed identidem omnium
>   ilia rumpens;   20
>
> nec meum respectet, ut ante, amorem,
> qui illius culpa cecidit velut prati
> ultimi flos, praetereunte postquam
>   tactus aratro est.

Furius and Aurelius, comrades of Catullus, whether he will make his way into the farthest Indians, where the shore is beaten by the loud-resounding Eoan wave, or the Hyrcani or soft Arabes, (5) or the Sagae and arrow-bearing Parthi, or the waters that seven-twinned Nile dyes, or whether he will stride across the lofty Alps, watching the reminders of mighty Caesar, (10) the Gallic Rhine, the dread water, and the farthest Britons, prepared to investigate together whatever the will of the gods will bring, proclaim a few, not good, words to my girl. (15) Let her live and flourish with her adulterers, three hundred of whom she holds together in her embrace, loving none truly but repeatedly rupturing them all. (20) Nor let her look, as before, for my love, which through her fault has fallen like a flower in the farthest meadow after it has been touched by a passing plough.

The first half of Catullus's extraordinary valedictory curse to Lesbia is taken up by a catalogue of place names that embrace the bounds of the known world, from *extremi Indi* (2) to *ultimi Britanni* (11–12). We escape in our mind's eye away from Rome's center into an experiential, sensory space that in its distances harbors the thunderingly resonant and the soft, the martial and the colorful, the lofty and the threatening. What Furius and Aurelius may apprehend with Catullus is what all travelers discover, the immediate sights and sounds of novel circumstances that bring refreshment and renewal as well as escape from the sameness or the tribulations of life's immediacies, or some combination thereof.

At the center of the poem, Catullus's would-be companions, and addressees, are imagined about to be sent on what would be a supreme test of any traveler with Catullus, the ultimate trial, namely to bring a lyric message to Lesbia that is also a *maledizione*. We share in an exposé of the hyperbolic obscenity of her sexual life—a spate of invective that we would expect Catullus to put into iambic verse—that is at the same time a delicate metaphorizing of her love. The literal geography of the most distant Britons becomes the flower in the farthest meadow, devirginated by Lesbia's brutal and voracious plough.

The voyager's external itinerary looks to sensory exactness, to a plethora of tactile experiences that tantalize the observer. The inner life of the poet, who at once adores and execrates, is built around paradox, where the generic miscegenation of lyric with invective underscores the exchange, and interchange, between flower and plough, animate and inanimate, female and male, delicate and helpless, cold and harsh. As we progress in the poem from travelogue to the destructiveness as well as the fragility and beauty of love, we move first to the sheer vulgarity of Lesbia's sexuality, then to the sphere of metaphor and symbol, as the speaker describes his affection. This progress takes us from physical to spiritual in a poem dealing with the bitter communication of a word-smith writing in Sappho's meter to a woman whose name complements Sappho's own.

Both Catullus 11 and C. 1.22 are therefore songs about song, but in making the transition from Lesbia to Lalage, we leave behind the problematics of eroticism and embrace the imagined realm of a sacrosanct poet fully devoted to the lyre and its authority. The passage from poem to poem can be illustrated *in parvo* by a further look at Catullus's final verse, *tactus aratro est* (24). The deflowering of Catullus's chaste, private, sequestered love, the forced, deadly relationship between *flos* and *aratrum*, as we have seen, brings poem 11 to a stunning finale. The play on the verb *tango* that ends Catullus's poem leads easily to the first word of Horace's ode, *integer*, an adjective formed from a combination of *in* and *tango*.[39] We are still in a world where virginity is a touchstone, but now it is one of ethics and the spirit, not of sexuality's figuration. Horace's affair with Lalage, which is to say with the lyric tradition from Sappho to Catullus, must be accompanied by an impeccable moral stance that complements the inviolability of the poet as well as the Orphic potential of his song.[40]

Here another resonance helps elucidate Horace's meaning and purpose. His initial verse as a whole—*Integer vitae scelerisque purus*—is a reminder of verses where the earlier poet addresses the gods for help in his unhappiness (76.19–20):

> me miserum aspicite et, si vitam puriter egi,
> eripite hanc pestem perniciemque mihi.
>
> Behold me in my misery and, if I have lived an untainted life, snatch
> this disease and blight from me.

As he does metaphorically at the conclusion of poem 11, Catullus here protests the spiritual innocence he feels in his relationship with Lesbia, whatever its physical component. Horace, as we have seen, uses reference to Catullus to emphasize his elimination of any immediate erotic dimension to his poem.

The same distinction holds true, with variations, for other reminiscences of Catullus in C. 1.22. Take, for instance, Horace's fifth verse (*sive per Syrtis iter aestuosas*), which is a bow to the parallel line in Catullus 7 (*oraclum Iovis inter aestuosi*). Catullus's advertence to space "between the oracle of sweltering Jupiter" and the tomb of old Battus forms part of an analogy detailing the infinite kissings of Lesbia that would satisfy "mad Catullus." Once more Catullan sensuality is referred to, only to be suppressed or transmuted.

Line 5 in Horace also looks to another fifth verse in Catullus, this time from the familiar poem 46: *Nicaeaeque ager uber aestuosae*. The parallel is strengthened by the fact that forms of the concluding words of 46.3–4, *aura* and *campus*, also are found at the ends of C. 1.22.17–18, and that 1.22.18—*pone me pigris ubi nulla campis*—is permeated with Catullus's music (46.4): *linquantur Phrygii, Catulle, campi. . . .*

Catullus's literal journey from Bithynia, actuated by the mind's excitement, becomes the imagined itinerary of the hallowed poet for whom even external nature at her most oppressive can present no dangers. In Catullus, as we follow the sequence from poems 46 to 31, the poet arrives home *curis solutis* (31.7), with the cares of travel behind him (and the pangs of yearning spent). By contrast, we find Horace imagined as setting out on an itinerary where physical threats mean nothing (and during which a lover's worries are also absent), *curis . . . expeditis* (C. 1.22.11), free from trouble. Once again Horace's figurative vision replaces Catullus's literal journey, which nevertheless inspired the later poet to produce one of his most witty and affecting songs about his carefree, persistent love affair with song.[41]

Before concluding, let us take a brief look at two further interchanges where the relation of time and place, this chapter's central theme, is an essential notion to our poets. The first set centers on the relationship of Catullus 2 with Horace C. 1.9. The ode opens with the speaker asking his addressee, and us, to view distant Mt. Soracte, covered with snow, as part of an exterior picture of winter chill that we must dispel by taking advantage of a world within, of the fire, and wine, that hearth and Sabine jug can offer. Do not worry about the future, says the speaker, which is in the hands of the gods, not us. Take advantage of the present and, while young and green, and while the whiteness of life's winter is still to come, enjoy love and dance. Our spring, not winter's stormy moment, forms the final, emphatic "now" of the poem's conclusion (C. 1.9.18–24):

> . . . nunc et campus et areae
>   lenesque sub noctem susurri
>   composita repetantur hora,   20
>
> nunc et latentis proditor intumo
> gratus puellae risus ab angulo
>   pignusque dereptum lacertis
>   aut digito male pertinaci.

Now let the Campus be your goal and the squares and at nightfall gentle whispers at the trysting hour, (20) now the pleasant laughter

from the inmost corner that betrays a girl and the pledge snatched
from her arm or from a finger that scarcely resists.

In the course of the poem, we move from winter to spring, from old age
to youth, from exterior to interior to exterior again. The final picture of
both the expanse and intimacy of springtime is brilliantly constructed,
with two sets of tricola building to a climax. Horace leads us, first from
the Campus Martius and generalized public spaces to a plurality of whispers, then from a particular girl's laughter to her arm and, finally, her
finger—an extraordinary reach that sweeps us from cityscape to lover's
hand and ring.

Though C. 1.9 is one of his most original and arresting odes, Horace
is again building on his poetic past. The first two stanzas, at the least,
have an ode of Alcaeus as their model.[42] But, as part of a phenomenon
that we have regularly seen, Catullus also is part of his heritage, in con-
structing a poem that once again smoothly mixes Greek and Roman elements. The bow to Catullus occurs at the poem's conclusion, three lines
before the end, the same position it holds in the earlier poet's work, the
last verses of poem 2 (11–13):

tam gratum est mihi quam ferunt puellae
pernici aureolum fuisse malum,
quod zonam soluit diu ligatam.

So pleasant it is to me as they say the golden apple was to the swift girl
that released her long-bound girdle.

Gratum . . . puellae becomes *gratus puellae*, and *pernici* suffers metamorphosis into Horace's concluding *pertinaci*, as the odist's final vignette of love-making looks back to Catullus's vision of Atalanta's loss
of virginity. The earlier poet's *malum*, the golden apple by means of
which Hippomenes (or Milanion) tempts and wins his inamorata, becomes the *pignus*, bracelet or ring, that Horace's *puer* snatches from his
puella as a lover's surety. But, whatever their differences, both poets are
creating final scenes of seduction with the focus on particularities, whether
it be apple and girdle in one case, or jewelry in the other.

But there is another connection. Horace's last detail, the girl's scarcely
resisting finger (*digito male pertinaci*), leads us back into the body of
Catullus's poem, where we watch Lesbia playing with her sparrow
(1–4):

Passer, deliciae meae puellae,
quicum ludere, quem in sinu tenere,

cui primum digitum dare adpetenti
et acris solet incitare morsus.

Sparrow, delight of my girl, with whom she is wont to play, to hold in
her lap, to offer to its eagerness the tip of her finger, and to arouse
sharp bites.

In this complex masterpiece, the sparrow is treated as a type both of
remedium amoris and of lover, for Lesbia as well as for the poem's
speaker. On the one hand, to play with the sparrow might bring relief
from the speaker's love pangs, just as (in his, we presume, wishful
thinking) it does for her, in her passion for him. But there is no doubt
that he would also see himself, at least in his mind's eye, playing with
Lesbia, not as toy but as beloved, claiming the sparrow's territory for
his own.[43]

The final analogy between the largely first-person speaker and Atalanta, which is also to say between the sparrow and the golden apple,
has several shades of meaning. It projects, among other possibilities, the
speaker's femininity as well as potential loss of virginity. But the resonance of *puellae* (1) in *puellae* (11) within the poem also centers our
thoughts on Lesbia as an Atalanta figure whose virginity will be lost by
playing with Catullus as sparrow.

Whatever the case, and other interpretations are also plausible, Horace helps us draw Catullus's poem together as we progress from Lesbia's finger, anticipating the sparrow-lover's bite, to the potential erotic
pleasure of "the speaker" as, or with, Atalanta, and from *malum* to a
pignus snatched from wrist or finger that, in the case of Horace's young
lovers, suggests the fulfillment of mutual pleasure.[44] And, as is often the
case elsewhere, Catullus joins one or both of the poets from Lesbos as
mutual influence, helping to shape Horace's genius.

A further example of the interaction of Catullus and Horace in poems
dealing with time and place is the later poet's reading of Catullus 9 in C.
1.36. First Catullus:

Verani, omnibus e meis amicis
antistans mihi milibus trecentis,
venistine domum ad tuos penates
fratresque unanimos anumque matrem?
venisti. o mihi nuntii beati!   5
visam te incolumem audiamque Hiberum
narrantem loca, facta, nationes,
ut mos est tuus, applicansque collum
iucundum os oculosque suaviabor.

o quantum est hominum beatiorum,   10
quid me laetius est beatiusve?

Veranius, in my mind of all my friends worth more than three hundred
thousand, have you come home to your household gods, and your
like-minded brothers and aged mother? You have come. O happy news
to me! (5) I will see you safe and sound, and hear you telling of the
places, deeds, and tribes of the Hiberi, as is your wont, and, clinging
to your neck, I will kiss your sweet face and eyes. Of all the very
happy men there are, (10) who is more joyful or happier than I?

Catullus draws us into a drama of anticipation beginning with a question
by which he teases both himself and his reader, who shares in the act of
speculation. Has Veranius arrived? Yes, he has, but not yet to Catullus,
whose emotional fulfillment lies in the future. As we have already seen,
the lover in poem 51, for example, can watch and attend to his beloved
(*spectat et audit*, 4).[45] Here the speaker must wait and imagine how, as
so often in Catullus, spiritual leads to physical, contemplation to action,
how, in this instance, seeing and hearing (*visam . . . audiamque*, 6) will
yield place to the erotic immediacy that they portend. Veranius's telling is
followed by "the speaker's" clinging, just as future beholding and listening give way, climactically, to the kissing of Veranius's face and eyes.

Depth of feeling is accompanied by magniloquence. Catullus complements the quadruple uses of the first-person pronoun and triple em-
ployment of the second with three appearances of *beatus*, all at verse
endings. And even the poet's contemplation of how he will absorb Veranius's storytelling is projected rhetorically through what we might call
the figuration of intimacy, with one line (6) featuring three examples of
elision, followed by another (7) having asyndeton as its basic rhetorical
device. Finally, even though the last lines are couched in the present
tense, the interrogative statement still leaves the reader on a note not of
fulfillment but of expectation as to what, in time soon to come, may
make the speaker more blessed than most ordinary creatures.

We find no better example of how this Catullan propensity for self-
revelation mutates into Horatian aloofness than in C. 1.36:

Et ture et fidibus iuvat
    placare et vituli sanguine debito
custodes Numidae deos,
    qui nunc Hesperia sospes ab ultima

caris multa sodalibus,   5
    nulli plura tamen dividit oscula

quam dulci Lamiae, memor
   actae non alio rege puertiae

mutataeque simul togae.
   Cressa ne careat pulcra dies nota,   10
neu promptae modus amphorae
   neu morem in Salium sit requies pedum,

neu multi Damalis meri
   Bassum Threicia vincat amystide,
neu desint epulis rosae   15
   neu vivax apium neu breve lilium.

omnes in Damalin putris
   deponent oculos, nec Damalis novo
divelletur adultero
   lascivis hederis ambitiosior.   20

It gives pleasure to appease with incense and music and the requisite
blood of a bullock the guardian gods of Numida, who, safe from
farthest Hesperia, shares many kisses with his dear comrades, (5) but
with none more than sweet Lamia, mindful of their childhood passed
with no one else as "king," and of their toga exchanged at the same
time. Let the beautiful day not want a mark of white, (10) nor let there
be restraint for the wine jug to hand, nor rest for feet following the
Salic tradition. Nor let tipsy Damalis surpass Bassus at Thracian
draughts, nor let roses (15) or long-lived celery or the fleeting lily be
lacking to the feast. All will fix their mellowing eyes on Damalis, nor
will Damalis, more entwining than wanton ivy, be plucked from her
new paramour. (20)

That Horace would have us think of Catullus 9 is clear enough from the
plot line alone—Numida has returned "from farthest Hesperia" just as
newly arrived Veranius will also tell of the western Hiberi among whom
he had lived.[46] The safety of both has been a concern to each speaker
(Veranius is now *incolumem*, Numida *sospes*). Both are deeply beloved
by the person responding to their arrival: Catullus's speaker kisses Veranius's "pleasant face and eyes," while "sweet Lamia" shares in more of
Numida's kisses than any other friend.[47]
   But the last parallel also points up a major, typical distinction between
the two poets. The Horatian narrator admits no involvement with any of
the emotional aspects of the tale he tells.[48] He may express delight in the
ceremony of sacrifice upon Numida's return, and urge that the subsequent

celebration not stint in wine, dance, or flowers. But he claims no share in the two erotic liaisons of which he tells, first, the male bonding of Numida with his *sodales*, especially Lamia, then the heterosexual union that is implied between Numida and Damalis in the poem's final stanzas. To be sure, he is an apparent participant in the festivity, and therefore also, we may presume, could be listed among the *sodales* who receive Numida's gestures of affection. Yet even the fact that such a detail is left to the reader's imagination—if Horace's speaker is to be counted among the *sodales*, he is absorbed into their nameless plurality (*caris . . . sodalibus*)—emphasizes the speaker's careful dispassion. He is interested in the ambiance of his plot and in the outlining of the two relationships that make up the ode's narrative progress, but he has no part in the latter.

Put another way, Catullus offers a strongly emotional, if one-sided, counterplay between the poem's "I" and "you," between "the speaker" and Veranius. Horace, by contrast, deflects this heightened self-involvement away from the speaker initially onto Numida and Lamia, then toward Numida and Damalis. And, as if to throw down the gauntlet to Catullus, the earlier poet's fourfold appeal to the first person and the triple attention to "you," in the fervid, circumscribed atmosphere that attests to the depth of his speaker's feelings, is replaced by the Horatian speaker's repetition of the name Damalis three times within six verses. Just as the ode's distant narrator averts any emotional involvement from himself, so also the homosexual implications of Catullus's poem, and their immediacy, are smoothly displaced in Horace's poem, first, toward the male bonding between Numida and Lamia that began in adolescence, and then, in an expected transition, to the former's present heterosexual intimacy with Damalis.

As is so often the case elsewhere, one reference here to Catullus is also strengthened by another, a gesture that in this instance wittily both confirms and spoofs Numida's last union.[49] In his final lines, Horace would have us think back to a moment in Catullus's first epithalamium where the chorus appeals to the god of marriage (61.31–35):

ac domum dominam voca
coniugis cupidam novi,
mentem amore revinciens,
ut tenax hedera huc et huc
    arborem implicat errans.   35

Call home its mistress, eager for her new husband, binding her mind with love, just as clinging ivy, wandering here, and here, entwines its tree. (35)

Horace takes the image of love, enfolding the bride's mind like ivy, and transfers it to Damalis herself. She is both lusty and as literally embracing as she is ambitious in character, eager for what she wants. What we might call a spiritual image in Catullus—love is like a vine enclosing one's thoughts—becomes on the surface insistently physical in Horace, as if to say that Horace, too, even here could put final stress on the immediately erotic when he chose. But we are dealing not with a *coniugis . . . novi* but with a *novo . . . adultero*, not with a new husband soon to suffer the restrictions of marriage but only with a new lover. Damalis, as a courtesan, could only take to herself a burlesque version of an epithalamium for it to have any applicability to her pretensions toward domesticity. Horace, therefore, on one level deflates the expansive rhetoric he employs to delineate the strong attachment of Damalis to Numida that the iteration of her name suggests, through the irony of generic parody, just as he mitigates the ardor of Catullan emotionality by studied narratorial distance. But in both clusters of references, Catullus exerts his special charm to elicit a typically Horatian masterpiece, at once indebted to his predecessor and thoroughly original.[50]

To conclude this chapter on the topics of time and place, let us turn to one of Catullus's most moving meditations on temporality, poem 101, an elegy on the death of his brother:

> Multas per gentes et multa per aequora vectus
> advenio has miseras, frater, ad inferias,
> ut te postremo donarem munere mortis
> et mutam nequiquam alloquerer cinerem,
> quandoquidem fortuna mihi tete abstulit ipsum,   5
> heu miser indigne frater adempte mihi.
> nunc tamen interea haec, prisco quae more parentum
> tradita sunt tristi munere ad inferias,
> accipe fraterno multum manantia fletu,
> atque in perpetuum, frater, ave atque vale.   10

Having journeyed through many peoples and over many seas, I come, brother, to these sad obsequies so that I might give you the last offering of death and address in vain your silent ashes, since fortune has taken you yourself from me, (5) alas, poor brother, unworthily snatched from me. Yet now, meanwhile, accept these offerings, which by the ancient custom of our fathers are bestowed as a sad gift for obsequies, deeply drenched with a brother's tears, and forever, brother, hail and farewell. (10)

Catullus's moving tribute to his brother is built around several words that, as they repeat and interlard themselves, give the elegy a special fervor. The speaker's brother is appropriately apostrophized at the poem's beginning, middle, and conclusion (*frater*, 2, 6, 10, accompanied by *fraterno*, 9) to form its essential structural element, but the repetitions of *mihi* (5–6) at the center and of *inferias* (2, 8) in a more framing position, along with forms of *miser* and *munus*, of *do* and its compound *trado*, help to give the poem its sense of ritual urgency. For the elegy fulfills many roles at once. It tells of the sorrowful speaker's presence at funeral rites offered by brother to brother, which is also to say of the gifts that form part of the ceremony and of the duties that carrying through the solemnity entails. Most movingly, it exemplifies one side of a dialogue that can never be resumed, an apostrophe to which no response is possible.[51]

Above all, however, the *donum* and the *munus* are the poem itself, the most appropriate gift a poet can offer, his condensed ritual of words, his verbal "task" and duty as a creative person to honor, however sadly, his world. In this case, the five couplets look back to an origin of elegiac poetry in ritual lament and focus that tradition on the present moment of sorrow. But the writing of such a threnody is also an act of remembrance. It tells of life overtaken by death and of someone dear torn forever away, but at the same time it pulls life from death and brings the beloved vividly before us. The poem immortalizes the moment of mortality and, here, the brother who is its victim, yet it also gives him through words a period of endurance beyond the negative claims of human time.

Many of these thoughts were in Horace's mind as he wrote the central ode of his fourth book (C. 4.8). It is the only other poem in his corpus that is in the same meter, the first asclepiadean, as C. 1.1 and C. 3.30, the framing odes of the first collection, and it is much concerned with the content and enduring quality of poetry and, in particular, of Horatian verse. I quote its opening lines:

> Donarem pateras grataque commodus,
> Censorine, meis aera sodalibus,
> donarem tripodas, praemia fortium
> Graiorum, neque tu pessuma munerum
> ferres, divite me scilicet artium   5
> quas aut Parrhasius protulit aut Scopas,
> hic saxo, liquidis ille coloribus
> sollers nunc hominem ponere, nunc deum.
> sed non haec mihi vis, nec tibi talium
> res est aut animus deliciarum egens: 10
> gaudes carminibus; carmina possumus
> donare, et pretium dicere muneri.

Gladly would I present the gift of bowls and shapely bronze to my
comrades, Censorinus, gladly present tripods, prizes for the bravery of
Greeks, nor would you carry away the least of the rewards, if only I
were affluent in the artistry (5) that either Parrhasius or Scopas
advanced, the one with stone, the other with liquid pigments, clever to
devise now a man, now a god.

But this is not my forte, nor does your station or your instinct crave
such delicacies. (10) You delight in songs. We have the power to offer
songs and are able to tell the worth of the reward.

Horace flaunts his gesture to Catullus here in his first word, *donarem*,
repeated prominently at the beginning of line 3. Their appearances,
and Catullus's use in his line 3, are unique in each poet for this form of
dono. The allusion is further confirmed by Horace's repetition of forms
of *munus* at lines 4 and 12, a word that we have seen Catullus repeat
at lines 3 and 8 of poem 101. We should note also that Horace's second use of the noun ends a line that begins with *donare*, the poet's
third adoption within twelve verses of a form of the verb *dono* to initi-
ate a line.[52]

If we follow out Horace's suggestion that we read the poems together,
what immediately stands out is the fact that the later poet is addressing
someone still alive, Censorinus, in contrast to Catullus's farewell to the
dead. Horace's poem goes on to treat explicitly what Catullus leaves
only implicit, namely the fact that life after death can be given as the
benison of great poets to those whom they choose to embrace as subjects
for their verse. Scipio, Romulus and other heroes, the ode goes on to say,
and by implication the poem's addressee, would be nothing unless writers had told of their accomplishments. For a moment, Horace's ode becomes a study in the difference between speech and silence. If the Muses
of Ennius didn't speak forth (*indicant*, 19) the praises of Scipio, and if
his pages were mute (*sileant*, 21), what would we now know of him? It
is the Musa (28, 29), working through the tongue of powerful poets (*lin-
gua potentium / vatum*, 26–27), that salvages what is worthy and noble
of the past for the future. Horace offers not an impossible immortality
for the human hero himself, but instead an assured future for the memory of his grand deeds, his creative legacy, as it were.

But the gist of what Catullus has to say is also at the core of Horace's
presentation. The earlier poet offers his poem as a very personal gift to
the departed, yet he also leaves us to infer that the process memorializes
both the brother himself as well as the moment of valediction. Horace,
by contrast, takes the idea of poetry's gift and illustrates its expansive,
public power to save even the great from oblivion. We leave Catullan immediacy of family affection and of private emotion and grief for a survey

of demigods and gods, and above all for a statement blazoning the claim that the authority of the imagination surpasses the tangible power held by the movers of history. But the multivalent meaning of the gift of poetry is already present in Catullus, and this truth his successor understood and honored.

CHAPTER TWO

Speech and Silence

In the preceding chapter, as part of the examination of our poets' uses of the categories of time and place, we looked at the opening lines of Catullus's poem 51, his reworking of Sappho 31, for their relation to C. 1.22. Its final stanza, original with the translator, also exerted a manifold influence on Horace (13–16):

> otium, Catulle, tibi molestum est:
> otio exsultas nimiumque gestis:
> otium et reges prius et beatas
>   perdidit urbes.[1]

> Leisure, Catullus, is troublesome for you. In your leisure you run riot and act uncontrollably. Before this, leisure has destroyed both kings and wealthy cities.

Catullus's poem, like Sappho's, is built around a series of rivalries, of a lover with the gods, of one lover with another in a triangular situation, of Catullus with Sappho, outdoing her while absorbing her own poem, especially in this last stanza, where the speaker distances himself from the hyperbolic setting into which he has imagined his alter ego. But even in writing his amatory biography, dealing with love's jealousies and potential destructiveness, Catullus the poet is also in love with Sappho, watching and capping her art from a craftsman's distance. The situation is emotional, no doubt, but it vivifies a different set of responses from the physical symptoms that lovers suffer, especially lovers in competition with each other.

Catullus himself offers a model, at once parallel and divergent, for these complementary sets of emotional responses in his preceding poem, which critics have long since seen must be read in close conjunction with its successor. If C. 2.16 and Catullus 51 can be viewed as the outer elements of a chiasmus, with differing meditations on *otium* at its double, complex center, then in Catullus's neighboring duo, *otium* is the bounding, and binding, abstraction. We begin poem 50 with two poets at leisure (50.1–6):

> Hesterno, Licini, die otiosi
> multum lusimus in meis tabellis,

ut convenerat esse delicatos:
scribens versiculos uterque nostrum
ludebat numero modo hoc modo illoc,   5
reddens mutua per iocum atque vinum.

Yesterday, Licinius, at our ease we played much in my writing tablets,
as it suited us to be self-indulgent: as we wrote our little verses, each of
us played now in this meter, now in that, (5) parrying one another as
we joked and drank.

And we end poem 51 with reflections on the ruinous aspects of *otium*,
after three preceding stanzas outlining a situation that could serve to
precipitate and then to help define them. A similar situation evolves in
poem 50, for what began as two poets at play turns immediately into a
one-sided love poem with Catullus affected by, and responding to,
Calvus's attractiveness (50.7–13):

atque illinc abii tuo lepore
incensus, Licini, facetiisque,
ut nec me miserum cibus iuvaret
nec somnus tegeret quiete ocellos,   10
sed toto indomitus furore lecto
versarer, cupiens videre lucem,
ut tecum loquerer simulque ut essem.

And from there, Licinius, I went away, set aflame by your charm and
your wit, so that neither did food give pitiable me any pleasure nor did
sleep cover my eyes in rest, (10) but, a prey to delirium, I tossed the
length of the bed, desiring to see the light so that I could speak with
you and be together with you.

Night figures centrally in each poem. In poem 50 it is a literal period of
erotic longing, in poem 51 it serves as a metaphor for love's menacing
omnipotence, in one of Catullus's most powerful and novel additions to
Sappho: *gemina teguntur / lumina nocte* ("and my eyes are covered with
twin night").[2] But there is, of course, the major difference that Sappho
endures to challenge Catullus purely through the force of words written
centuries past, whereas Licinius Calvus, one of Rome's foremost contemporary poets, is, at least to his friend, much alive.

   Calvus plays at once the separate roles of Lesbia and Sappho in the
subsequent poem. In the first, as they write back and forth, and fall in
love, poet with poetry and then with poet, for Catullus's speaker they
become mutually inclusive. In the second, Sappho, creator of erotic verse
in archaic Greece, serves as a stimulus for Catullus to depict his own

amatory situation, to use the provocation of the earlier writer to help him describe the complex affectiveness stirred by his own lady of Lesbos. But both poems are united around the hazards of *otium*, which, here for Catullus, suggests a time not of relief from life's challenges but of readiness to be implicated in them, especially if one were prone to the writing of brilliant erotic verse.

Both of these poems, and several others of Catullus, are in the intellectual background of one of Horace's most engaging odes, C. 1.32:

> Poscimus, si quid vacui sub umbra
> lusimus tecum, quod et hunc in annum
> vivat et pluris: age, dic Latinum,
>   barbite, carmen,
>
> Lesbio primum modulate civi,   5
> qui ferox bello tamen inter arma,
> sive iactatam religarat udo
>   litore navim,
>
> Liberum et Musas Veneremque et illi
> semper haerentem puerum canebat   10
> et Lycum nigris oculis nigroque
>   crine decorum.
>
> o decus Phoebi et dapibus supremi
> grata testudo Iovis, o laborum
> dulce lenimen mihi †cumque† salve   15
>   rite vocanti.

It is our prayer, if at leisure we played anything with you under the shade, which might survive both for this year and for many: come now, give forth a Latin song, o lyre, first tuned by the citizen of Lesbos (5) who, though bold in war, yet, whether amid arms or whether he was mooring his storm-tossed boat to the wet shore, sang of Bacchus and the Muses and of Venus and the boy always clinging to her (10) and Lycus, graceful with dark eyes and dark hair. Hail, o lyre-shell, who graces Apollo and delights the banquets of Jupiter on high, o sweet soothing of my cares (15) whenever in due prayer I call on you.

That Horace is thinking of Catullus from the poem's start, and that his poem is also to be a love poem of sorts, as well as a poem about poetic *aemulatio*, is made clear from the imitation of *otiosi . . . lusimus* from the first two lines of poem 50 in *vacui . . . lusimus* from Horace's opening verses. We will watch similarities and differences, as we trace other references back and forth, but one of the latter is made clear at the beginning, in the change from *otiosi* to *vacui*.

That *vacuus* in Horace suggests a freedom from erotic tribulations that Catullus's *otiosus*, with its implications of readiness for amatory adventures and misadventures, does not, is confirmed by an earlier passage from Horace, with its own Catullan gloss.[3] At C. 1.6.17–20, after a *recusatio* to Agrippa saying that the telling of his epic deeds should be left to Varius, the Horatian speaker says of himself:

> nos convivia, nos proelia virginum
> sectis in iuvenes unguibus acrium
> cantamus vacui, sive quid urimur,
>   non praeter solitum leves.

> We sing of banquets, of the fights of maidens with trimmed nails
> fiercely attacking boys, we, whether unattached or whether on fire,
> light-hearted as usual.

As the line endings attest, in verses 19–20 Horace is looking back at Catullus 72.5–6 to effect both parallelism and distance:

> nunc te cognovi: quare etsi impensius uror,
>   multo mi tamen es vilior et levior.

> Now I have found you out. Wherefore, though I am deeply on fire,
> nevertheless you are much cheaper and more fickle to me.

Catullus works in black and white, as his speaker looks at past versus present and at his own depth of affection as opposed to Lesbia's mere words. While he senses his own burning, more and more weightily, she is in equal measure more untrustworthy. Horace gently twists his source, who, he hints, might do with a little of the odist's brand of *levitas*. The Horatian speaker, whether free of love or involved, is in any case *levis*, flexible whatever his situation, which is to say never yielding, in Catullan fashion, to an intensity that can only spell trouble. This is the Horace that we encounter at the start of C. 1.32, free of love and yet ready for play that reminds us of both *lusimus* and *ludebat* at the start of Catullus's poem 50. Paradoxically, we are to experience a form of love poem from the imagination of someone who claims not to be in love.

This combination of erotic and non-erotic can be found absorbed and varied in the notices to Catullus that follow. The phrase *quod et hunc in annum / vivat et pluris*, for example, looks back to the final lines of Catullus 1, where he pleads for the Muse's interest in his book (9–10):

> . . . <o> patrona virgo,
> plus uno maneat perenne saeclo.

> O patron virgin, may it remain enduring more than one generation.

The parallel *quod* clauses, with their kindred invocations in the present subjunctive, the repetition of *plus*, and the etymological play on *perenne* and *annum*, find Horace appealing to an appropriate moment in Catullus, apparently the opening poem in his collection, when thinking of the longevity of his own *Latinum carmen*. He begins with prayer to his lyre, whereas Catullus concludes by addressing the muse, in Roman fashion, as his protectress. But the endurance of poetry, as book or song, as something to be read or heard, is a theme both poems share.

More often than not, however, Horace's references to Catullus look to highly charged moments of personal feeling in the earlier poet that, as a regular occurrence with Horace's borrowings, are deflected or sublimated by him. The phrase *lusimus tecum*, for example, which opens Horace's second verse, picks up the words *tecum ludere*, which introduce the ninth line of Catullus's second poem (and which are themselves a reflection of *quicum ludere* from that poem's second line). In Catullus we are watching a sparrow, playing with which—such is the speaker's presumption—relieves his girl of her pangs of ardor and would do the same for him, if only he had the privilege. Whatever the intricate erotic interassociations in Catullus, they are replaced in Horace by a poet sporting with his lyre, which is to say having a love affair with a metonymy for poetry itself.

The same differentiation holds true for an acknowledgment that Horace makes to the concluding lines of Catullus 31 (11–14):

> hoc est quod unum est pro laboribus tantis.
> salve, o venusta Sirmio, atque ero gaude,
> gaudete vosque, o Lydiae lacus undae,
> ridete quidquid est domi cachinnorum.[4]

> This is alone worth such great trials. Hail, o lovely Sirmio, and rejoice
> in your master, and rejoice also, you waves of the Lydian lake, laugh
> whatever giggles there are at home.

The proximity of forms of *labor* (which, in Catullus, picks up *labore* at 31.9) with the command *salve*, in connection with the double apostrophe commencing with the interjection *o*, all within the final four lines of each poem, once more draws Catullan verses into Horace's context.[5] In Catullus's case the addressee is a place, Sirmio on Lacus Benacus, but for the course of the poem, from the initial apostrophe to the peninsula as *ocelle* to its final salutation as *venusta*, belonging to Venus, we are observing, in however metaphoric a fashion, one lover dealing with another, at a moment when the cares of longing are now past and the speaker finds rest on the bed that had been his desire. Once again, in the change of contexts, Catullan eroticism is absorbed into Horatian emphasis on matters of mind.[6]

We must also look at parts of two adjacent similes from Catullus 68, where the lovesick speaker compares the help that Allius has given him in finding a way to bring him and his mistress together, first to a stream that bestows refreshment on its landscape, then to a calming wind that Castor and Pollux send to threatened sailors in response to their prayer. The water offers (61–64):

> dulce viatori lasso in sudore levamen,
>   cum gravis exustos aestus hiulcat agros,
> ac velut in nigro iactatis turbine nautis
>   lenius aspirans aura secunda venit.

> Sweet comfort to a wayfarer, sweating and tired, when oppressive heat
> forces open the parched field, or like the arrival of a favorable breeze,
> breathing quite gently, to sailors tossed in a dark storm.

Horace turns Catullus's *dulce . . . levamen*, which brackets his line 61, into *dulce lenimen*, which opens C. 1.32.15. And, though Horace apparently invents the word *lenimen*, nevertheless he has found an impetus for his neologism in Catullus's *lenius* (64). The connection is further advanced by the echo of the intervening *iactatis . . . nautis* (63) in Horace's *iactatam . . . navim* (7–8).[7]

The connection with Catullus here has a degree of complexity that Horace's references to poems 2 and 31 lack because the odist eases us, via Catullus, from concrete to abstract. Catullus's similes are expansive metaphors for satisfaction in love after a period of yearning. Horace assimilates his predecessor's figuration of eroticism and turns it in two directions. We find it in the historical situation of Alcaeus, singing of Bacchus, the Muses, Venus, and his beloved Lycus, even when at war or mooring his tempest-tossed ship, which is to say pursuing the life of the imagination, whatever his external situation.[8] We are dealing again, as in the case of Catullus, with the circumstances of a poet in love, and with the writing of amatory verse. But here Horace also attaches Catullus's language to his speaker in love not with a beautiful boy but with the lyre, which, palpable though it be, is also, as we earlier observed, a metonymy for song—a speaker in love, in other words, with the lyric muse and her music.

But there is a still further level of sophistication. Horace, as the climax of his list of the contents of Alcaean song, would have us concentrate, as no doubt the archaic poet also did, on the figure of Lycus. He does so, among other means, by the emphatic repetition of *nigris / nigro*, which is also a stunning act of differentiation because the quantity of the initial syllable changes from long to short, as we move from one use to the next. We watch, and we hear, in the poet's words and melody, both sameness and subtle differences in the boy's physical charm. But there is another noteworthy repetition. The last word that Horace uses to describe Lycus is *decorum*, "graceful." This is immediately followed by the noun, *decus*, applied to the lyre and to the honor that it brings to Apollo. But the intimacy between adjective and noun, especially when their combination serves directly to link the last two stanzas, allows abstract and concrete, Lycus and lyre, beloved boy and metonymy for song, to shade into each other. Beauty and grace complement both the youth and the music that tells of him, be it in the form of Alcaeus's love poetry, or of Horace's verse that tells of both. Eroticism, too, touches Horace's muse, as boy and *barbitos*, Alcaeus and Horace, merge together.[9]

Catullus, too, plays a key, if unexpressed, role in this last amalgamation, especially when we think of the part his poems 50 and 51 serve in the generation of C. 1.32. In both Catullan works, the challenges and rivalries between poets, of Catullus first with Licinius Calvus, then with Sappho, are a major theme. The pattern of imitation that Horace follows here is typical of one of the general ways in which he treats Catullus. We will see it, for instance, in the poems addressed to Virgil, especially C. 1.24 and C. 4.12. There, though Horace's great contemporary is both addressee and intellectual pivot, the poetry of Catullus is much in the background as an influence. The same is true for Alcaeus. C. 1.14 offers a good example where direct imitation of Alcaeus is mediated by a series of indirect considerations of Catullus.[10] We find a parallel pattern in C. 1.32, where the Greek poet and his verses are the poem's central subject. Rivalry as well as emulation are certainly implicit as Horace plays Alcaeus's Greek *barbitos* but tells a Latin song. Here, too, Catullus's poetry is a crucial ingredient in the mix of Horace's own creativity. One poet is named, but the other is pervasively present as a spur to his successor's muse.[11]

Though, as we have seen, Alcaeus is several times called upon directly by Horace, allusion also on occasion brings him immediately before the reader. We have seen C. 1.14 as a case in point. C. 1.18 furnishes another example. Here, again, as in C. 1.32 and elsewhere, Catullus also figures importantly as influence:

> Nullam, Vare, sacra vite prius severis arborem
> circa mite solum Tiburis et moenia Catili.
> siccis omnia nam dura deus proposuit neque
> mordaces aliter diffugiunt sollicitudines.
> quis post vina gravem militiam aut pauperiem crepat?　　5
> quis non te potius, Bacche pater, teque, decens Venus?
> ac ne quis modici transiliat munera Liberi,
> Centaurea monet cum Lapithis rixa super mero
> debellata, monet Sithoniis non levis Euhius,
> cum fas atque nefas exiguo fine libidinum　　　　　　10
> discernunt avidi. non ego te, candide Bassareu,
> invitum quatiam nec variis obsita frondibus
> sub divum rapiam. saeva tene cum Berecyntio
> cornu tympana, quae subsequitur caecus amor sui
> et tollens vacuum plus nimio gloria verticem　　　　15
> arcanique fides prodiga, perlucidior vitro.

Plant no tree, Varus, in preference to the sacred vine, around Tibur's mellow soil and the walls of Catilus. For the god has ordained that everything be oppressive for the sober, nor in any other way do biting cares take flight. After wine-drinking, who complains of the harshness of soldiering or of poverty? (5) Who does not rather prefer you, father Bacchus, and you, graceful Venus? Yet, lest anyone leap beyond the bounds of a modest Liber, the contest fought out by the Centaurs with the Lapiths over wine gives us warning. Bacchus's harshness to the Sithonians gives warning when, zealous with desire, they demarcate right and wrong by the narrow line of their lust. (10) Bright Bassareus, I will not shake you if unwilling, nor will I expose to the light of day your emblems clothed in variegated leaves. Repress the fierce drum along with the Berecyntian horn that blind Self-love follows after, and Vainglory, lifting its empty head aloft on high, (15) and Faith that betrays a secret, more transparent than glass.

The ode's initial verse is largely a paraphrase of a verse by Alcaeus quoted by Athenaeus—μηδὲν ἄλλο φυτεύσῃς πρότερον δένδριον ἀμπέλω.[12] ("Plant no other tree before the vine")—also in the greater (or fifth) asclepiadic meter. We do not know what followed in Alcaeus, but two differences stand out between Horace and what we possess of his original, namely the emphasis on the holiness of the vine (*sacra*) and the prominence of the addressee's name, as the second word of the poem. This

Varus is likely to be the Cremonese P. Alfenus Varus, eminent statesman and jurist who, at the time of the writing of the *Carmina*, would have been at least in his fifties.[13] It is also plausible that he was the addressee, then much younger, of the only work also written in greater asclepiads by his fellow Transpadine, Catullus, poem 30:

> Alfene immemor atque unanimis false sodalibus,
> iam te nil miseret, dure, tui dulcis amiculi?
> iam me prodere, iam non dubitas fallere, perfide?
> nec facta impia fallacum hominum caelicolis placent.
> quae tu neglegis ac me miserum deseris in malis.   5
> eheu quid faciant, dic, homines cuive habeant fidem?
> certe tute iubebas animam tradere, inique, <me>
> inducens in amorem, quasi tuta omnia mi forent.
> idem nunc retrahis te ac tua dicta omnia factaque
> ventos irrita ferre ac nebulas aereas sinis.   10
> si tu oblitus es, at di meminerunt, meminit Fides,
> quae te ut paeniteat postmodo facti faciet tui.

Alfenus, forgetful and treacherous to your fellowship of comrades, do you have no pity, hard-hearted, on your sweet little friend? Do you have no hesitation, faithless one, now to betray, now to deceive? The impious deeds of deceitful men do not please the gods. This you disregard, and abandon lovesick me in my troubles. (5) Alas, tell me, what should men do, or in whom should they have trust? For surely, unjust creature, you commanded me to hand over my life, luring me into love as if everything would be safe for me. Yet now you draw yourself back and allow the winds and airy clouds to bear off all your words and deeds. (10) But, if you have forgotten, the gods remember, Faith remembers, who will see to it that hereafter you regret your deeds.

On the surface the poems appear dissimilar. Horace brings more polish to a difficult meter that Catullus leaves rough-hewn, a deliberate reflection, perhaps, of the speaker's agitated state. The same can be said for the remarkable amount of repetition in Catullus's poem, betraying an immediately personal involvement absent from Horace's rationalizing speaker. We move from an invective to a paraenetic poem. The first finds a suffering speaker both openly attacking and publicly cursing someone who has lured him into a liaison, only to prove faithless in word and deed. In the second, the didactic speaker exhorts his addressee to a life of moderate drinking, but his words work by innuendo also, leaving the reader to wonder whether there was a tiff at some recent *convivium*.

Were the rites of Bassareus, who while *candidus* also makes men candid, in fact wrongly revealed? Was some nameless individual, perhaps even the poem's recipient, guilty of self-love and a breach of trust? In other words, where Catullus is directly, expansively emotional in response to personal hurt, Horace is the didactic teacher, working through implication to project his message.

The same distinctions also arise when we think of the difference between the *sodalicium* around which Catullus's poem is built and the events at a hypothetical *convivium* that are Horace's immediate concern. Like the occasion offered by the writing of poetry detailed in poem 50, inclusion in a band of *sodales* offers the opportunity to go beyond mere *amicitia* in personal relations and to develop an intimacy that, when ruptured, causes the hurt that is the source of the poem's outburst. Horace's recipe for the proper *convivium*, by contrast, speaks against the overindulgence in wine that can lead to brawling between bridal parties at the marriage of Hippodameia and Pirithous, or to incest among the Sithonians, to situations where avidity and lust hold sway and where Venus is no longer *decens*.

As so often, Catullus deals openly with passionate feelings, putting into verse the most private, sensitive responses to experience. Horace gives what is apparently an impersonal lecture not only on moderation in behavior but also on restraint: in holding private what should remain so (even to the point of keeping the reader guessing why Varus should receive this particular poem); in shunning self-advertising, which is blind to the ostentation that others see; and in avoiding the breach of trust, transparent when opacity—and silence—should have been its characteristics.

But Horace's capping of Catullus, by rounding off the name of Alfenus Varus as bond between the two poems, suggests that he wished there to be a rapport between them, a dialogue both completing and complementary, with each highlighting important aspects of the other. Two themes are salient. One is the idea of memory. This stands out in Catullus by the powerful juxtaposition and chiasmus at line 11 (*di meminerunt, meminit Fides*), in Horace by the repetition of *monet* at the same metrical position in adjacent lines (8–9). Catullus's emphasis lies, as his diatribe runs its course, on those who remember when lovers forget, and who bring vengeance on the perjurer who uses words to deceive (we move from *false* to *fallere* and *fallacum* within four lines) and disregards their truths. Horace's counselor takes the more engagèd role of serving to remind, of twice appropriating the lessons of myth to supply exemplars for present conduct. But in either case, recollection, whether a passive or an active experience, is a pivotal notion in each poem.

The second complementary theme with which both poems are engaged centers on the notion of *Fides*. *Fides* and its adjectival compound *perfide* stand out at three verse endings in Catullus's twelve-line poem (3, 6, 11), whereas transparent *Fides*, betrayer of secrets, is the central figure of Horace's final line. In the first poem, trust is a determining element in the expectations of Catullus's speaker, and its breach, rendering meaningless former statements and actions, is a form of treachery. For Horace, *Fides* is essential for those sharing in the *convivium*, whether on a particular occasion or in the larger gathering we call life. To publicize what has been seen or said in private, to expose the secrets of religion or to divulge the confidences of a friend, is the ultimate in disloyalty. So, whether we are dealing with the emphases of Catullan eroticism, the *amor* between the speaker and Varus, or with Horace's concern with *amor sui* gone awry, or, put more positively, with caring conduct between individuals in a larger moral trajectory, fidelity figures prominently as a bond between people, and between poets.

Proper behavior at a *convivium* is also an important consideration in another ode where the influence of Catullus is deeply felt, C. 1.27:

> Natis in usum laetitiae scyphis
> pugnare Thracum est: tollite barbarum
>   morem verecundumque Bacchum
>   sanguineis prohibete rixis.
>
> vino et lucernis Medus acinaces   5
> immane quantum discrepat: inpium
>   lenite clamorem, sodales,
>   et cubito remanete presso.
>
> voltis severi me quoque sumere
> partem Falerni? dicat Opuntiae   10
>   frater Megyllae, quo beatus
>   volnere, qua pereat sagitta.
>
> cessat voluntas? non alia bibam
> mercede. quae te cumque domat Venus,
>   non erubescendis adurit   15
>   ignibus. ingenuoque semper
>
> amore peccas. quidquid habes, age
> depone tutis auribus. a miser,
>   quanta laborabas Charybdi,
>   digne puer meliore flamma.   20

quae saga, quis te solvere Thessalis
magus venenis, quis poterit deus?
  vix inligatum te triformi
    Pegasus expediet Chimaera.

It is Thracian to fight with goblets created for the use of pleasure.
Away with the barbaric custom and keep bloody brawls distant from
our modest Bacchus. The Persian sword is vastly out of harmony with
wine and lamps: (5) tone down your impious shouting, comrades, and
stay with elbows steady. You wish me to share in the harsh Falernian?
Let the brother of Megylla from Opus tell from what wound, (10)
from what arrow, he perishes in happiness. You have no such wish? I
won't drink under other terms. Whatever passion tames you does not
burn you with flames for which you should blush, (15) and your
indiscretion is always with a freeborn love. Come now, entrust whatever has come your way to safe ears. Poor creature, in what a
Charybdis you are struggling, boy worthy of a better flame! (20) What
witch, what magician with herbs from Thessaly, what god will be able
to bring you release? Scarcely Pegasus will unprison you from the
bonds of the threefold Chimaera.

Horace's ode is unusual in that the narrative story line and the narrative present are evolving at the same time.[14] We are witnesses to a
drama in progress. At the beginning, the speaker is a commanding
presence, with four imperatives proclaimed by their apparently sober
colleague to his fellow conviviasts, demanding that they call a halt to
any incipient violence inappropriate to their gathering. Then the dramatic action begins to unfold, with its pauses and demarcations. The
speaker is asked to drink. He will, if he learns who the lover of
Megylla's brother is. Given the information, he exclaims on the horror
of the boy's situation.

The poem's final stanzas are built around a series of teases, of the audience within the story line and of the reader. The conviviasts at least
know what the reader doesn't: the identity of the brother of Opuntian
Megylla. But both they and the reader remain in the dark about the girl
who is causing the trouble. We thus move in the course of the poem from
shouting and physical battling to silence, and to knowledge, attained by
the speaker alone and shared only by innuendo. But, as we move from
literal action to highly figurative description, we are drawn into another
domain of potential violence that we only learn of by the culminative
thrust of wrought language. Oxymoron (the happiness that comes from
wounds, and arrows that serve as metonymies of love's presence), para-

dox (wine that is harsh, fires that don't redden, monsters of the watery deep that enflame[15]), and analogies from myth all conspire to educate the reader by indirection into what he can never absorb at first hand: as we learned in C. 1.18, *Fides* and its accompanying circumspection are vital ingredients for participants in a gathering of wine-drinkers.

We never find out the name of either boy or girl, but by the conclusion of the poem we have learned from the speaker a lot about them both. She is akin to a devouring whirlpool or to a fire-breathing, dragon-coiled monster, he to an Odysseus or a Bellerophon who must confront the fiendish. Horace, therefore, with consummate wit, combines climactic hyperbole with unyielding obliquity to reveal much about characters of whose names we remain ignorant.[16] But, as shouting turns to silence in the story line, literal brawling yields to a spiritual violence adumbrated only by the heaping up of metaphoric language. Nevertheless, in its own form of humorous paradox, the poem manages to speak forth loudly and clearly what it chooses not to communicate straightforwardly.

Two poems of Catullus here serve as stimuli for Horace's imagination. The first is poem 6:

> Flavi, delicias tuas Catullo,
> ni sint illepidae atque inelegantes,
> velles dicere nec tacere posses.
> verum nescio quid febriculosi
> scorti diligis: hoc pudet fateri.   5
> nam te non viduas iacere noctes
> nequiquam tacitum cubile clamat
> sertis ac Syrio fragrans olivo,
> pulvinusque peraeque et hic et ille
> attritus, tremulique quassa lecti   10
> argutatio inambulatioque.
> †nam inista prevalet† nihil tacere.
> cur? non tam latera ecfututa pandas,
> ni tu quid facias ineptiarum.
> quare, quidquid habes boni malique,   15
> dic nobis. volo te ac tuos amores
> ad caelum lepido vocare versu.

Flavius, you would wish to tell Catullus, nor would you be able to remain silent, about your sweetheart, unless she were charmless and lacking elegance. But you are fond of some fever-wracked whore. You are ashamed to let on about this. (5) For your couch, silent in vain, reeking of flower-garlands and Syrian oils, shouts out that you don't lie there for celibate nights—and the pillow rubbed uniformly on this side and on that, and the shaken creaking (10) and commotion of the vibrating bed. It's no good being silent about those foibles of yours. Why? You wouldn't display such fucked-out flanks if you weren't up to something outlandish. Wherefore, tell me whatever you're up to, whether good or bad. (15) I wish to invite you and your beloved into heaven with charming verse.

The assuming of the phrase *quidquid habes*, with an imperative, from 6.15 into C. 1.27.17 shows that Catullus's poem is behind that of Horace, and that the latter would have us watch the interconnections and ponder the differing craft of each.[17] Both are poems built around the notions of noise and quiet, talk and silence, of information withheld and revealed, suppressed and offered. Horace's brilliance is to begin with the disruptive *clamor* of babble immediately experienced and rendered in detail (we hear of cups, wine, lamps, a scimitar, elbows), and then to change to calm communication rendered purely by implication abetted by heightened figuration.

Catullus starts with, and maintains throughout the poem, the distinction between speech and speechlessness, only to expose the futility of the latter. *Tacere* (3, 12) and *tacitum* (7) run in counterpoint to *dicere* (3), *fateri* (5), *dic* (16), and the final *vocare* (17), and the latter wins, with Catullus in the process also letting loose a witty series of innuendoes. The personified couch shouts out (*clamat*, 7), like Horace's celebrants, but, instead of being silenced by the demands of a vexed speaker such as Horace's, it continues to be full of life. Miraculously, like a good Roman orator, it has *argutatio* (11), adroitness of utterance, and, as Catullus cleverly fills out his line with assonance and alliteration, it possesses *inambulatio* (11), the ability to keep an audience's attention by proper pacing up and down. In brief, Catullus celebrates sound, the hubbub of conversation, the noise of sexual encounters, the final liberating call to immortality.

Horace plays with his readers by having his protagonist learn a name that is not made known to us. In Catullus, we never find out who Flavius's *scortum* is either, though at least we become acquainted from the initial apostrophe with the male side of the erotic duo. The closest that Horace chooses to come is through the locution *Opuntiae frater Megyllae* (10–11). Nevertheless, for all the external evidence that should bring about disclosure—Flavius's bodily symptoms, a bed with the talents of a rhetor—we are still dealing with innuendo. The couch, for all its skills, cannot speak like a human, and Flavius is never given an opportunity to respond to "Catullus's" prodding. There is no dialogue here as there is, though implicitly, in Horace. The poem initiates a plot but leaves its completion to the reader.

In sum, in Horace the undifferentiated noise with which the poem opens, and Catullus's love of sound-making, are replaced by the speaker's call for calm and by his discriminating reaction to words that we never hear. "Horace" grabs the attention of his brawlers, and the imagination of his readers, by skillfully hinting at what he has learned but can never tell.[18] Nevertheless, though direct communication is impossible, an enormous amount is revealed by figuration. If negative commotion is curbed at the poem's start, we are lured, however deviously, into a domain of passionate, potentially destructive emotion by its conclusion. Violence can enter the symposium only by metaphor.

In Catullus, indirection also holds sway, but here at least the evidence for lovemaking is brought candidly before our eyes. If Flavius should respond, then we will know the truth! Yet Catullus ends his poem, which is itself one large provocation for Flavius to reply so that the poet can exercise his own magic power of utterance still further, with one extraordinary speech act and the promise of another. Flavius's girl may be *illepidae*, but she will be maneuvered into *lepido versu*, which is to presume that she will become *lepida* in the process of being written about.

If Flavius does tell what the speaker requests, it will result in the latter's own "calling," the ability to name names, and to use words, to immortalize. Horace only accomplishes what "you wish" (*voltis*, 9) or elicits what Megylla's brother would wish in response (*voluntas*, 13). The results are splendidly startling. Catullus, by contrast, will effectuate what "I wish" (*volo*, 16), provided he is given the information that he needs (one cannot immortalize, any more than one can curse, without a name). Catullus, as we noted, craves dialogue: an answer from Flavius will elicit even more potent words from him. Horace first suppresses noise, then dialogic speech itself. Catullus will make even more notorious what he is already publicizing, and, as usual in Catullus, sexual energy is described forwardly, in a graphic, unmediated manner.

As we move from bedchamber to symposium, "Horace," who does learn what he wants, will hold the exactness of his knowledge a private secret, as he must, while nevertheless using his formidable powers as a poet also to suggest here to the reader's imagination an extensive amount about eroticism. And naturally enough, Horace's teasing non-exposé, which comes only as close to breaking the banquet's bond of secrecy as his wit will allow, also arouses its own form of desire on the part of the reader.

Another quintessential Catullan poem, 27, makes a brief but distinct appearance in C. 1.27:

Minister vetuli puer Falerni
inger mi calices amariores,

ut lex Postumiae iubet magistrae
ebrioso acino ebriosioris.
at vos quo lubet hinc abite, lymphae,   5
vini pernicies, et ad severos
migrate. hic merus est Thyonianus.

Boy, attendant of the ancient Falernian, pour me more bitter goblets, as
the law of mistress Postumia, more drunken than the drunken grape,
commands. But you, water, ruin of wine, away from here wherever you
want, (5) and make your way to the sober. Here is pure Bacchus.

As at the start of Horace's ode, we are concerned with wine and wine-
drinking. We are also in a world of hierarchies of power and of a commanding speaker. The four imperatives of the odist's opening two stanzas
are paralleled in the three that dot Catullus's seven-line poem. Horace's
speaker puts himself in authority over his *sodales*. Catullus's, who is himself subject to the dictates of Postumia, mistress of the revels, first orders
the *puer*, who is both slave of the old man Falernus and pourer of his
transformed self, to offer him wine that is quite pungent.[19] Then, as the
poem draws to a close, he asks waters, the whole tribe of them, to make
their way to the land of the *S(s)everi*, lest his wine be diluted.

We have, in other words, a study *in parvo* of the differentiation between our two poets revolving around a similar theme. Catullus's concentration centers on his demand for wine that is at its most natural, potent
state, with nothing extraneous to corrupt it. We find him elsewhere making a similar statement about the more life-troubling condition of his
love, as he addresses the gods (76.19–20):

me miserum aspicite et, si vitam puriter egi,
    eripite hanc pestem perniciemque mihi.

Behold me in my misery and, if I have led an untainted life, snatch this
disease and blight from me.[20]

In whatever circumstances, be it the drinking of wine or the endurance
of an amour gone awry, authenticity and innocence, sometimes carried
to such a point that their loss borders on the fatal, are Catullus's proclaimed touchstones. By contrast, moderation rules Horace's world. It is
not that he wishes wine away from his existence, the way Catullus does
water, only that it should be imbibed temperately, lest it disrupt the calm
aura of the symposium where the consumption of wine should be such
as to stimulate the wit and reveal the truth, but not to pass the bounds,
in the words of C. 1.18, "of a Liber [Freer] who knows restraint" (*mod-
ici Liberi*, 7).

Horace also works his moderating influence on Catullus's text. In the sentence *voltis severi me quoque sumere / partem Falerni*? (C. 1.27.9–10), and in particular in the phrase *severi Falerni*, the later poet seems to be offering a summary of Catullus's sympotic verses, from *vetuli Falerni* (1) to *ad severos / migrate* (6–7). Were we to take Horace literally, we would expect an adjective like *amarus* or, more likely, *austerus*, the word Pliny uses, to describe a dry Falernian.[21] Since *severus* would be unique with such a meaning, Horace wittily proposes a paradox that makes sense only after a reading of Catullus. His Falernian, instead of being an ancient vintage, will partake of a characteristic Catullus comes near associating with water and water drinkers. It will be sober and, to give the word a still more moralistic ring, both serious and rigorous.

Horace's initial stanzas depict a *convivium* that has gotten out of control.[22] In such a context, if Horace drinks, it will be a Falernian that will restore order to the proceedings, one that is both strict and restricting, a wine with associations that could be complemented by water and therefore serve as proper accompaniment for a symposium ruled by moderation. For Horace, then, *severus*, as a qualifier of wine, is an active, performative adjective. It is austere itself and has the effect of making its drinkers austere. It tempers both itself and the proceedings in which it shares. And its oxymoronic sense—we are concerned with wine that is a teetotaler—forms a characteristic of the poet and poetry in which it shares, being circumspect, like the symposium and its narrator, who in his conduct remains, to a proper degree, unexplicit and non-revelatory.

Severitas is as much an anathema for Catullus as it is essential for Horace. For the earlier poet, with his penchant for the essential, wine's lack of dilution goes without saying, and the *severi*, creatures who, in their aged version as *senum severiorum* (5.2), carp at, or do not even comprehend, erotic extravagance, are suitable receivers of the banished *lymphae*. Horace's call for calm and moderation, by contrast, deliberately confounds wine and severity, stimulus and its management. He omits any consideration of the excited center of Catullus's poem, with its repetitions revolving around the grape itself at the core of the poem (*ebrioso acino ebriosioris*, 4), and instead merges what Catullus keeps carefully separate from each other—wine and stringency—in order to create a metaphorical touchstone for C. 1.27 and, from one angle at least, for his poetry as a whole.

The language of Catullan emotionality in poem 27 is also absorbed by Horace into C. 2.11, an ode likewise devoted to wine-bibbing. The subject here is not what initiates C. 1.27, the disciplining of a roistering group of *sodales*, but the celebration of the moment, in the face of life's cares, and of the passage of time. Why not quaff wine, as we lie at ease in the shade, our locks perfumed (18–20):

> . . . quis puer ocius
>   restinguet ardentis Falerni
>   pocula praetereunte lympha?

What slave will hasten to temper the goblets of burning Falernian with water flowing by?

Again we have present a *puer*, while *Falerni* and forms of *lympha* likewise appear at line endings. Catullus's *vetuli*, as attribute for the vintage, is replaced not by *severus*, as the wine magically becomes stern just like the speaker who reproves his brawling comrades, but by *ardentis*, at once fiery and ardent, that, paradoxically, needs to be quenched before being imbibed. Once more moderation in drinking is Horace's theme, by contrast to Catullus's taking his wine, like his life, neat. For Horace, wine with passion spent, or at least allayed, is suitable accompaniment for the poised appearance of the courtesan Lyde at the end of the poem, "her hair bound back into a decorative knot, like a Spartan woman's" (*in comptum Lacaenae / more comam religata nodum*). The melding, rather than the disjunction, of wine and water typifies his regular reception of Catullus, whether toning down the unruly, as in C. 1.27, or, as here, limiting wine's fervor, first literally, then metaphorically, by the water of equanimity.

One further appearance of Catullus 27, this time in C. 1.38, will take us into the final topic of this chapter, beginnings and endings, as we look at demarcating poems where we would expect the challenge between poets to be prominent. Let us begin with the concluding poem, the *sphragis*, or "seal," to the first book of odes:

> Persicos odi, puer, adparatus,
> displicent nexae philyra coronae,
> mitte sectari, rosa quo locorum
>   sera moretur.
>
> simplici myrto nihil adlabores   5
> sedulus curo: neque te ministrum
> dedecet myrtus neque me sub arta
>   vite bibentem.

I hate Persian elaboration, boy. Crowns woven from linden bast give me no pleasure. Away with pursuing where the late rose lingers. I don't want you officiously to add something to the simple myrtle: (5) the myrtle is neither unbefitting for you, the server, nor for me as I drink beneath the tight-knit vine.

The two brief scolions, one seven, the other eight lines long, are united by the apostrophe in the opening line of each, to the *puer* who is designated *minister* in Catullus's first word and *ministrum* in Horace's sixth line, and by a speaker who is drinking the wine that the boy serves. Both are poems of likes and dislikes, of acceptances and dismissals, of presence and absence, here and there. Catullus would have us bid farewell to *lymphae*, Horace to *coronae* and the recherché *rosa*. The *lymphae* receive from the speaker their order to depart en masse (*quo lubet hinc abite*, 5); crowns and rose form part of an imperative to the wine-pourer (*mitte sectari . . . quo locorum*, 3–4). Both are poems about what is welcome or unwelcome for a speaker, standing in for a poet, as he drinks wine, in the case of Horace at least, by himself in the appropriate setting of a vine-arbor, the source of the wine itself that the didactic speaker himself is imbibing with the assistance of his servant.

But we expect something richer from the concluding poem of the initial sequence in a superlative collection of lyrics. A further comparison of the two poems may offer a suggestion. The speaker of Horace's poem is two things at once, if we watch him watching Catullus. First, he is a poet imitating a poet, someone knowing another wordsmith's creation and refining it to his own specifications. Second, if we superpose one narrative on the other and give full play to the personification of *vetulus Falernus*, whose servant Catullus addresses, then Horace is also a surrogate for "old Falernus," waited upon by his own young self as pourer. In other words, through Catullus he is both poet and wine, singer of vinous songs and the wine that inspires them.

The *puer*, listening to the wine-poet's lecture, stands in for the poetry and the poetry-book that C. 1.38 brings to a conclusion. It is he who must learn about, and embody, writing that eschews the over-elaborate, the recondite and the exotic, in favor of what is simple and tautly constructed. He must exchange wreaths held together by linden bast for Venus's myrtle that, for Horace elsewhere, symbolizes spring (C. 1.4.9) and youth (C. 1.26.18), whose crowns grace symposia (C. 2.7.25) and whose leaves miraculously protect stripling poets (C. 3.4.19). And, if we turn again to the Catullan background, he must absorb the earlier poet's uncompromising world of antonyms, of wine versus water, purity versus corruption, Bacchic frenzy and the structuring of ordered verse, into his own mind-set, one that thrives on poise and grace, woven into a garland of poems.[23]

Direct mention of Catullus is pointedly absent in two places where Horace dwells on his own achievement as lyric bard. One is another bounding poem that brings to a proud end the whole initial collection (C. 3.30):

Exegi monumentum aere perennius
regalique situ pyramidum altius,

quod non imber edax, non aquilo impotens
possit diruere aut innumerabilis
annorum series et fuga temporum.   5
non omnis moriar multaque pars mei
vitabit Libitinam: usque ego postera
crescam laude recens, dum Capitolium
scandet cum tacita virgine pontifex:
dicar, qua violens obstrepit Aufidus   10
et qua pauper aquae Daunus agrestium
regnavit populorum, ex humili potens
princeps Aeolium carmen ad Italos
deduxisse modos. sume superbiam
quaesitam meritis et mihi Delphica   15
lauro cinge volens, Melpomene, comam.

I have brought to fulfillment a monument more lasting than bronze,
and loftier than the regal mass of the pyramids that neither gnawing
rain nor the violent north wind nor the countless sequence of years
and the flight of time can destroy. (5) I shall not completely die, and a
large part of me will shun Libitina. I will grow ever fresh with future
praise, so long as the priest will climb the Capitolium with the silent
maid. It will be said, where the unruly Aufidus roars (10) and where
Daunus, needy of water, ruled over rural folk, that I, powerful from a
lowly origin, was the first to have spun Aeolian song to Italian measures. Accept my pride won by your merits, Melpomene, (15) and
kindly encircle my locks with the laurel of Delphi.

In boasting of his position as premier poet of Greek lyric writing in
Latin, as the first—to retranslate *deduxisse* and *modos*, doing fuller justice to their ambiguity—"to have led Aeolian song in triumph to Italian
beats," Horace invents for himself, in the sphere of literary creativity, a
role of *princeps* parallel to that of Augustus in the realm of politics.[24] In
making such a proclamation, he, on the surface at least, neglects the accomplishment of Catullus, especially of poems such as 11, 30, 34, and
51, which in meter, and often content, recall the work of the lyric poets
of archaic Greece.

Yet one word, *perennius*, offers evidence that Catullus was in fact on
Horace's mind. It occurs in line 10 of the poem that opens the earlier
poet's gathering of poems, at least as we have it:

Cui dono lepidum novum libellum
arida modo pumice expolitum?
Corneli, tibi: namque tu solebas
meas esse aliquid putare nugas

iam tum, cum ausus es unus Italorum   5
omne aevum tribus explicare cartis
doctis, Iuppiter, et laboriosis.
quare habe tibi quidquid hoc libelli
qualecumque, quod, <o> patrona virgo,
plus uno maneat perenne saeclo.   10

> To whom am I giving this new, charming little book, just now polished
> with dry pumice? To you, Cornelius, for you were wont to consider
> my trifles something, even then when, unique among the Itali, you
> dared (5) to unfold all time in three volumes, learned, by Jupiter, and
> painstaking. Wherefore consider as your own this little book, whatever
> it is, whatever its value, which, o patron virgin, may it remain
> enduring more than one generation. (10)

Horace pays Catullus the great compliment of honoring him in a way
that he becomes part of Horace's own act of structure. Elements of Horace's inner scaffolding are clear enough. Let me offer two. The first is
meter. C. 1.1 and C. 3.30 are the only two poems in the initial collection
of lyrics in which Horace uses the first asclepiadean. The second is the
figure of Maecenas. He is the dedicatee of the opening poem and the receiver, pointedly as we saw, of the penultimate ode of the same gathering. The last poem is left for Horace and for the due pride he takes in his
achievement. By attending to the final line of Catullus's first poem in the
opening verse of the *sphragis* of his masterpiece of odes, Horace therefore expands his design to include all of Catullus, exclusive of meter,
within its scope. So while announcing publicly his own uniqueness, the
later poet also tells his reader that his great predecessor is in fact not
only on his mind, but also part of a larger patterning of Latin literary
history to which he lends authority.

Nor do the similarities between the two poems rest with one word.
Both are meditations on temporality. Horace's poem ends with a prayer
to Melpomene to crown him with Apollo's laurel, which is to say to give
her approval to his presumption that the symbols of poetic immortality
are appropriately his. Catullus concludes by asking the muse, in the form
of a nameless *patrona virgo*, that the contents of his *libellus* live on for
one further generation.[25] Both have touchstones against which to measure their attainments vis-à-vis the passage of time. For Catullus, with his
pretense at humility, it is the unique Cornelius Nepos and his history that
treats all time in three books—a world of numbers and of universals.
How is a poet of trifles to compare his work to that of someone who con-
trols the past (and is spoken of in the past) except to ask, by contrast to
Cornelius's comprehensiveness, for a small stake in the future?

But Catullus may be more mischievous than I am allowing him. The adjectives that he allots to Cornelius's work, *doctus* and *laboriosus*, are ones that his contemporary audience and his later readers would apply as readily to the poet himself. Perhaps in ironizing against himself, writer of frivolities that might survive for a bit, he is also gently mocking his addressee, learned embracer of all past history.[26] Perhaps time was on the poet's side: after all, we possess a generous amount of Catullus's work and Nepos's *Chronicon* is lost. Perhaps, too, he would expect us to make the transfer I suggest, and, in becoming the *doctus poeta* that he was, also to allow him the dominion over temporality that he modestly declines but perhaps knew would be his. Horace's yardsticks for survival, bronze and the pyramids in their bulk, for their mere physicality are more vulnerable to the passage of years than what we would expect for the written works of a historian who tells of, and therefore to a degree masters, time. So also his pride is more open than Catullus's. Nevertheless, he has given us more than a hint that his inspirers, and challengers, were not just the poets of Aeolia, but his great Latin predecessor as well.

We must turn from the odes to the first book of epistles for one final instance of Horace's direct suppression of Catullus while subtly acknowledging his presence. In the collection's next-to-last poem, *Epi.* 1.19, Horace spends some time pondering the question of his originality.[27] First calling himself *princeps* again (21), he continues on to boast of his primacy (*primus*, 23) in the writing of *iambi*, which is to say the *Epodes*, and of how he "tempered" Archilochus in his transference from Greek to Latin. There follow references to Sappho and Alcaeus. Of the latter he says (32–33):

> hunc ego, non alio dictum prius ore, Latinus
> volgavi fidicen.
>
> I, the lyricist of Latium, have made him known, never sung before by the lips of others.

It is true that he doesn't say the same of Sappho, perhaps out of respect for Catullus's two poems in sapphic meter, 11 and 51. Yet, Horace leaves the impression that Alcaeus stands for the poetry of Lesbos and therefore for both the salient figures of archaic Greek lyric.

Nevertheless, that he has been thinking here of Catullus is made clear by the acknowledgment of line 3 of his poem 69, dealing with a lover's offering—*non si illam rarae labefactes munere vestis* ("Not though you may cause her to falter by a gift of diaphanous cloth")—at *Epi.* 1.19.38, where the phrase *tritae munere vestis*, also at the end of the hexameter, is applied to a gift that a politician might use to garner votes.[28] But, as if to make amends for the direct omission here, Horace clearly brings Catullus to his reader's mind in the next poem, the "seal" poem for his first book of epistles, the next collection to follow, some three years later, upon the publication of the first three books of odes in 23. The poet imagines his book as a young, handsome slave who yearns for the city (*Epi.* 1.20.1–5):

> Vortumnum Ianumque, liber, spectare videris,
> scilicet ut prostes Sosiorum pumice mundus;
> odisti clavis et grata sigilla pudico,
> paucis ostendi gemis et communia laudas,
> non ita nutritus: fuge quo descendere gestis.

> You seem, my book, to cast your eye at Vortumnus and Janus, clearly
> in order that you might offer yourself for sale, polished by the pumice
> of the Sosii. You hate the keys and the seals that please the chaste. You
> complain that you are shown to only a few, and praise the public arena,
> though not reared for it. Be off, down whither you yearn to descend.

The poem continues on with the life story of the book-whore, discarded by a satiated lover, thumbed by the vulgar, escaping to, or imprisoned in, the provinces, teaching the alphabet to schoolchildren. But the book will have another charge: to tell the world about its creator, his background, his personality, and, finally, his age (26–28):

> forte meum siquis te percontabitur aevum,
> me quater undenos sciat inplevisse Decembris,
> conlegam Lepidum quo duxit Lollius anno.

> If anyone chances to ask you my age, let him know that I completed
> my forty-fourth December in the year when Lollius drew Lepidus as
> consul.

If Catullus is bypassed in the speaker's literary biography of the preceding epistle, his presence is strongly felt as a multivalent structuring device in the final poem, with its conclusion telling the poet's life story. Horace is again thinking, as we have seen him do on several previous occasions, of the opening lines of Catullus's first poem:

> Cui dono lepidum novum libellum
> arida modo pumice expolitum?

The first two lines of each poem interact with one another: Catullus's modest *libellus* becomes a full-scale *liber*, while *arida . . . pumice expoli-*

tum turns into *pumice mundus*. Catullus's suggestive hint at personification in the beautifying of his little volume suffers elaboration in the slave-prostitute-book, who both incorporates Horace's words and outlines his *curriculum vitae*.[29] It is the word *lepidum* that undergoes the more astonishing transformation. It makes its appearance not in connection with the *liber* but as the cognomen of Quintus Aemilius Lepidus, consul of the year 21, whose name appears in the poem's final hexameter. Charm is associated not with a personification at the opening of the poem but with a real person at its conclusion, a person who forms a specific part of the speaker's self-definition. Allusions to Catullus 1 therefore serve to help Horace construct a double frame. They outline *Epi.* 1.20 in and of itself, and they demarcate their poetry books as the first and last poems, respectively.

Finally, we must recall *C.* 1.38 and the role Catullus played in its engendering, especially through his poem 27. There, too, we found a *puer* who was at once slave and poetry-book, also suffering a lecture from his master-creator, now in a lyric's compressed form. *C.* 1.38 speaks of a refined poetics, and *Epi.* 1.20 tells, in serio-comic fashion, of a book's tangible and spiritual destiny, but both are concluding poems. From their place of prominence they not only help lend shape to their books, they offer commentary on the style and content of what has gone before. Catullus provides impetus for both.

CHAPTER THREE

Helen

In the previous chapters we surveyed notions of the temporal and the spatial as well as of utterance and its inhibition as means to adjudicate the interaction between Catullus and Horace. We now turn from abstract to concrete, as in separate chapters we watch two figures who help focus our attention on a series of interconnected poems by each writer. The first is Helen of Troy.

Three adjacent odes in the first book of *Carmina*, 15–17, however diverse their subject matter in appearance, have important elements in common.[1] The clearest unifying factor is their distinctive associations with Helen. The first of the trio is essentially a narrative poem:

> Pastor cum traheret per freta navibus
> Idaeis Helenen perfidus hospitam,
> ingrato celeris obruit otio
>   ventos ut caneret fera
>
> Nereus fata: "mala ducis avi domum   5
> quam multo repetet Graecia milite
> coniurata tuas rumpere nuptias
>   et regnum Priami vetus.
>
> heu heu, quantus equis, quantus adest viris
> sudor, quanta moves funera Dardanae   10
> genti. iam galeam Pallas et aegida
>   currusque et rabiem parat.
>
> nequiquam Veneris praesidio ferox
> pectes caesariem grataque feminis
> inbelli cithara carmina divides,   15
>   nequiquam thalamo gravis
>
> hastas et calami spicula Cnosii
> vitabis strepitumque et celerem sequi
> Aiacem: tamen heu serus adulteros
>   crines pulvere collines.   20

non Laertiaden, exitium tuae
genti, non Pylium Nestora respicis?
urgent inpavidi te Salaminius
    Teucer, te Sthenelus sciens

pugnae, sive opus est imperitare equis,   25
non auriga piger. Merionen quoque
nosces. ecce furit te reperire atrox
    Tydides melior patre:

quem tu, cervus uti vallis in altera
visum parte lupum graminis inmemor,   30
sublimi fugies mollis anhelitu,
    non hoc pollicitus tuae.

iracunda diem proferet Ilio
matronisque Phrygum classis Achillei:
post certas hiemes uret Achaicus   35
    ignis Iliacas domos."

When the treacherous shepherd was carrying his hostess Helen
through the waters on his Trojan ships, Nereus stilled the swift winds
with unwelcome calm that he might prophesy harsh fate: "With an
evil omen you are carrying home (5) her whom Greece will seek back
with many a soldier, joined by oath to break your marriage and the
ancient kingdom of Priam. Alas, alas, how much sweat for horses,
how much for men is at hand, how many deaths you are posing for
the Dardan race. (10) Already Pallas is readying her helmet and aegis,
her chariot and her rage. Fierce because of Venus's protection, you
will comb your hair in vain and strum on the unwarlike lyre songs
pleasing to women, (15) in vain in your marriage chamber will you
avoid the weighty spears and the darts of Cretan reed, the roar of
battle, and Ajax quick to pursue. Though late, yet sometime, alas, you
will smear your adulterous locks with dust. (20) Don't you notice
Laertes's son, the ruin of your race, not Pylian Nestor? Fearlessly
Teucer of Salamis presses after you, after you Sthenelus who knows
about combat, or if there is need to guide his horses, (25) no
sluggard of a charioteer. You will also recognize Meriones. See, dread
Tydides, braver than his father, rages to discover you. Feebly you will
flee him with panting breath, like a deer forgetful of its pasture (30)
when it has seen a wolf in another part of the valley—what you
didn't promise to your beloved. The anger of Achilles's fleet will
postpone the day for Troy and the Trojan mothers. Nevertheless,

after the allotted winters, Greek fire (35) will engulf the homes of
Ilium."

The ode's initial stanza places us in the midst of the sea journey from
Greece to Troy on which Paris abducts Helen, wife of his host Menelaus.
Nereus causes the winds to cease so that, for the remainder of the poem,
the god could harangue the "treacherous shepherd" about the consequences of his perfidy to himself and to his homeland. Foreground movement comes to a halt for the narrator to offer one long apostrophe—the
word "you" appears as pronoun or within verbal forms in every stanza
except the last—that in effect does not so much summarize heroic deeds
at Troy as catalogue the gods and heroes, from Athena to Achilles, who
will soon focus their menace on Paris. The poem essentially stands as
a lyric documentation of the first of a continuum of actions leading
inevitably to the burning of Troy, to which the final quatrain is dedicated.[2]

Though nominally a narrative of events to come, Nereus's speech carefully balances future with present. The repetition of words like *quantus*,
together with the uninterrupted focus on the second person, steadies us
to face the immediacy of events. Moreover, the personal involvement of
Nereus in the story that he tells, as he both chastises and commiserates
with his hapless listener (the iterations of *heu* at lines 9 and 19 are especially moving), underscores the subjective intensity here of Horace's lyric
art, even when dealing with an event shrouded in myth.

The second poem in the trio, 1.16, brings in Helen vicariously. The
ode is on the surface an act of repentance by the speaker for the writing
of some iambic poetry (*criminosis iambis*, 2–3; *celeres iambos*, 24) directed against his girl. Its core is a consideration of the destructive power
of anger (*irae*, 9 and 17), while the conclusion is a prayer that she restore
herself to him if he continues to make the requisite change from harsh to
mild, which is to say from the writing of iambic poetry to that of lyric.

The poem was recognized in antiquity as a παλινῳδία in imitation of
what were apparently two recantations on the part of the sixth-century
poet Stesichorus. According to a tradition famously initiated by Plato,[3]
Stesichorus was blinded for having calumniated Helen, by accusing her
of going to Troy "on the well-benched ships" and therefore of both
causing and sharing in the war subsequent to her abduction by Paris.
The poet's sight only returned when he retracted his supposed vituperation.[4]

The third ode in the sequence, C. 1.17, finds us in the Sabine hills with
the speaker offering an invitation to Tyndaris, which is to say Helen,
daughter of Tyndareus, now in the guise of a lyre-playing guest-friend, or
even potential lover, of the speaker. She is to join him in his retreat, rich

in the glories of the countryside, and share the world of his *musa* by singing of Penelope and Circe (we are now in the context of the *Odyssey*) in the manner of Anacreon. Once within the speaker's sanctuary, she will escape the threat of Cyrus's violent hands and become as lacking in fear (*nec metus*, 24) as the animals who share in this magic landscape (*nec metuunt*, 8).

Though the figure of Helen is the surest connecting link between this extraordinary trio of odes, much else besides serves to unify the group. There is copious lexical overlap among all three poems as well as a careful chain of verbal interconnections. Let me offer a few examples. The ruin that Odysseus plans for Paris's Trojan race (*Laertiaden exitium tuae / genti*, C. 1.15.21–22) anticipates the disaster, which we hear about in the next poem, that wrath brings upon Thyestes (*Thyesten exitio gravi*, C. 1.16.17); and the description of Diomedes as *melior patre* (C. 1.15.28), better than his father Tydeus, looks ahead to the subsequent poem's opening address—*o matre pulcra filia pulcrior* ("O daughter, fairer than your mother fair"). In this respect, the first word of the final stanza of 1.15, *iracunda*, has special force. The fleet of Achilles is angry because its leader is angry. This serves as a reminder of the first word of the *Iliad*, and therefore of the epic as a whole, but also as a foretaste of the poem to come, with its emphasis on the destructiveness of *irae*.[5]

If anger connects poems 15 and 16, the idea of change links 16 and 17. The speaker of 16 will forego fury for friendship at the end of that poem (*mutare*, 26). At the start of C. 1.17, Faunus will exchange Arcadia for the poet's Sabine setting (*mutat*, 2), and will serve thereby as a model for the transition that the speaker trusts Tyndaris will make. Helen once journeyed with Paris from Sparta to Troy, with dire consequences. Horace's Tyndaris, by contrast, will abandon the incipient violence of a world elsewhere for the poet's arcadia of calm and song.[6]

All three poems can likewise be viewed as exemplifying a figurative aspect of change, replacement, and alteration based on genre. Horace's commentator Porphyrio tells us, without offering specific evidence, that in C. 1.15 Horace is imitating an ode of Bacchylides in which Cassandra predicted the advent of the Trojan War. Stesichorus, whose "serious Muses" (*graves Camenae*) Horace mentions at C. 4.9.8, would also be a likely candidate as an important influence on Horace here. This is a feasible suggestion, first, for the combination of epic themes in lyric verse that typifies his work, and second, because it anticipates his overriding presence in the subsequent ode.[7] Certainly the poem itself serves not only as an example of the lyricizing of epic themes, but also of the tension, in the future life of Paris, between the two genres.

At C. 1.6.10 Horace speaks of his allegiance to the "Muse who has power over the unwarlike lyre" (*inbellis . . . lyrae Musa potens*), a loyalty that will not allow him to sing in epic the praises of Caesar and Agrippa. Paris, strumming "songs on an unwarlike lyre" (*inbelli cithara carmina*, C. 1.15.15), is in a parallel position, with the difference that he is supposedly a warrior, not a poet-singer. For Paris in his context, under the patronage of Venus, to chant songs pleasing to women is in fact to feminize himself and to leave the deeds worthy of epic to the men who will soon prove to be his, and Troy's, undoing. Horace encloses epic within his own lyricizing, but in the same process tells a tale where amatory passion, and its imaginative outlet in lyric song, is incompatible with what, at least here, are the destructive energies that a Homer documents.

If we turn to C. 1.16, we find that the generic mutation around which this poem is built lies in the tension between iambic and lyric poetry, which is to say in this instance between invective poetry steeped in anger and poetry of affection and affiliation. Horace's juxtaposition of these two odes, however, may be meant to bring with it a touch of humor, especially coming after Nereus's relentlessly negative catalogue of Paris's enemies in the preceding poem:

O matre pulcra filia pulcrior,
quem criminosis cumque voles modum
    pones iambis, sive flamma
        sive mari libet Hadriano.

non Dindymene, non adytis quatit   5
mentem sacerdotum incola Pythius,
    non Liber aeque, non acuta
        sic geminant Corybantes aera,

tristes ut irae, quas neque Noricus
deterret ensis nec mare naufragum   10
    nec saevos ignis nec tremendo
        Iuppiter ipse ruens tumultu.

fertur Prometheus addere principi
limo coactus particulam undique
    desectam et insani leonis   15
        vim stomacho adposuisse nostro.

irae Thyesten exitio gravi
stravere et altis urbibus ultimae
    stetere causae, cur perirent
        funditus inprimeretque muris   20

hostile aratrum exercitus insolens.
conpesce mentem: me quoque pectoris
    temptavit in dulci iuventa
        fervor et in celeres iambos

misit furentem: nunc ego mitibus   25
mutare quaero tristia, dum mihi
    fias recantatis amica
        opprobriis animumque reddas.

O daughter fairer than your fair mother, bring about whatever demise
you choose for my slanderous iambs, whether it be by means of flame
or through the Adriatic Sea. Neither Dindymene, nor the dweller in
Delphi's shrine equally sets trembling the mind of his priests, (5) nor
Bacchus, nor do Corybantes so clash their cymbals, as bitter anger,
which neither the Noric sword daunts nor the ship-breaking sea (10)
nor fierce fire, nor Jupiter himself, descending in fearful uproar.

Prometheus, when forced to add a segment culled from anywhere
and everywhere to our primal mud, is said also to have attached the
violence of the mad lion to our disposition. (15) Anger laid Thyestes
low in grievous ruin and has remained the primary reason why lofty
cities have utterly perished and a haughty foe has stationed a hostile
plough on their walls. (20) Restrain your spirit: in the sweetness of
youth, passion of heart afflicted me also and drove me, raging, toward
swift iambs. Now I seek to exchange harsh for mild, (25) provided,
seeing that I have recanted my insults, you become my friend and
return me your mind.

We start off with an enormous compliment from the speaker to his
Helen—*O matre pulcra filia pulcrior*—one that Ovid caps in *Heroides*
16. Paris is writing to Helen, but the words are Venus's (85–86):

"nos dabimus, quod ames, et pulchrae filia Ledae
    ibit in amplexus pulchrior illa tuos."

"We will bestow on you something that you can love, and the daughter
of beautiful Leda, herself more beautiful, will come to your embrace."[8]

Nevertheless, by adopting the stance of Stesichorus, Horace's speaker
ironizes Helen's part in the Trojan War out of existence. He thus not
only does away with the Homeric tradition of Helen at Troy but also
gives the lie to the subject matter of the preceding poem. The martiality
of *C.* 1.15 is replaced in *C.* 1.16 by the catalogue of horrors that *irae* can
bring into being. But just as the ghost of Stesichorus brooding over the

poem makes Helen and war discordant entities, so the change from iambic to lyric verse mollifies the pernicious aspects of anger that had previously ruled the speaker's mind.

C. 1.17 also exhibits many characteristics in common with the preceding poems:

Velox amoenum saepe Lucretilem
mutat Lycaeo Faunus et igneam
    defendit aestatem capellis
        usque meis pluviosque ventos.

inpune tutum per nemus arbutus   5
quaerunt latentis et thyma deviae
    olentis uxores mariti
        nec viridis metuunt colubras.

nec Martialis haediliae lupos,
utcumque dulci, Tyndari, fistula   10
    valles et Usticae cubantis
        levia personuere saxa.

di me tuentur, dis pietas mea
et musa cordi est. hic tibi copia
    manabit ad plenum benigno   15
        ruris honorum opulenta cornu.

hic in reducta valle caniculae
vitabis aestus et fide Teia
    dices laborantis in uno
        Penelopen vitreamque Circen.   20

hic innocentis pocula Lesbii
duces sub umbra, nec Semeleius
    cum Marte confundet Thyoneus
        proelia, nec metues protervum

suspecta Cyrum, ne male dispari   25
incontinentis iniciat manus
    et scindat haerentem coronam
        crinibus inmeritamque vestem.

Swift Faunus often exchanges Lycaeus for lovely Lucretilis and ever wards off fiery heat and rainy winds from my goats. Harmlessly

through the safe wood the wandering wives of the smelly husband
search for lurking arbutus (5) and clumps of thyme, nor do the female
kids fear green vipers or the wolves of Mars whenever, Tyndaris,
(10) the valleys and the smooth rocks of reclining Ustica have
resounded with the sweet pipe.

The gods protect me, my piety and inspiration are dear to the gods.
Here for you from kindly horn Abundance, rich in the glories of the
countryside, will pour forth to the full. (15)

Here in a withdrawn valley you will avoid the swelterings of the
Dog-star and you will tell on Tean lyre of Penelope and deceitful Circe,
in turmoil over one man. (20) Here in the shade you will quaff
goblets of harmless wine from Lesbos, nor will Semeleian Thyoneus
embroil battles with Mars, nor, as object of jealousy, will you fear that
forward Cyrus lay unrestrained hands on one scarcely his equal, (25)
and tear the garland that clings to your hair and your undeserving
garment.

Homer is again part of the speaker's world, this time, as we saw, in the
form of the *Odyssey* rather than the *Iliad*. And, even though the subject
matter is erotic—the mutual love of Penelope and Circe for Odysseus—
nevertheless Tyndaris/Helen is to sing of it on a Tean lyre, namely in the
manner of Anacreon. Once more, different genres are juxtaposed. In
particular, once again epic is, as it were, domesticated to lyric, and once
again any threatening elements, here in the person of Cyrus and his
propensity for physicality, are absent. Helen and her lyric song are safe
in Horace's sequestered vale and an enhancement of it.

There may be a touch of humor here, too, as complement to the light-
ening of genre. Though at *Epi.* 1.16.10 Horace mentions a flock (*pecus*)
in connection with his Sabine farm, the first three stanzas of *C.* 1.17 offer the only detailed mention of what we might call animal husbandry in
Horace's poetry. We move from she-goats (*capellis*, 3), those "wives of a
smelly spouse" (*olentis uxores mariti*, 9), to female kids (*haediliae*, 9).
All are protected in this magic environment from any danger, be it from
the elements, such as heat or rainy winds, or from inimical fauna such as
snakes and wolves. But goatherds are implicitly present as well, because
the rocks reverberate with the sound of the "sweet pipe" (*dulci fistula*,
10). In fact, we find ourselves, suitably enough in a poem much concerned with poetry, introduced into the domain of pastoral song, a domain that would have been familiar to all of Horace's readers from the
Eclogues of Virgil and of which he offers an incisive vignette at *C.*
4.12.9–12, a poem dedicated to his fellow poet and one with which we
will later be concerned. If we were to choose an appropriate symbol for
pastoral poetry, it would be the reed pipe.

The presence of such music and music-making would be apropos for C. 1.17 alone were it not for two further details. By bringing Helen into his world, the speaker becomes implicitly a figure for Paris, poet-seducer of a lyre-playing Helen, drawn into a setting compatible with both. But Horace would also have us remember the striking way that he introduces Paris to us in C. 1.15, with its first word, *pastor*.[9] It was as tender of herds on Mt. Ida that the Trojan youth was asked to make his famous judgment between Hera, Athena, and Aphrodite when, by opting for the goddess of love, he gained Helen as prize. The latter-day Sabine herder, Horace, guarding "my goats" (*capellis meis*) and associating himself with the sound of the reed pipe, will indeed, we trust, lure his own Helen into his version of pastoral, which in turn will harmonize with her own talent. But there will now be no Trojan War as a result. Just as the speaker in the preceding poem renounces iambic invective for love-lyric, so here Homer's grandeur is tamed to the lyre's gentleness. Whatever violence Tyndaris might have experienced in another sphere is banished from the poet's precinct of pastoral and lyric melody.

As we have noted elsewhere, it is a working principle with the lyric poetry of Horace that when the poets of archaic Greece are mentioned, either explicitly or by implication, through allusion or from comments in the scholiastic tradition, then the work of Catullus will also often be part of the intellectual background. In this case, where we have Homer, Stesichorus, Anacreon, and Bacchylides as potential influences, we would also expect to find Horace's great Republican forbear present. Let us turn first to C. 1.16, where the immediate impact of Catullus is most strongly felt. Then we will look at the adjacent odes.

When Horace himself thinks of the iambic tradition, it is to Archilochus that his mind turns,[10] and his proud boast, in connection with his accomplishment in the *Epodes*, is that (*Epi.* 1.19.23–25)

> . . . Parios ego primus iambos
> ostendi Latio, numeros animosque secutus
> Archilochi, non res et agentia verba Lycamben.
>
> I was the first to show to Latium the iambs of Paros [birthplace of Archilochus], following the rhythms and the spirit of Archilochus, but not the matter and the language hounding Lycambes.[11]

When Porphyrio, in his comment on C. 1.16.22–24, thinks of the use of iambic poetry *ad maledicendum*, for abuse or slander, it is to Catullus that he turns for an example of invective writing. He cites a poem, knowledge of which comes only from his mention (fr. 3 Mynors): *At non effugies meos iambos* ("But you will not escape from my iambs"). He could presumably have turned to poems still extant in the Catullan corpus, such as 40, whose opening lines suggest the hostile force of the poet's *iambi*:

Quaenam te mala mens, miselle Ravide,
agit praecipitem in meos iambos?

What unfortunate turn of mind, poor little Ravidus, drives you
headlong against my iambs?

Or we have 54.6–7, where the ire of the addressee, in all probability Julius Caesar, will be aroused against Catullus's iambs, innocent because veracious:

irascere iterum meis iambis
inmerentibus, unice imperator.

You will be angry again at my undeserving iambi, one-of-a-kind
sovereign.

But there are two poems in the Catullan corpus that have direct bearing on C. 1.16, both of which in different ways are concerned with iambic verse.
    The first is poem 36, a witty address to the *annales Volusi*, the epic chronicle of a certain Volusius, the sheets of whose poetry will replace Catullus's own in fulfilling a vow of the poet's girl (3–8):

nam sanctae Veneri Cupidinique
vovit, si sibi restitutus essem
desissemque truces vibrare iambos,   5
electissima pessimi poetae
scripta tardipedi deo daturam
infelicibus ustulanda lignis.

For she vowed to holy Venus and to Cupid that, if I were restored to
her and ceased to brandish fierce iambs, (5) she would offer the
choicest writings of the worst of poets to the limping-footed god to be
roasted on unlucky logs.

The poem continues with a fulsome, mock-hymnic apostrophe to Venus to approve the vow, and concludes with a final invitation to Volusius's disreputable trash to round matters off and "make your way into the fire" (*venite in ignem*, 18).[12]
    Both Catullus 36 and C. 1.16 revolve around the notion of a poet having to make amends for producing iambs insulting to his girl, both by

ceasing to write such invective and by disposing of the offending verse. The act of annihilation on the part of the girl, upon which Catullus expands, Horace leaves simply by reference to alternative methods of burning by fire or drowning in water (3–4):

> . . . sive flamma
> sive mari libet Hadriano.

In Catullus we have fire mentioned twice, in the form, first, of Vulcan's ill-starred timber on which to burn the criminally guilty verse, then of the final flames. There is no mention of water, but Horace's *mari Hadriano* as the place, or means, of putting an end to the dread verse may have been inspired by Catullus's mention of Durrachium, the "inn of the Adriatic" (*Hadriae tabernam*, 15), among the extensive list of places where Venus finds suitable habitation.

At this point Horace leaves his offending *iambi* behind for the poem's central subject, the injurious evils of *irae*. Only when he abandons abstract for concrete and returns again, at the ode's finale, to the iambs themselves do we find a further aspect of commonality between the two poems. The abandonment of *iambi*, fierce for Catullus, criminal and swift for Horace, is the precondition for the pairs of lovers to become reconciled to each other. In the case of Catullus, it is the restoration of himself to his *puella* that is in question (*restitutus essem*, 4). He has been so chagrined by her behavior that he has abandoned her, leaving as their only point of contact the iambic weapons that are his source of menace. For Horace, his iambs, and the youthful fervor that engendered them, are what has driven his girl away. He asks that she "return her spirit" (*animum . . . reddas*, 28). This is the same verb that, at line 16 of his poem, Catullus had used for the proper "discharge" of his vow to the goddess of love and her child (*redditum . . . votum*). He returns to his girl, and the vow is appropriately "returned" to Venus.

Here, too, interplay of genres is worth watching. Catullus uses an iambic meter, hendecasyllabics, for his poem as part of its humor because, although the relinquishment of invective is part of the poem's plot, vituperation can still be the order of the day, since the poet's addressee is the *annales Volusi*, not his girl, as is the case with Horace. Nevertheless, as poet seeks out other poetry to replace his *electissima* with someone else's, it is to epic, or epic-like, verse, not to poetry akin to his own, that Catullus turns (at 95.7–8 the *annales Volusi* are compared to the *Zmyrna* of Cinna, to the former's great disadvantage). Horace, because he is apostrophizing his girl, can only use the lyric of forgiveness as a gesture of change, when proposing the renunciation of iambic verse. Perhaps, too, this disavowal of past performance can be seen in Horace's use of the meter of Alcaeus to demonstrate an aversion from Stesichorus and from the *tristia* for which he must make amends. In sum, Catullus can cleverly fulfill his mistress's vow by substituting a bad poet's bad epic for his calumniating iambs. Horace can complete his recantation by changing his tune, as it were, within his own putative poetic production, from iamb to lyric, from Stesichorean slander to Alcaic love-song.

The second Catullan poem that powerfully influenced Horace here is 42, one of his wittiest and most famous. It consists of an address to hendecasyllables, in hendecasyllabic meter, asking them to take the initiative themselves to demand back their writing tablets, which a "base adulteress" (*moecha turpis*, 3) refuses to turn over to the speaker. What follows is a miniature drama in which the speaker takes the lead in putting the personified verses to work to regain their property,[13] and in which we learn a great deal about the whore by indirection, as we did about the *puella* in poem 36, even though there the lackluster, overwritten verses of the *annales Volusi* are apostrophized. The hendecasyllables in 42 first must learn who the creature is (7–12):

> . . . illa quam videtis,
> turpe incedere, mimice ac moleste
> ridentem catuli ore Gallicani.
> circumsistite eam, et reflagitate   10
> "moecha putida, redde codicillos,
> redde, putida moecha, codicillos!"

She whom you see strutting repulsively along, grinning annoyingly the
way a mime-actress would, with the muzzle of a Gallic whelp.
Surround her and demand back from her: (10) "Stinking adulteress,
give back our writing-tablets, give back, stinking adulteress, our
writing-tablets."

The first *flagitatio*, in which the speaker-poet and his creatures join in shouting their demands, has no positive result. So, in the hope of at least bringing a blush "from the iron face of the dog" (*ferreo canis . . . ore*, 17), they pursue the invective by repeating the same lines in a higher voice, as if iteration and increased volume will join with the words themselves magically to effect the desired end. When this effort, too, fails, the only recourse is a change of style, on which the poem ends (21–24):

> sed nil proficimus, nihil movetur.
> mutanda est ratio modusque nobis,
> siquid proficere amplius potestis:
> "pudica et proba, redde codicillos."

> But we're making no headway. She isn't moved at all. We must change
> our method and mode, if you can somehow gain a better issue:
> "Chaste and upright, give back our writing-tablets."

Alteration of tone, illustrated in the brilliant assonantal leap from *putida*
to *pudica*, when the *moecha* now hears what the speaker imagines that
she will like, even though his veracity is questionable, produces a laugh
for the reader sharing in the entertainment. The outcome of the "plot" is
never revealed.

In C. 1.16 Horace reveals his debt to this tour de force in ways both
particular and general. The most specific reference occurs in the last
three lines, which offer a canny commentary on the parallel three lines in
Catullus (C. 1.16.25–28):

> . . . nunc ego mitibus
> mutare quaero tristia, dum mihi
>   fias recantatis amica
>   opprobriis animumque reddas.

A form of the verb *muto* initiates the antepenultimate line in each poem.
In the final verses, Catullus's *proba* is absorbed into, and suffers witty
metamorphosis through, *opprobriis*, and the verb *reddere*, which appears six times in Catullus's twenty-four lines, most pointedly as the
poem's next-to-last word, gains even more prominence in Horace for its
final position.[14]

We will probably never know what influence the palinodes of Stesichorus exerted on Horace as he wrote (the one surviving fragment offers little help). But Catullus's poem we have before us, and the weight the earlier poet carries is important to trace, if only to clarify the differences
between the two. The assimilation of *proba* into *opprobriis* can serve as
synecdoche for more general observations. Catullus's adjective, though a
clever way of telling the *moecha* what she is not, reverses the *opprobria*,
the insults that he and his cohort of invective lines have hurled at her until this point in the poem. Whatever the diverse ways in which the listener
within the poem and the reader outside may interpret the final line, it
serves as a retraction of what has been said before. In other words, it is a
form of palinode. The miracle of Catullus's poem is that it is at once an
invective poem and a recantation, however parodic. The change in the
content and tone of the spoken addresses to the *moecha* serves to illustrate the typological distinctions. The mutation of one, over the course
of the poem, anticipates the mutation of the other.

Horace also ends on a speculative note: Will the addressee give back her
soul to the speaker any more than the adulteress will return the writing

tablets? By turning to lyric as the vehicle for his poem, Horace makes a gesture that Catullus ignores. Whatever the intellectual tergiversations of 42, its sweep remains hendecasyllabic, which is to say that, whatever the apparent change of tone at the end, the framework of invective remains. By writing in lyric that specifically replaces an iambic past, Horace makes it clear in generic terms that his recantation takes palpable form in its means of expression. When Catullus uses *modus* at the end of his poem, he is attending to the manner in which he is performing, to the tone of his utterance. Horace, in line 2 of his ode, expands, varies, and enriches this same word in offering to his girl the opportunity to dispose of his negative iambs. For him, the *modus* spells the "finale" of an ill-conceived poetic adventure. But it also suggests that the end of one poetic mode is the beginning of another, one that may have a happier outcome.

Horace himself, in epode 17, offers further commentary on the relationship of the two poems that furnishes as well a direct transition between them. We come in on the protagonist at the mercy of the witch Canidia. He prays that she stop torturing him, admits that he was wrong in questioning her power, and promises expiation. Her reply, which concludes the poem, offers him little hope, one reason perhaps being that sarcasm permeates his attempt to mollify her, an attempt that flaunts its own mendacity (*Epodes* 17.37–45):

> effare: iussas cum fide poenas luam,
> paratus expiare, seu poposceris
> centum iuvencos, sive mendaci lyra
> voles sonare: "tu pudica, tu proba   40
> perambulabis astra sidus aureum."
> infamis Helenae Castor offensus vice
> fraterque magni Castoris victi prece
> adempta vati reddidere lumina:
> et tu—potes nam—solve me dementia.   45

Speak out: ready to make expiation, I will faithfully pay the penalties you order, whether you will demand a hundred bullocks, or whether you will wish to resound on lying lyre: "You, chaste, you, upright, (40) will parade, as a golden constellation, among the stars." Castor, angered by the circumstances of Helen's defamation, and the brother of mighty Castor, won over by prayer, gave sight, which they had taken away, back to the bard. So do you—for the power is yours— release me from my madness. (45)

Another of Horace's ancient commentators, Pseudo-Acro, in his comment on the opening line of C. 1.16, quotes lines 42–44 as offering explicit explanation of the parallel to Stesichorus that Horace leaves the reader to assume as intellectual background for his ode. But the direct notice of Catullus 42 in line 40 confirms not only that the epode looks backward to Catullus's poem, but that *C.* 1.16 does so as well.[15] Catullus seems as primary a touchstone on which Horace tests his ingenuity as Stesichorus.

The speaker's consideration of the "lying lyre" (*mendaci lyra*) brings to the surface the prevarication at the end of 42 of Catullus's persona, who flatters his subject into believing what he has led us to understand is an untruth. The lyre is mendacious on two counts. First, it utters lies. Second, it is false symbolically, giving vent to lyric statement—"You parade through the heavens as a golden constellation"—when in fact its utterance is in the iambic tradition.[16] Yet the mention of *lyra* also duly serves as another means of transition between Catullus 42 and *C.* 1.16, because, in this tripartite progression, by the time that we reach the ode, we do in fact have a true lyric expression that puts behind it both Catullus's invective and the epode's less than candid pretense at lyric discourse within an iambic context.

The epode mediates between Catullus 42 and *C.* 1.16 in another way. There has been much debate about the root meaning of the name Canidia. Perhaps Horace had several etymologies in mind, all of which resonate in the poems where she is mentioned.[17] But in the context of epode 17 and its Catullan heritage, none stands out more pointedly than a connection with *canis* ("dog"). Horace's mining of 42.24 at *Epodes* 17.40 reminds us that the chief characteristic of the *moecha*, when confronted by the speaker and his powerful verse-allies, is her dog-like face. At line 9, we remember, she is "grinning with the muzzle of a Gallic whelp" (*ridentem catuli ore Gallicani*), and at 17, the hendecasyllables try to elicit a blush "from the iron face of the dog" (*ferreo canis . . . ore*)—in vain, of course, because she lacks both modesty and its close companion, shame.

But there is no figure in ancient literature with whom the attribute "dog-faced" is more strikingly associated than with Helen of Troy, strikingly because such a characteristic is so at odds with her physical beauty. In all four Homeric appearances of the analogy, Helen is speaking of herself. At *Iliad* 6.344 and 356 she describes herself to Hector as a dog (κύων), and at both 3.180, as she talks with Priam, and *Odyssey* 4.145, with her husband Menelaus, she sees herself as "dog-eyed" (κυνῶπις), which is to say as someone visibly lacking in shame.[18]

Implicitly, therefore, in epode 17, because of the speaker's self-equation with Stesichorus at 42–44, Canidia serves as a figure for Helen, in however perverse a form. In particular, she is able to cure his "blindness" if he

voices the correct apology. And the whole of C. 1.16, as we have
seen, is on one level a further working out of the analogy between the
speaker as Stesichorus and the addressee as Helen, more beautiful than
her beautiful mother because, among other reasons, half divine. The invective tone of Catullus 42 and epode 17 is purged by the time that we
reach C. 1.16, with its detached rumination on the negative capabilities
of anger framed by the warmth of its request to the *filia pulcrior*. Nevertheless, Catullus 42 is on a par with epode 17 as a source for the later
Horace's inspiration, as dog-faced Helen suffers, in C. 1.16, a final,
ameliorating transformation from *moecha* to *amica*, a transformation
also reflected in the extraordinary poetry that documents this metamorphosis.

Helen as *moecha* also appears in another Catullan poem that has
bearing on the first of the Horatian triad we have been examining. The
only direct mention of Helen in the Catullan corpus occurs at 68.87–88,
in connection with her rape and the ensuing conflict:

> nam tum Helenae raptu primores Argivorum
> coeperat ad sese Troia ciere viros.

> For then, because of the rape of Helen, Troy had begun to summon to
> itself the chief men of the Greeks.

The particular context for warring is elaborated at 101–4:

> ad quam tum properans fertur <lecta> undique pubes
> Graeca penetralis deseruisse focos,
> ne Paris abducta gavisus libera moecha
> otia pacato degeret in thalamo.

> At that time youth of Greece, [chosen] from everywhere about, is said
> to have hastened to [Troy], leaving behind their homes' hearths, lest
> Paris, enjoying the adulteress he had abducted, pass unconstrained
> leisure in a wedding-chamber at peace.

One of the key words here for students of Catullus is *otia*, because the
poet uses it so memorably in poem 51. There, as we have seen, it stands
out for its appearance in triple anaphora in a concluding stanza that is
unique with Catullus vis-à-vis his Greek original (13–16):

> otium, Catulle, tibi molestum est:
> otio exsultas nimiumque gestis:
> otium et reges prius et beatas
> perdidit urbes.

> Leisure, Catullus, is troublesome to you. In your leisure you run riot
> and act uncontrollably. Before this, leisure has destroyed both kings
> and wealthy cities.

Catullus here posits a scenario, familiar in his poetry, where the detached, percipient speaker addresses a "Catullus" so deeply involved in a
situation that he does not appreciate its hazards. In this case, it is his
own adulterous relationship with Lesbia that poses a danger.[19] The poem
as a whole, appropriately a translation from Sappho, both deepens the
threatening physicality of its Aeolic model and ends with a dynamic act
of abstraction that has the effect of hammering home to the naïve addressee the peril that he is in. The speaker's passionate dispassion should
not only bring "Catullus" to his senses but also establish a similar distance for one presently "acting without restraint."

The references to *otium* in the two Catullan poems serve as commentary on each other. As befits its powerful, essential act of generalization,
poem 51 leaves in a deliberately vague plural who, or what, might be the
"kings and wealthy cities," destroyed for becoming engulfed in ominous
circumstances akin to those with which the "Catullus" of poem 51 is involved. Poem 68 presents an obvious example. It is the moments of adulterous leisure shared by Paris and Helen—and *otium* and its adjective
otiosus are elsewhere, as we have seen, associated by Catullus with
erotic enterprise—that will cause the downfall of a specific king, Priam,
and his particular city, Troy.[20] This is the frightening inheritance of the
protagonist of poem 51.

Beatas urbes may anticipate mention of *altis urbibus* in the subsequent poem (C. 1.16.18), just as the latter's central notion, *irae* (C.
1.16.9 and 17), may hark back to *otium* as Horace's abstraction of
choice to exemplify a vice that can destroy cities (we remember that
"the angry fleet of Achilles," *iracunda . . . classis Achillei*, is the final instrument of Troy's downfall in the preceding poem, C. 1.15.33–34). But
it is primarily C. 1.15 that resonates with our Catullan poems. Take, for
instance, Nereus's opening words to the Trojan adventurer (C.
1.15.5–8):

> . . . "mala ducis avi domum
> quam multo repetet Graecia milite
> coniurata tuas rumpere nuptias
>   et regnum Priami vetus."

Lines 5–7 could serve as summary of the excerpts we quoted earlier
from Catullus 68, and the final phrase replaces Catullus's *reges* (51.15)
while looking specifically to Troy's aged ruler. Moreover, the subsequent

description of Paris's unmartial lyre-playing also glances back to Catullus (C. 1.15.14–18):

> . . . "grataque feminis
> inbelli cithara carmina divides   15
>   nequiquam thalamo gravis
>
> hastas et calami spicula Cnosii
> vitabis."

Horace divides, and varies, Catullus's *pacato thalamo* (68.104), repeating the second word, which he uses here for the only time in his career, and replacing *pacato* with *inbelli*, the peaceful wedding chamber, soon to be disrupted by war, with the unwarlike, feminized Paris and his lyre, in a setting more suitable for masculine heroes and epic deeds.[21]

Finally, we have the link between Catullus's four interacting uses of *otium* in poem 51 and the *ingrato otio* with which Nereus overwhelms the speedy winds in the opening stanza of C. 1.15, thus setting the narrative stage for his speech. The synchysis at 3–4—*ingrato celeris . . . otio / ventos*—suggests that winds and quiet are incompatible entities. Leisure is unpleasant to the winds because it is unwonted and goes against the grain of their nature. But, in the larger context of C. 1.15, and especially when examined against the Catullan background, the phrase *ingrato otio* looks also to Paris, Helen, and Troy. The *otium* of calm at sea is "unpleasant" to Paris because it postpones the *otium* of the future at Troy, the time of "songs pleasant for women," of leisure for love without limit. But the reader is expected to remember Catullus's *libera otia* and their potentially ruinous results, some of which Horace goes on to detail.

For Catullus, *otium* prepares the way for, or merges with, destructive sexuality. What begins as *gratum* may soon become its opposite. We think, for instance, of the *ingrato amore*, the thankless, unrequited, quasi-deadly love from which the speaker prays for relief at 76.6. Some of this same tone spills over into the opening of Horace's ode. The *otium* of Paris and Helen will presumably become *gratum* when they reach Troy, but the time of bliss will be fleeting. The adulterous journey from Sparta, the mise en scène for Horace's great ode, will elicit in response another journey from Greece to Troy, one this time bent on anger and revenge. If the *ingrato otio* of unexpected calm at sea leads to a time of (*gratum*) *otium* at Troy, this will in turn prove as destructive as it is short-lived, a still point that mimics the ill-boding lull from which C. 1.15 takes its start, with the sea god's frenzied prophecy powerfully anticipating the fervid deeds of which it tells.

We have previously discussed the further meanings of *otium* for Catullus and Horace, especially in connection with the idea of poetic rivalry.[22] Here I would like only to take note of the one moment where Horace is deliberately alluding directly to the end of Catullus 51, namely the opening stanzas of *C.* 2.16, mentioned earlier:

> Otium divos rogat in patenti
> prensus Aegaeo, simul atra nubes
> condidit lunam neque certa fulgent
>   sidera nautis,
>
> otium bello furiosa Thrace,   5
> otium Medi pharetra decori,
> Grosphe, non gemmis neque purpura ve-
>   nale nec auro.

> Someone trapped in the open Aegean asks the gods for peace, as soon as a black cloud has buried the moon and the sure stars do not gleam for sailors, Thrace wild in war asks for peace, (5) the Parthians, handsome with their quiver, ask for peace, not to be bought, Grosphus, with gems or purple or gold.

What follows is a poem not on the destructiveness of Catullan *otium* but on the abstraction as a necessary form of calm and quiet, defined here by Horace as lack of external ambition and as an unshaken sense of inner security in which the possessor lives a life-style that is "slender," whether that be illustrated in the modesty of one's exterior presentation—a gleaming saltcellar on a slender (*tenui*, 14) board—or of one's interior simplicity and lack of elaboration, the slender (*tenuem*, 38) spirit of the Greek muse that the speaker-poet can claim as his own, the spiritual tranquility that lies at the core of Horace's creativity.

By deliberately beginning where Catullus ends, by placing a triple anaphora at his poem's start, Horace pointedly asks us to read the two poems as a sequence and therefore to watch the differences between himself and his predecessor. Catullus's extraordinary gesture of originality in his concluding stanza, a final breaking from the Sapphic tradition, only adumbrated in the preceding segment of the poem, that serves to comment on it from the double vision of lover as poet and poet as lover, is picked up by Horace in an equally astonishing burst of originality. This novelty is highlighted by the challenge Horace offers Catullus in the words of a speaker who examines the meaning of *otium* from a series of new angles, foreign to the earlier poet's ordinary usage.

Both poems are meditations on self-distance. Catullus pulls himself aloof in his final stanza to ponder the potential disaster facing the "Catullus" that he apostrophizes, imagined to be suffering from the same symptoms whose ruinous possibilities he has just clinically described, with the help of Sappho. Horace detaches himself from Catullus's detachment, and holds up the poem not as an act of self-consciousness or of candid self-revelation, but as a mirror of Grosphus to Grosphus. An already self-aware speaker lectures Grosphus, the "javelin," whose aims in life are questioned and revalued as the poem evolves from general to particular.[23] For Catullus, *otium* activates a combination of eroticism and creativity whose intensity can readily turn deadly. For Horace, at least here, *otium* is the counterbalance to energy misused, the indwelling calm and self-mastery that serves as one defining characteristic of the Horatian muse.[24]

Taken together, the two poems form an extended chiasmus that pivots on the two sets of anaphora of the word *otium*, which at once converge and diverge. Catullus looks first at the details of physical symptoms, culminating in the terrifying, non-Sapphic phrase, "My eyes are covered by twin night" (*gemina teguntur / lumina nocte*). He then in his final, novel quatrain expands particular to universal, one person's private emotional drama to history's more general sweep, with the individual "Catullus" blending by synecdoche into the larger domain of kings and wealthy cities. With Horace we enter a world where blackness and fury, duly reminiscent of Catullus but now placed away from humankind in nature's celestial doings, merely typify the threatened existence of the misguidedly ambitious for whom *otium* becomes a necessity when their lives are in peril. Though Grosphus is apostrophized in the second stanza, impersonal generality largely prevails through the course of the ode. It is only in the final stanzas that universal slides into particular, and the chiasmus is completed as Grosphus and the speaker take over and bring the poem to an end, Grosphus with his riches, his interlocutor with his slim muse and aloof stance.[25]

Let me in conclusion turn back to our Horatian trio to look at one last notice by Horace of Catullus, this time from *C.* 1.17 back to Catullus 35. The only occasions in each poet's oeuvre where the phrase *inicere manus* occurs are at 35.9–10 and *C.* 1.17.26 respectively. The two appearances of this Roman technical sign for possession ("to lay hands on") seem diverse. In the first situation, a girl is imagined throwing her hands around the neck of Caecilius to delay his setting out to visit the speaker, something the apostrophized papyrus is expected to command. In the second, Tyndaris is to be shielded, in the speaker's sequestered environment, from Cyrus and the violent hands that he might otherwise lay on her. Each poem has a trio of protagonists. In Catullus, the narrator and his stand-in, the papyrus-poem, want Caecilius to come to them, though his girl holds him back. In Horace, the speaker invites Helen to join him in a setting that forbids Cyrus entry.

But one factor links these invitation poems gracefully together: both are concerned with poets and poetry. The first line of poem 35 represents Caecilius as *poeta tener*, a writer of love-poetry who is himself a lover, perhaps with implications of femininity. He is in the process of writing a *Dindymi domina* (14), or *Magna Mater* (18), which, though unfinished, has the goddess of love inspiring it, if we can judge from the adverb *venuste* (17). Catullus acknowledges both its quality and its erotic force by claiming for the girl, who has fallen in love with Caecilius because of the charm of his verse, an intelligence greater than Sappho's muse (*Sapphica puella / musa doctior*, 16–17). But if the *puella* surpasses one of the masters of archaic Greek lyric, presumably we are meant to understand that "Catullus" outdoes both the girl and her Greek poetic touchstone in his understanding of, affection for, and parallelism with Caecilius. After all, his poem 63 offers bountiful evidence that the "mistress of Dindymum" also fascinated him as a topic,[26] as did its central figure Attis, who is twice called *tener*, like the poet who writes about him.[27] Both poetry and, presumably, sexuality render it appropriate that Caecilius make the journey to Catullus and thereby confirm their equivalence.

We may say much the same for Helen and "Horace." She is invited as lover into the poet's world because she is also to some degree an allegory for Greek poetry, singing Anacreon's version of the *Odyssey*'s eroticism. She is taming epic to lyric, as Horace, in the tradition of Stesichorus and Bacchylides, does in *C.* 1.15. But she is also accomplishing her mission in a Latin setting. Her arrival in the Sabine hills hints at something of the lyric poet Horace's accomplishment not only in these three splendid odes but in his total lyric corpus as well, as he leads "Aeolian song to Italian measures" (*Aeolium carmen ad Italos / . . . modos*, *C.* 3.30.13–14). This is exactly what the singer Helen will do, as she quaffs the harmless wine of Lesbos in the shadow of Lucretilis and Ustica, for she, after all, is Horace as well as his recreation.

CHAPTER FOUR

Virgil

We move now from the realm of Greek myth to contemporary Rome, from one of Homer's most extraordinary creations to Virgil, five years Horace's senior and another master poet of the Augustan age. It may seem at first paradoxical to devote a chapter to Virgil when dealing with the influence of Catullus on Horace, but the three odes that the latter addresses to his friend, C. 1.3, 1.24, and 4.12, all exemplify a principle we have found operative elsewhere in dealing with the patterns of Horace's allusivity. He will often make direct, or indirect, mention of one poet—Alcaeus, say, or Sappho, or Stesichorus—while at the same time drawing on Catullus, often elaborately. In the case of the three poems offered to Virgil, apostrophe makes the presence of the poet, to whom immediate attention is given, particularly forceful. He happens in this case to be not only an acquaintance of Horace but also another of Rome's greatest practitioners of the poet's craft. He, more than most others, would presumably appreciate the extraordinary finesse of his friend's art.

Let me begin with the latest to be issued, C. 4.12, published around 13 BCE, some six years after Virgil's death, but when written we can only guess. Horace would have us imagine his friend alive, with the ode serving as an invitation from one poet to the other to come and drink the lyricist's wine. The poem has aroused some controversy because Horace's proclamation of Virgil as "hanger-on of noble youth" (*iuvenum nobilium cliens*, 15) and mention of his "zest for cash" (*studium lucri*, 25) seem in dubious taste, especially since the addressee would not have been alive at the time of the ode's publication. But humor permeates the poem. It presumably brings with it the self-knowledge that is often its companion and serves as the tonal complement to the wine-bibbing that will stave off, at least momentarily, the inexorable pressures of time:

Iam veris comites, quae mare temperant,
inpellunt animae lintea Thraciae,
iam nec prata rigent nec fluvii strepunt
    hiberna nive turgidi.

nidum ponit Ityn flebiliter gemens   5
infelix avis et Cecropiae domus

aeternum opprobrium, quod male barbaras
    regum est ulta libidines.

dicunt in tenero gramine pinguium
custodes ovium carmina fistula   10
delectantque deum, cui pecus et nigri
    colles Arcadiae placent.

adduxere sitim tempora, Vergili.
sed pressum Calibus ducere Liberum
si gestis, iuvenum nobilium cliens,   15
    nardo vina merebere.

nardi parvus onyx eliciet cadum,
qui nunc Sulpiciis accubat horreis,
spes donare novas largus amaraque
    curarum eluere efficax.   20

ad quae si properas gaudia, cum tua
velox merce veni: non ego te meis
inmunem meditor tinguere poculis,
    plena dives ut in domo.

verum pone moras et studium lucri   25
nigrorumque memor, dum licet, ignium
misce stultitiam consiliis brevem:
    dulce est desipere in loco.

The breezes of Thrace, companions of spring, who soothe the sea, now billow the sails, now meadows are no longer stiff and streams do not snarl from swelling with a winter's snows. The hapless bird, groaning in her lament for Itys, builds her nest, (5) an undying disgrace to the house of Cecrops because she cruelly avenged the brutish lusts of kings. In the tender grass, the guardians of fattening sheep sing songs on the pipe, (10) and gladden the god who takes pleasure in the flocks and black hills of Arcadia.

The season has aroused thirst, Vergilius. If, my protégé of noble youth, (15) you are anxious to broach Bacchus pressed at Cales, you will win the wine with unguent. A small jar of unguent will entice the cask, which now reclines in Sulpicius's vaults, expansive at giving fresh hopes and adroit at purging the bitterness of cares. (20) If you are in a rush for these festivities, come quickly with your barter. I have no thought, like a wealthy man whose house is full, to dye you, giftless, in

my cups. But put aside delays and ambition for gain, (25) and, mindful
of the blackening flames, while the chance remains, blend fleet folly
with your wit: it is sweet to be, opportunely, unwise.

The poem is about temporality. We find ourselves, in the first stanza,
watching ships at sea as they take advantage of spring's breezes. We listen,
in the second and third quatrains, to the nightingale, as she builds her
nest, and to the music of shepherds' songs that delight Pan. Only in the
fourth stanza, with the appearance of Virgil, do we hear of the thirst that
the season brings, which must be counteracted. If, and only if, the visitor
brings a jar of unguent—the speaker claims not to be "a rich man in an
opulent dwelling"—will he receive wine in return. And with the drinking
of wine, and with the joys that it brings, one can practice the folly, and de-
sipience, that blot out thoughts of the incipient fires that loom for all.

Though the exigencies of time are ever in the poem's background—we
will return later to their prominence as a theme—the plot of the poem is
built around two potential journeys. The first is of Virgil to the speaker's
convivium, the second, which is dependent on a positive reply to the invitation, is the completion of the wine's itinerary that has taken it from
Cales in Campania to Rome's Sulpician warehouses, prepared, finally, to
reach the host's dwelling and to be poured into the goblets that friend
will offer friend.

Horace's wit is ever-present as the two voyages converge. For an instance, the line in which we are introduced to Virgil (13)—*adduxere
sitim tempora, Vergili*—is a forthright bow to the third book of his
Georgics, lines 482–83, where we learn that one of the symptoms of the
devastating Noric plague manifests itself

> . . . ubi ignea venis
> omnibus acta sitis miseros adduxerat artus.

> when the fiery thirst, coursing through all their veins, had caused their
> pitiable limbs to contract.

Horace drolly turns his friend's horrific picture around. For Virgil, thirst
occasions the contraction of the limbs of his diseased animals. For Horace, the season has imported thirst into their midst, but the symptom is
now the object, not the generating subject, and we are dealing not with
the imminence of death, but with its, at least momentary, sequestering.
But just as the compound verb *adduxere* (13) leads quickly to its more
simple form *ducere* (14), so the advent of thirst can be immediately
counteracted by the arrival of Bacchus, who must be escorted to the
gathering.

Wine's advent is also treated to the poet's wit. We begin with the paradox of *pressum . . . Liberum* (14), the "Freer" who has to be "confined"
in order to fulfill his role. Then we move to the jug itself. The verb *eliciet*
(17) reminds us of its use at C. 2.11.21 in connection with the harlot
Lyde, who must be lured from her dwelling to grace another *convivium*,
while *accubat* (18), describing the jug at rest waiting other instructions,
abets the personification.[1]

The phrase *non ego te meis / . . . poculis* (22–23) adds a further dimension by recalling a similar expression at C. 4.9.30–31, *ego te meis /
chartis*. There, *chartae* refer to the poet's writings, which have power to
circumvent the obliterating force of silence, and to immortalize Lollius
and his achievements. But poetry and wine are for Horace ever complementary entities. To drink the speaker's wine, to accept his invitation to
the *convivium*, is to share in his intelligence and his imagination, and,
here, to drink in his thoughts on how to survive, at least briefly, the hazards of time's passage. The verb *tinguere* gives the injunction a diverting
turn. Horace's form of amusement—to "entertain" is one dictionary's
translation of the verb[2]—offers the metaphorical spectacle of his satu-
rating Virgil with wine, perhaps even dyeing him red in the process!
And this leads to the wine-pouring poet's final metaphorical command:
to mingle, at least for the moment, folly with discernment and guid-
ance, so as to produce something *dulce*, the sweet brew that centers its
receiver's thinking on a direct here and now, capable, at least for the period of insobriety, of washing away, in its Lethaean flow, the "bitter-
nesses of care."

It has long been noted that Horace has in mind here the thirteenth
poem of Catullus, a witty invitation to his friend Fabullus to come dine,
as long as he brings the dinner:[3]

> Cenabis bene, mi Fabulle, apud me
> paucis, si tibi di favent, diebus,
> si tecum attuleris bonam atque magnam
> cenam, non sine candida puella
> et vino et sale et omnibus cachinnis.   5
> haec si, inquam, attuleris, venuste noster,
> cenabis bene; nam tui Catulli
> plenus sacculus est aranearum.
> sed contra accipies meros amores
> seu quid suavius elegantiusve est: 10
> nam unguentum dabo, quod meae puellae
> donarunt Veneres Cupidinesque,
> quod tu cum olfacies, deos rogabis,
> totum ut te faciant, Fabulle, nasum.

You will dine well chez moi, my Fabullus, in a few days, if the gods are
good to you, if along with yourself you bring a handsome, large meal,
together with a shimmering girl, and wine and salt and every kind of
laughter. (5) If, I say, you bring these, my charming friend, you will
dine well. For the money-bag of your Catullus is full of spider-webs.
But in return you will receive unadulterated love, or something more
pleasant or choice: (10) for I will give you an unguent that the Venuses
and Cupids gave to my girl. When you give it a sniff, you'll beseech the
gods that they make you all nose.

Both poems are in part built around the language of economics, of
barter and exchange, of monetary give and take, of rich versus poor
and the costly versus the inexpensive. Horace emphasizes the point
with the etymological play between *merebere* and *merx*, which the
fourth-century commentator Tiberius Claudius Donatus connects as
follows: *merere est aliquid mercedis pro labore sumere* ("to earn is to
receive some commodity in return for one's effort").[4] Horace takes up
Catullus's point only to reverse it. Fabullus will receive an unguent so
olefactorily satisfying that he will want to suffer metamorphosis into
the organ of scent itself, if, that is, he brings the dinner and all its trap-
pings, including its wit. Virgil, by contrast, will convey the sweet-
smelling nard-oil, only a tiny jar of it, but that is sufficient to elicit
from his poet-host an abundance of wit in the form of one of ancient
Italy's best wines, stored in a jar and waiting for the command to be
broached.

We are dealing, of course, with questions of value and evaluation.
Catullus's unguent is as much more estimable than the banquet and its
fixtures that Fabullus will need to bring to gain it in response, as Horace's multivalent wine, his literal and metaphoric vintage, is to Virgil's
small container of nard. But we need to look further at how each poet
deals with the rhetorical figure of παρὰ προσδοκίαν, when the opposite
of the reader's expectations comes about. Catullus's poem is built around
this device, most regularly found in comedy. The general notion—that an
unguent is more than proper recompense for a magnificent dinner—is
fleshed out with particulars in such a way that our presumptions are always being humorously undercut. If the gods are good to Fabullus, he
will bring the whole dinner. Catullus's wallet is full, full of spider-webs.
He will receive in return something pure (*meros*), but not the wine that
Fabullus (or the reader of Catullus[5]) might expect, but an abstraction,
amores. Finally, and funniest of all, we wait until the last word of the
poem to find out the greatest improbability—that Fabullus will want to
suffer mutation from his present self into one grand example of synecdoche, a single, total organ of sensation.

The most extraordinary aspect of Horace's own wit here is the transference of Catullus's special verbal playfulness to his own poem, but with its significance extended. The earlier poet's lexical cleverness depends on Fabullus's, and the reader's, understanding for its appreciation. Understanding of Horace's facetiousness depends not only on Virgil's, and our, amusement at his wit, but also on his, and our, relishing the dialogue between poets that makes its richness possible. Not only is Horace's own poem structured around an event presented παρὰ προσδοκίαν—that a small container of unguent will lure forth an expensive jar of wine—but its relation to Catullus's thirteenth poem has its own element of the unexpected. Catullus's miraculous unguent, with its powerful, climactic effect, is diminished, in Horace's elegant verses, to a small receptacle that will lure forth the rich wine of the poet's creativity.

Perhaps Virgil might find unexpected any implicit accusatory tone in such phrases as *iuvenum nobilium cliens* (15). If so, it is lightened by the honor Horace pays him by addressing him in a poem that would allow full play to his own rich awareness of conversations among poets, of the exchanges of Horace with him that dot the lyric poet's corpus, but also of the give-and-take between Horace and Catullus in which Virgil, too, plays a part and which adds a vital level of play to a poem where humor is a crucial comrade to wine in helping to deflect thoughts of mortality.

Catullus can also be discerned behind Horace's formulation of time's negative aspects. At 68.18, for example, Catullus describes the love-goddess Venus as she "who mixes sweet bitterness with cares" (*quae dulcem curis miscet amaritiem*). Horace separates Catullus's powerful oxymoron into two segments. The first is found at 19–20, where he speaks of the *amara curarum* that his wine will wash away, the second at 27–28, when his own oxymoronic mixture (*misce*) of folly and sagacity brings a sweet (*dulcem*) result. In the process, Horace reminds us, for one final time in his lyric corpus, of how regularly he both absorbs and deflects the focus on sexuality that dominates much of Catullus's poetry into his own writing by regularly contextualizing any reference to it in settings such as the *convivium*. By so doing, Horace once again tempers Catullus's eroticism in favor, here, of a bond between poets, adjusting to temporality's varied harshness through the amiability of wine.

But Catullus makes a still more dramatic entrance into Horace's ode by means of its initial verse. *Iam ver* are likewise the opening words of what we have already seen to be one of Horace's favorite Catullan poems, 46. The odist strengthens the notice, first, by the anaphora of *iam*, a figure, we recall, that Catullus uses, also with *iam*, twice in the space of eight lines. Horace also immediately adds the word *comites* that appears in Catullus's line 9 as he bids farewell to his "sweet gatherings of comrades" (*dulces comitum . . . coetus*). It is as if Horace wished that Virgil—and we, his readers—have in mind, as he and we begin his final apostrophe to his fellow poet, a summary essence of one of their great predecessor's small masterpieces.

There, as we have seen, Catullus brilliantly correlates spring and mind, the arrival of the season's gentle freshness and its effect on the poet, which is to contemplate his flight to the cities of Asia and thence home. Horace's allusion signals us that he, too, is embarking on a journey-poem, and that its originality is partially to be observed from, and measured against, Catullus's accomplishment. Horace guides us on a mental itinerary from Thrace to Athens and Arcadia in which we take note of spring breezes, a nightingale's song, and the piping of shepherds, before tracing the anticipated advent of Virgil, and wine, to the speaker's abode. But entering each of the initial three stanzas is a somber note, which contrasts with the eager energy with which Catullus's speaker addresses Catullus and prepares us for the fact that Horace's progress will be both literal and figurative, taking us from place to place but also on our human course from birth to the funeral pyre.

In the first stanza, our reading of Catullus schools us to expect the Zephyr, wind from the west that silences heaven's madness with its gentle breezes. Instead, Horace paradoxically peoples his spring with *animae Thraciae*, gusts from Thrace. This would mean for the ancient reader the north wind, bringing with it not reinvigorating warmth but a furtherance of winter's chill. Perhaps, too, Horace would have us remember his own use of *Thracio . . . vento* at *C.* 1.25.11–12, where it is associated with Thrace's river Hebrus, "companion of winter" (*hiemis sodali*, 19), to help form a picture of the courtesan Lydia as she is imagined soon to pass ungracefully into desiccated old age.[6] Catullus 46 dwells on spring alone and its effects on nature, and on the poet looking at himself. For Horace, by contrast, the season carries within itself the incipience of its own demise, containing, as well as anticipating, winter to come.

Death and birth cohabit the second quatrain. The nightingale places her nest by recurring instincts in the spring, but Horace would have us also recall the ever-enduring scandal of Procne's tale of lust, mutilation, vengeance, and metamorphosis. Here, too, Catullus plays a small but significant part. Songs that the poet chants at the death of his brother will be as continuous as the love he bears him (65.11–14):

> . . . at certe semper amabo,
>   semper maesta tua carmina morte canam,
> qualia sub densis ramorum concinit umbris
>   Daulias, absumpti fata gemens Ityli.

> But certainly I will always love you, I will always sing sad songs for
> your death, like what the woman of Daulis sings under the branches'
> thick shade, mourning the death of Itylus torn from her.[7]

Catullus's is the only previous mention of Itylus/Itys in preserved Latin
literature. The iteration of the name coupled with the proximity of
gemens in each case, the only uses of the participle by each poet, assures
a direct bow by Horace to his predecessor. He thus associates spring not
only with the eternally tragic story of Procne, living forever as a swallow,
but also with another poet's unceasing singing of that tale, as he mourns
his own familial misfortune. Once again beneath Horace's dialogue with
Virgil lies his colloquy with Catullus, on this occasion reinforcing the
note of sadness and loss that runs through the ode.

Finally we have the third stanza, devoted to the music of man, the human singing of shepherds that brings pleasure to Pan. Yet there are hints
that Poussin's tombstone motto—*Et in Arcadia ego*—can be applicable to
our reading of Horace. The poet's use of *nigri* to describe the hills of Arcadia anticipates the adjective's reappearance shortly later as attribute of
death's black flames (*nigrorum ignium*, 26).[8] We might note also the most
recent appearance of Pan, *deus Arcadiae*, in Latin literature, at line 26 of
Virgil's tenth and final eclogue. There we find him at the point of climax
of a list of visitors who have come to mourn with the lovesick Gallus,
whose comfort lies in the Arcadians' chanting his sad tale to the accompaniment of their reed pipes (*Eclogues* 10.31–34):

> tristis at ille "tamen cantabitis, Arcades," inquit
> "montibus haec vestris; soli cantare periti
> Arcades. o mihi tum quam molliter ossa quiescant,
> vestra meos olim si fistula dicat amores!"

> But in sadness he speaks: "Nevertheless, Arcadians, you will sing this
> tale to your mountains. You alone are skilled at singing. O how gently
> my bones then would rest if one day your pipe would sing of my
> loves!"

Once more, melancholy lies scarcely beneath the surface in the music of
spring that Horace conjures up for his friend to ponder.

Thus Virgil again enters Horace's poem, this time with a reminder of
how poignant the bittersweetness of pastoral lament can be, especially in
a season of renewal. But it is Catullus, ever in the background, who
helps us embark on this journey on which, for Horace, spring brings
with it the presentiment that death is in the offing. It is through reminders of Catullus's own suffering, at the hands of the fickle goddess of

love, or from his association of himself with death, as he constantly grieves for his brother just as the nightingale ever laments her son's loss, that we see with clearer eyes Horace's own forebodings, to be shared with his poet friend and for a moment to be surmounted by them both. And, finally, it is with the help of Catullus and his poetry, by witty consideration of its wit, that Horace musters the humor that makes the drinking of his poetic wine, now as then, such a bracing counteractive to time's demands.

As we work backward, the second ode that Horace addresses to Virgil is C. 1.24. It is both *epicedium* and *consolatio*, a lament for the passing of Quintilius Varus, a critic of consequence and Horace's friend, and an act of condolence to the great poet who was likewise the deceased's intimate:

> Quis desiderio sit pudor aut modus
> tam cari capitis? praecipe lugubris
> cantus, Melpomene, cui liquidam pater
>   vocem cum cithara dedit.
>
> ergo Quintilium perpetuus sopor   5
> urget; cui Pudor et Iustitiae soror
> incorrupta Fides nudaque Veritas
>   quando ullum inveniet parem?
>
> multis ille bonis flebilis occidit,
> nulli flebilior quam tibi, Vergili.   10
> tu frustra pius, heu, non ita creditum
>   poscis Quintilium deos.
>
> quid? si Threicio blandius Orpheo
> auditam moderere arboribus fidem,
> num vanae redeat sanguis imagini,   15
>   quam virga semel horrida
>
> non lenis precibus fata recludere
> nigro conpulerit Mercurius gregi?
> durum: sed levius fit patientia
>   quidquid corrigere est nefas.   20

What restraint or control should there be to yearning for so dear a person? Teach sad songs, Melpomene, to whom the father gave crystalline voice along with the lyre. And so unceasing sleep presses upon Quintilius. (5) When will Restraint and untainted Trust, sister of

Justice, and naked Truth find anyone his equal? He died wept by many
good men, wept by none more than by you, Virgil. (10) With vain
piety you ask the gods for Quintilius, alas not entrusted to life on such
terms. So? Even were you to control the lyre, heeded by the trees, more
seductively than Thracian Orpheus, would life then return to the
empty shade (15) that Mercury, ungentle to open the gates of death to
prayer, with his dread wand has once penned amid his black flock? It
is hard, but whatever is wrong to alter is more easily borne with
patience. (20)

Horace's valediction against immoderate mourning is addressed to a
poet who had not long since written of the mythic power of the Orphic
voice to civilize and, nearly, to charm life from death.[9] It would no doubt
be a hard truth for the author of the *Georgics* to accept, but mere human
poets, for all their ability to immortalize in words the deeds of a man
worthy of continued renown, cannot bring life back to a body claimed
by death. Mercury, death's banker, knows no bartering for his merchan-
dise. It has been loaned to the world of the quick for a set term, and on
set terms, only.[10]

Catullus again has a share in helping us to clarify some of the particular points that Horace is making. The phrase *tam cari capitis*, for instance, prominent because of the enjambment whose sense is concluded
at the opening of the poem's second line, comes from Catullus 68. I give
its immediate context (119–24):

> nam nec tam carum confecto aetate parenti
>   una caput seri nata nepotis alit,   120
> qui, cum divitiis vix tandem inventus avitis
>   nomen testatas intulit in tabulas,
> impia derisi gentilis gaudia tollens
>   suscitat a cano volturium capiti.

Not so dear [as Protesilaus was to Laodamia] to her father, undone
with age, is the head of his late-born grandchild whom his only
daughter nurses, (120) found only just in time [as heir to] his
grandfather's wealth, when he has entered his name in a duly
witnessed will. By doing away with the perverted joy of a kinsman
now made a butt of jokes, he removes the vulture from [the old man's]
hoary head.

Catullus's graphic simile is part of a series of three that reinterpret and
qualify the depth of Laodamia's passion for Protesilaus. These particular
lines take a turn familiar to readers of Catullus, where love's vehemence

is viewed in terms of strong, but non-erotic, bonds between family members. The detailing lends the simile special force, as does the inclusory effect of the reflection of *carum caput* in *cano capiti*. This repetition highlights the relationship between grandfather and grandson through figuration, since *caput* serves as both synecdoche and metonymy, standing at once for the human body and for the life that animates it.[11]

Horace accepts the figuration and places it as a prominent reminder of a Catullan poem, his admiration for which is reflected in many adaptations. But this prominence also sets into relief two major differences here between the two poets. The first is the not-unexpected elimination of any overt sexual intimations in the poem. If *desiderium* has erotic overtones, they are highly nuanced. Second, the implication that one *caput* both contains life for itself and sustains that of another is absent from Horace's vivid portrayal to Virgil of blood leaving Quintilius's body once and for all. The economic imagery of barter and exchange, which we have traced in the word *creditum* and in the name Mercurius, can be seen as a metaphorical reflection of the literal riches that, in Catullus's analogy, a child's birth can keep within a family. But for Horace, the body's value is fleeting at best, and subject to reclaiming by Mercury when its time is up. Here, at least, there is no relief from the exigencies of death.

The fifth poem in the Catullan corpus, a poem that we have already seen to be much beloved by Horace,[12] is also richly influential here, especially with its memorable differentiation between daily and human time (4–6):

> soles occidere et redire possunt:
> nobis cum semel occidit brevis lux,
> nox est perpetua una dormienda.

> Suns can set and return. When once our brief light has set, it is one continuous night of sleeping.

As often in the relationship between the two poets, it is not so much one impressive image or striking lexical usage that links work with work as a plethora of vocabulary scattered throughout a poem. Here we begin with the transformation of *nox est perpetua una dormienda* into *perpetuus sopor urget*, one eternal obliteration of day and light, through which we must remain asleep with senses annihilated, into the continuous oppression of Sleep, which anticipates the black flock among which we are cribbed by the rod of Mercury, the psychopomp. The appearance of *occidit* at line 9 might be understood simply as "die" if the recurrence of the words *redeat* and *semel* shortly later, in adjacent lines (15–16) as

they are in Catullus, did not give it also the further resonance of "set."
No blood will return to his now-insubstantiated image, once his body
has dipped into the darkness of death.

Nevertheless, however much the poems overlap, the final gist of Horace's consolatory ode is quite other than what Catullus proposes. The
earlier poet's meditation on life's brief passage precedes a plea for num-
berless kisses, whose continuous counting will magically countervene the
gossip of the loveless aged as well as the speaker's apothegm on human
transcience. Horace, by contrast, is facing death squarely and making
Catullus's concise moment of abstraction his central, all-consuming
theme. For Catullus, frenzied sexuality may temporarily obscure time's
lethal presence. For Horace, once death has arrived, there is no escaping
its importunity.

There remain two further poems of Catullus to discuss in relation to
Horace's ode, both from the segment of the Catullan corpus written in
elegiac couplets. The first of these, 96, follows a by-now-familiar pattern
in which reference, or even address to, one poet, in this case Virgil,
cloaks the enriching presence of Catullus. This model here takes a novel
turn because the poem in question is itself a consolation directed to
another poet, on this occasion Licinius Calvus, grieving for the loss of
his wife:

> Si quicquam mutis gratum acceptumve sepulcris
>   accidere a nostro, Calve, dolore potest,
> quo desiderio veteres renovamus amores
>   atque olim missas flemus amicitias,
> certe non tanto mors immatura dolori est   5
>   Quintiliae, quantum gaudet amore tuo.

> If anything attractive or welcome can befall a silent grave from our
> grief, Calvus, from the yearning by which we renew old loves and
> weep for friendships long lost, surely her untimely death is not so
> much a sorrow (5) for Quintilia as the joy she experiences from
> your love.

That Horace was thinking of Catullus's couplets is clear from the conspicuous echo of the phrase *quo desiderio*, which opens Catullus's third
line, in the first words of his ode, and the name of Calvus's departed con-
sort, Quintilia, slides easily into that of the friend whom Virgil mourns.
What may have moved Horace most, as he thought of Catullus while he
wrote, is that, just as Catullus was bringing comfort to Calvus, his fellow
poet and good friend, so Horace was attempting the same for his friend
and superlative colleague, Virgil. But the purposes of each are dissimilar.

We possess two fragments of Calvus's poetry that most likely come from an *epicedium* serving as his own expression of the loss of Quintilia. Propertius, in a poem that carefully places Calvus in the line of Roman elegists between Catullus and Gallus and that links their three amours, Lesbia, Quintilia, and Lycoris, gives eloquent testimony to its force (2.34.89–90):

> haec etiam docti confessa est pagina Calvi,
>   cum caneret miserae funera Quintiliae.

> These [love songs] the page of learned Calvus also has disclosed,
> when he sings of the death of sad Quintilia.

But Catullus himself pays his friend's verses the greatest compliment. If the assumption is correct that Calvus's fragment 16—*forsitan hoc etiam gaudeat ipsa cinis* ("Perhaps her ashes themselves may receive joy from this")—comes from his *epicedium*, then Catullus's conclusion,

> certe non tanto mors immatura dolori est
>   Quintiliae, quantum gaudet amore tuo,

both imitates and transcends Calvus's expression. By replacing subjunctive with indicative, it exchanges possibility for certainty while at the same time it transmutes the metonymic ashes of our human remnant back into Quintilia herself, the wife who is imagined miraculously to rejoice in poetry's, and a poet's, manifestation of love. In reflecting on Calvus's potential ability, and need, to communicate his affection to his deceased wife and to have her experience it, Catullus turns his peer's wish into actuality. He thus wills away a major force of death by proclaiming that emotion can be received by the dead as well as offered by the living. Linkage exists between our sublunar world and the hereafter, says Catullus, if the dialogue is initiated by poets possessed of the imagination's power to replace the evanescent with the immortal.

Horace's coopting of this powerful interchange underscores the remarkable difference between it and the dialectic of his relationship with Virgil in C. 1.24. As Catullus's poem builds on Calvus, there occurs an intensification of emotion with a parallel heightening of poetry's presumed ability to challenge death. As we observed earlier, throughout all his poetry, the need for communication, and interconnection, regularly between speaker and addressee but taking other guises as well, is an omnipresent element. In his first poem, a book merges the poet and his dedicatee; in the second and third, a sparrow links the speaker and Lesbia; a yacht is the speaker's bond between foreign parts and home in the fourth. But to plot a conversation between the living and the dead, between survivor and departed, is one of his most challenging undertakings.

Horace, by contrast, builds his poem around the impossibility of such an enterprise. Through the agency of Melpomene, he mourns for Quintilius, as does Virgil, who laments as no one else. But the later poet, unlike Catullus, bounds rather than expands emotionality by suggesting, as the core of his ode, not only that there must be limits put to Virgil's grief, but also that even his Orphic magnetism, his power and the power of his words, could not establish a connection between the living and the dead, not to speak of bringing the defunct back to life. On one level, Horace seems to say, he will not play Catullus to Virgil's Calvus, nor will he claim here for song anything beyond a circumscribed role as manifestation of suitable sorrow. His exhortation to Virgil is directed toward restraint, not toward any reliance on impassioned song to break the bonds of hell. Nevertheless, by couching through allusion his dialogue with Virgil at least partially in terms of Catullus's dialogue with Calvus, he adds, as it were, a historical as well as a literary dimension to his accomplishment. However different his message might be, he embraces his Roman poetic past in a richly parallel manifestation, to add to the forcefulness of his own project.

Horace glances at Catullus one further time. Six selections subsequent to the address to Calvus we find another poem, 102, which begins with the same words as 96:

> Si quicquam tacito commissum est fido ab amico,
>   cuius sit penitus nota fides animi,
> meque esse invenies illorum iure sacratum,
>   Corneli, et factum me esse puta Arpocratem.

> If anything was ever entrusted by faithful to silent friend, whose loyalty of mind was known to the full, you will find me bound by their code, Cornelius, and believe that I have become Harpocrates.

It may not be coincidental that here, too, as in C. 1.24, we have the noun *fides* in one line followed by a verse including a form of the verb *invenio* in the same metrical position, preceded by two words, each of which is elided. If so, Horace's eye and ear may have led him from one instance of *si quicquam* to another nearby, and to a further instance of conversation between friends. Moreover, if the Cornelius in question is Cornelius Nepos, receiver of the first poem's *libellus*, then we are dealing again with one writer engaged with another of consequence, this time the author of biography, history, and, on the evidence of Pliny the Younger, light verse.[13]

Let us turn now to Horace's first poem to Virgil, C. 1.3, the placement of which is particularly salient. It comes as the third in an opening sequence that begins with a dedication to the poet's patron, Maecenas, and continues with a eulogy of the emperor Augustus:

Sic te diva potens Cypri,
　　sic fratres Helenae, lucida sidera,
ventorumque regat pater
　　obstrictis aliis praeter Iapyga,

navis, quae tibi creditum　　　　　　　　　　　　　5
　　debes Vergilium: finibus Atticis
reddas incolumem, precor
　　et serves animae dimidium meae.

illi robur et aes triplex
　　circa pectus erat, qui fragilem truci　　　　　　10
commisit pelago ratem
　　primus, nec timuit praecipitem Africum

decertantem Aquilonibus,
　　nec tristis Hyadas, nec rabiem Noti,
quo non arbiter Hadriae　　　　　　　　　　　　15
　　maior, tollere seu ponere volt freta.

quem mortis timuit gradum,
　　qui siccis oculis monstra natantia,
qui vidit mare turbidum et
　　infamis scopulos Acroceraunia?　　　　　　　20

nequiquam deus abscidit
　　prudens Oceano dissociabili
terras, si tamen impiae
　　non tangenda rates transiliunt vada.

audax omnia perpeti　　　　　　　　　　　　　25
　　gens humana ruit per vetitum nefas,
audax Iapeti genus
　　ignem fraude mala gentibus intulit;

post ignem aetheria domo
　　subductum macies et nova febrium　　　　　30

terris incubuit cohors
  semotique prius tarda necessitas

leti corripuit gradum.
  expertus vacuum Daedalus aera
pennis non homini datis;   35
  perrupit Acheronta Herculeus labor.

nil mortalibus ardui est:
  caelum ipsum petimus stultitia neque
per nostrum patimur scelus
  iracunda Iovem ponere fulmina.   40

May the goddess who holds sway over Cyprus, may the brothers of
Helen, bright stars, and the father of the winds, with the rest fettered
except for Iapyx, guide you, o ship, who owe back the Virgil you have
in trust: (5) I pray that you return him sound to the lands of Attica and
that you keep safe the half of my soul. That man had core of oak and
triple bronze around his heart (10) who first entrusted his frail bark to
the fierce waves. He was not terrified by the Southwest wind vying
with the North, nor by the dismal Hyades nor the wrath of Notus,
than whom there is no more powerful master of the Adriatic, (15)
whether his desire is to roil or calm the waves. What approach of
death did he fear who with dry eyes beheld the monsters of the deep,
who beheld the swollen sea, and Acroceraunia, with its notorious
cliffs? (20) Vainly did the provident god separate the lands with the
divide of Ocean if nevertheless wicked boats leap across waters they
ought not to touch. The human race, boldly enduring everything,
rushes ahead through forbidden crime. (25) Boldly did the offspring of
Iapetus through evil deceit bring fire to humankind. After fire was
removed from its heavenly home, leanness and a new troop of fevers
brooded over the earth, (30) and the slow inexorability of death,
hitherto remote, quickened its pace. Daedalus made trial of the empty
air on wings not given to man. (35) The effort of Hercules broke
through Acheron. Nothing is too steep for mortals: in our folly we
seek heaven itself, nor, because of our criminality, do we allow Jupiter
to set aside the thunderbolts of his anger. (40)

The addressee of the ode is actually the ship taking the writer on a voyage to Greece, while the ode itself is a varied form of propempticon
wishing the traveler a safe journey and a speedy return. The warm bond
between the two poets comes clear in Horace's famous characterization
of Virgil as *animae dimidium meae*, "the half of my soul" (8). It is no

accident that the first of several divinities to whom the speaker prays for assistance in the poem's opening lines is Venus, goddess born of the sea, and therefore would-be protectress of those who confront its hazards, yet also goddess of love (and mother of Aeneas). The poem quickly turns impersonal as Virgil, present-day sailor, yields place to the first seafarer. However, because the latter is made here to follow an itinerary similar to Virgil's, through the Adriatic and past the treacherous promontory of Acroceraunia, Horace suggests commonality in their experiences, as each confronts the terrors of the deep.

The ode now moves away from the individual histories of Virgil and his unnamed prototype and into a diatribe, first against navigation itself, then against all over-reachers—Prometheus, Daedalus, and Hercules are singled out—for the trouble they foisted on the world in the wake of their impious ambitions. Only in its final stanza does the poem become oriented again to the human world, as the speaker utilizes the first person to draw us all together as perpetrators of such folly. It is we who in our iniquity "foolishly seek heaven itself," and we who, from our criminality, "do not allow Jupiter to lay aside the thunderbolts of his anger" (*neque . . . patimur . . . iracunda Iovem ponere fulmina*, 38–40)—words to which we will return. The one comfort to Virgil, if comfort it be, is that the inventor of seafaring, and the poet who imitates him, are only parts of a universal "we," all guilty of attempting to exceed mankind's god-given limitations.

Details reminiscent of Catullus dot Horace's brilliant lecture, which has few if any equals in his corpus for its unrelieved negativity.[14] But the Catullan work that most caught Horace's imagination as he wrote is his longest and most complex, poem 64, an epyllion that takes its start by telling of the expedition of the Argonauts. This leads to a description of the marriage of Peleus and Thetis at which the Fates sing their praises while detailing as well the horrors that their son Achilles perpetrates both before and, paradoxically, after death. During its course, by means of the device of ekphrasis, we are told the story of Ariadne and Theseus, which takes up more than half the poem in which it is embedded. The whole concludes with an epilogue contrasting man's pious life of old with his present decadence. If readers of *C.* 1.3 are correct in maintaining that Horace is in fact allegorically warning Virgil, embarked now, as his curriculum progresses, on writing the *Aeneid*, about the perils of composing epic, then it is apropos that his thoughts turned to the poem of Catullus that both deals with myth's expansiveness and ends with a twelve-line jeremiad on the reasons for human decline.[15]

For his special purposes, Horace summarizes Catullus' larger intellectual plot, which takes us from the manufacture of the *Argo*, the first ship, to the wedding of Peleus and Thetis. This was the last occasion in myth at which humans and gods celebrated together, a ceremony at which Prometheus is present, showing off the wounds he received for the stealing of fire, but which was boycotted by Apollo and Diana for unstated reasons, no doubt in part because the union meant the birth of bloodthirsty Achilles and the end of a harmonious time in man's relationship to divinity. The lengthy digression on Ariadne's desertion by Theseus and on Aegeus's suicide resulting from his son's forgetfulness only further exemplifies the moral corruption that elicits Catullus's concluding contrast between then and now.

Catullus's Argonauts are sailing toward *fines Aeeteos* (3), the land of Aeetes, Virgil toward the bounds of Attica (*finibus Atticis*, 6).[16] The word *robur*, rare in each poet, drawn on by Catullus to describe the initial sailors as "the flower of Argive youth" (*Argivae robora pubis*, 4), is adopted by Horace to symbolize the hardy courage (*robur*, 9) that characterized his anonymous first venturer onto the deep. Primacy is, of course, a determining ingredient to each tale (64.11; C. 1.3.12), as are the *vada* on which the boats embark (64.6; C. 1.3.24). Likewise, daring is essential for this as well as, in Horace, other foolhardy endeavors (*ausi sunt*, 64.5; *audax*, C. 1.3.25 and 27).

At this point, Horace's allusiveness jumps to the end of Catullus, leaving admirers of his lyric concentration to supply for themselves what they will of the particulars of the earlier poet's more expansive narrative. Let me offer one detailed example of what Horace gleaned from Catullus's conclusion. We are watching a world now "dyed with unspeakable crime" (*tellus scelere est imbuta nefanda*, 397).[17] Both *scelus* (39) and *nefas* (26) are used prominently by Horace. Their importance for Catullus is underscored shortly later by their repetition in his vignette of the impious mother and of the more general consequences of her behavior (403–6):

> . . . ignaro mater substernens se impia nato
> impia non verita est divos scelerare penates.
> omnia fanda nefanda malo permixta furore
> iustificam nobis mentem avertere deorum.

> An impious mother, stretching herself beneath her unknowing son, feared not, in her impiety, to implicate the gods of the household in her crime. All our doings, right and wrong blended in evil madness, have turned from us the righteous thoughts of the gods.

Not only do *scelerare* and *nefanda* emphasize words already common to both poets, *impia* (twice), *omnia*, and *malo* add further to the overlap.

Finally, let us look at the concluding lines of each poem. For Catullus, it is the gods who no longer wish to have a share in the life of mortals (64.407–8):

quare nec talis dignantur visere coetus,
nec se contingi patiuntur lumine claro.

Wherefore they do not deign to visit such throngs, nor do they suffer
themselves to be touched by brilliant light.

For Horace, by contrast, the king of the gods does intervene in human
affairs, but negatively, and it is we who are the cause (38–40):

> . . . neque
> per nostrum patimur scelus
> iracunda Iovem ponere fulmina.

Horace, then, condenses and concentrates the story of the *Argo* and its
ethical aftereffects, material upon which Catullus enlarges from a variety
of angles during the course of his longest poem. The lyric poet leads from
particular to general, from Virgil to an anonymous first voyager whose
ambitions, along with those of his fellow aspirants toward a heroism that
violates human limitations, provoke the wrath of the gods. But it is not in-
ept on Horace's part to conjure up for the reader, as part of the intellectual
background of his brilliant ode, Catullus's pessimistic treatment of the
Argonautic adventure. This is especially true if Virgil was in fact deeply involved with the hazards of his own multivalent epic enterprise, which plots
his hero's course from Troy to the foundation of Rome and its future.

Let us leave Virgil behind to conclude with a look at C. 3.27, one of
Horace's longest odes, which, though nearly twice the length of C. 1.3,
serves as its careful counterbalance as the collection nears its close.
It, too, is a propempticon, this time addressed to a girl named Galatea,
about to depart, like Virgil, on a sea journey. Here, too, the speaker offers a wish for the voyager's well-being along with a reminder of the
treacherousness of marine travel. On this occasion, however, Horace offers us his most expansive narrative poem, for its final two-thirds tell the
tale of Europe's adventures, picaresque and erotic, with her bull-lover,
Jupiter.[18]

Horace offers us a series of clues connecting the two poems. The perils
of the Adriatic figure in both, and only in these two odes do we find
mention of Iapyx, the northwest wind.[19] Moreover, at exactly the same
stanza in each poem (25–28), we hear of the boldness connected with
such nautical enterprises. In the first poem, it is the human race and
Prometheus who are both *audax* (25, 27), the latter bringing fire to mortals "by evil deceit" (*fraude mala*, 28). In the later poem, it is, of course,
Europe who is *audax* (28), and the *fraudes* that she confronts (27) are
those not of a thief at work but of the ocean seething with monsters.

The presence of Catullus 64 in the background is also an important unifying factor for the two odes, but in this instance the parallelism is dramatically illustrated. The core moment of Catullan influence here is the segment in 64 devoted to the story of Ariadne and Theseus. Within it, what many critics see as the most striking, as well as weighty, section of the poem is the seventy-line lament that the heroine delivers upon the realization that she has been deserted by her lover (132–201). In C. 3.27 Horace offers an equivalent in the more than thirty-line speech of Europe (34–66), at once blaming herself, bemoaning her fate, and wishing for vengeance on her errant *inamorato*. She proclaims herself ready to be the prey of wild animals, to commit suicide or to become the servant of a barbarian mistress.

By giving her a lengthy speech, Horace seems to be making good for leaping over the Ariadne-Theseus episode, which is to say more than half of Catullus 64, in C. 1.3, in his sharp focus on its beginning and end. It is also as if Horace were saying to the reader that he, too, can produce for us a suffering heroine's lament with all of its abrupt changes of mood and topic, a lament that also proportionally dominates the narrative in which it is embedded. To look at a few details: the only use of the word *singultus* ("sob") by each poet comes, for Catullus, at the line before Ariadne's monody begins (131) and, for Horace, when Europe's speech is over, in Venus's command to her to stop wailing (74). For both, lamentation is the order of the day.[20] Their respective fathers figure prominently from the opening words of each one.[21] Both see themselves as potential booty for animals.[22] One of Horace's rare mentions of the symptoms of sexual passion in the *Carmina* is the word *furor* he gives to Europe at line 36. She is *victa furore*, just as Ariadne styles herself *caeca furore* (197).[23] And the list continues on.[24]

Likewise, the surrounding narrative offers numerous instances of rapport between the two poems. Catullus introduces his story with two uses of the phrase *quae simul* (64.12 and 31), which Horace employs at C. 3.27.33, and the words that there immediately follow—*centum tetigit potentem / oppidis Creten* ("[As soon as] she reached Crete, powerful with its hundred cities")—may well have their roots in Ariadne's prayer at 64.171–74:

> Iuppiter omnipotens utinam ne tempore primo
> Cnosia Cecropiae tetigissent litora puppes
> indomito nec dira ferens stipendia tauro
> perfidus in Cretam religasset navita funem.

> Almighty Jupiter, would that in the first place the Attic ships had never
> reached the shores of Cnossos and that the faithless voyager, bringing

the dreadful offering to the savage bull, had not tied his ships on [the shores of] Crete.

Moreover, if we look at the conclusion of Catullus 64 quoted earlier, Europe's definition of her misfortune as *pietas . . . victa furore* (35–36) finds a plausible source not only in Ariadne's phrase *caeca furore* but also in the narrator's bleak look at the contemporary world, where, as we saw, a mother, *impia* twice over, is only one particular element in a general indictment of a time when the speakable and the unutterable are "blended with evil madness" (*malo permixta furore*, 405).[25]

But there is a tone of less than high seriousness in Horace's ode of which we should also take due note. Its first four quatrains, with their meticulous look at the omens that greet the impious setting out on a trip—hooting owl (*parra*), pregnant dog, wolf, fox, snake, raven (*corvus*), crow (*cornix*)—exaggerate the Roman penchant for augury. Especially because of the emphasis on song, in the "singing" (*recinentis*) owl and the "chanting" (*oscinem*) raven,[26] we sense the speaker parodying himself as *providus auspex*. There is a further level of humor in these opening lines. The only other appearance of the word *parra* in Latin poetry occurs in Plautus's *Asinaria* in a passage where the slave Libanus is trying to figure out how to steer the "bark of his cleverness." I quote lines 258–61 of his soliloquy:

unde sumam? quem intervortam? quo hanc celocem conferam?
impetritum, inauguratumst: quovis admittunt aves,
picus et cornix ab laeva, corvos, parra ab dextera
consuadent.

Where shall I get [the money I need]? Whom shall I swindle? Where shall I steer this launch of mine? I've got my favorable omen, my favorable auspices. The birds let me steer it where I'd like— woodpecker and crow on the left, raven and owl on the right urge me on.

Horace's speaker may be sending Galatea on her way with a positive omen, but in doing so he is embarking on his own launch of wit. By framing it in terms parallel to those of a clever Plautine slave, embarking on a wily enterprise, Horace's narrator becomes a type of *servus auspex*, the thoroughgoing somberness of whose subsequent tale, and that of its Catullan progenitor, the reader is now prepared to call in question.

If we look at the story of Europe with a view to comic elements in its presentation, and especially with its role as a response to the grimness of C. 1.3 in mind, then Jupiter can be visualized as in fact a prototype of the first boat and Europe of the first sailor. She entrusted herself (*credidit*) to the treacherous animal, heading from Phoenicia to Crete, just as Virgil was entrusted (*creditum*) to the ship ready to depart for Greece.[27] She calls Jupiter a *monstrum* (49), which to her means both a beast and bestial, the animal incorporation of evil for (apparently) deserting her. The Catullan reader, however, would also remember the earlier poet's depiction of the *Argo*, at 64.15, as a *monstrum* to its initial viewers. It would appear both enormous in size and a prodigy as well, unique as the first object of its kind that is also embarked on a venture of epic proportions.

Europe's extended lament, whose only parallel in the Horatian corpus is the much shorter warning speech of Hypermestra to her husband at C. 3.11.37–52, has elements of exaggeration about it, once again suggesting that Horace is not only imitating Catullus's Ariadne but parodying her, and her creator, as well, for the amusement of his readers.[28] For instance, the notion of the deserted heroine being devoured by creatures of the wild, a notion that Ariadne projects in one phrase (*"dilaceranda feris dabor alitibusque / praeda,"* "I will be given as prey to beasts and birds to rend apart," 64.152–53), takes up the better part of two stanzas in Europe's lament (49–56). Not only are the predators specified as lions and tigers, they also pointedly receive the last word in each of their respective stanzas. And in her account, she is no ordinary, reluctant piece of booty, but naked, which is to say gratifyingly available for the lions, and a morsel both succulent and comely for the tigers!

Europe also just happens to have handy in her equipage the *zona*, whose loosening and release symbolize her loss of virginity, to put to good use now in implementing her potential suicide by hanging. Its presence suggests another level of parody, this time based on genre. When Europe's complaint is finished, we find that Venus has been present all this time along with her son Cupid, his bow unstrung because it has already served its purpose. Venus speaks the final cautionary words of revelation to Europe, that she is now the "wife of invincible Jupiter" (*uxor invicti Iovis*, 73). But before she does so, the narrator gives us a glimpse of the goddess in her familiar pose of "smiling treacherously" (*perfidum ridens*, 67). We learn, too, that she has finally had enough of the game she has been playing (*lusit satis*, 69).

The end of her sport means the end of the poem. But the phrase also recalls the words of Catullus's singer, who includes himself with the virgins he commands to close the house door, at the end of his first marriage song (61.225): *lusimus satis* ("We have had sufficient play"). This is to say that both wedding ceremony and the ceremony of words that tells of it are coterminous and have reached their conclusions. In the case of C. 3.27, the reflection of Catullus tells us that we have also been witnessing an epithalamium of sorts. A bull-god is the past and future husband—the animal has already been "much beloved" (*multum amati*, 47)—and Europe is already his wife, according to Venus (73). She will find that her rescuing Bacchus has been present for a while, but in a disguise not usual for an incipient bridegroom.[29]

C. 3.27, therefore, offers both a careful complement to and a contrast with C. 1.3. Both odes draw deeply on Catullus 64 for inspiration, the former in several particulars, the latter in general sweep as well. Ode 3.27 seems to spoof Catullus's high seriousness, but in doing so it also stands back from the apparently relentless gloom of C. 1.3, granting witty relief from its ever-deepening invective by parodying many of its themes. If so, the later poem fulfills one of Horace's usual roles in dealing with Catullus. It lightens the earlier poet's intensity by urging recollection on the reader, and, in the act of reminding, stands as exhortation toward a self-distance that treats life's difficulties with detachment, resignation, and, yes, humor. In so doing, he is poking fun at the unsmiling self he displayed in C. 1.3. He also may be urging Virgil, who would be aware of his implicit involvement in C. 3.27 because of its parallelisms to C. 1.3, to take the hectoring of the earlier poem, and its applicability to him, with a dash of wit. The duet of poems therefore falls nicely into the pattern we have traced in the other odes to Virgil, urging him to accept life, especially life as it faces death, with acquiescence (for what else can one do?) and humor (as the best antidote for too large a dose of reality). And Catullus's poetry is an ever-present, not to say essential, force in this evolution.

CHAPTER FIVE

Genres and a Dialogue

In the previous chapters we explored the presence of two themes—the association of time with place, and of speech with sound—and of two figures, one drawn from Greek myth (Helen), the other from contemporary Rome (Virgil), that are all central to our discussion of Horace's reception of Catullus. Here we look at two genres, the hymn and the wedding song, or epithalamium, by means of which the Augustan poet absorbed and varied the inheritance of his predecessor. As a postlude, which will also serve in part as summary, we will turn to a set of poems where the rhetorical presentation of lovers speaking in turn both forges a bond between and acts to distinguish our authors.

Let us turn first to the hymn. Though there are other moments in Catullus, such as the address to Venus in poem 36, that share in elements of the hymn, his only full-fledged example is poem 34:

> Dianae sumus in fide
> puellae et pueri integri:
> <Dianam pueri integri>
>   puellaeque canamus.
>
> o Latonia, maximi   5
> magna progenies Iovis,
> quam mater prope Deliam
>   deposivit olivam,
>
> montium domina ut fores
> silvarumque virentium   10
> saltuumque reconditorum
>   amniumque sonantum:
>
> tu Lucina dolentibus
> Iuno dicta puerperis,
> tu potens Trivia et notho es   15
>   dicta lumine Luna.
>
> tu cursu, dea, menstruo
> metiens iter annuum,

rustica agricolae bonis
　　tecta frugibus exples.　　　　　　　　　　　　　　　20

sis quocumque tibi placet
sancta nomine, Romulique,
antique ut solita es, bona
　　sospites ope gentem.

We, chaste boys and girls, are in the service of Diana, let us sing
[Diana, chaste boys] and girls. O daughter of Latona, (5) mighty
offspring of mightiest Jupiter, to whom your mother gave birth near
the olive of Delos, so that you might be mistress of mountains and of
green forests, (10) of hidden glens and resounding streams: you are
called Juno Lucina by those in the pangs of childbirth, you are called
powerful Trivia (15) and Luna with light not your own. As you measure out the course of the year in your monthly route, you fill up the
country dwellings of the farmer with good produce. (20) Be blessed by
whatever title you please, and, as was your wont of old, keep safe the
race of Romulus with good resource.

We move smoothly from the virginal singers to the parentage and birth
of the virginal goddess of Delos. There follow three stanzas devoted to
her attributes, as patroness of wild nature, of birth, in her chthonic form
(Trivia), and in her heavenly manifestation (Luna). In the latter guise,
her monthly appearance guides the year to produce riches for the farmer.
We end, appropriately, with prayer, a prayer for the well-being of the
Roman people.

Several themes unify the hymn. One is the poet's attention to birth and
generation, taking us from Diana's engendering (*progenies*, 6) to the race
of Romulus (*Romuli . . . gentem*, 22–24), with reminders on the way
that she is both a goddess of childbirth as well as one who brings to
fruition the agricultural world's annual gestation. Following a parallel
pattern, we advance from wild nature to the earth tamed by man into
productivity. We also follow a developing chronological pattern, from
the atemporal realm of mountains, woods, and streams to the farmer's
unchanging dependence on a yearly calendar, to Roman man in historical time, a project that takes us from Romulus to the present moment of
prayer that Diana continue her sustenance of the Romans as she had in
the past (*antique*, 23). Catullan eroticism can only be sensed vicariously
here, as we anticipate the time when the chorus will no longer be virginal, and consider the implicit sexuality in the virgin goddess's role as
light-bringer and protector of childbirth.[1]

We will trace the influence of Catullus's poem on several Horatian odes,

but there is one upon which we would expect it to be especially prominent, the *Carmen saeculare*.[2] Scholars will probably never discover the ex-
act occasion, but Catullus 34 reads as if it were performed at a specific ceremony where singers prayed for Diana's ongoing support of Rome. Of
Horace's several hymns, only the *Carmen saeculare* is in this respect parallel, because it was written for public execution on June 3 of 17 BCE, during the celebration of Augustus's *Ludi Saeculares*. It, too, is dedicated to
Diana, but now the honors are equally shared with her twin, Apollo.

Horace's opening line both gives initial prominence to Apollo as
god of light and announces the poem's acknowledgment of Catullus:
Phoebe silvarumque potens Diana ("Phoebus and Diana, with power
over woods"). The apostrophe is followed shortly in both poems by a
statement on the chorus's part of the chastity of its youthful members,
divided between male and female, and by the unifying "we," in Catullus
through song (*sumus*, 1; *canamus*, 4), in Horace through prayer (*preca-
mur*, 3). In the hymn to Diana we hear nothing further of the chorus as
it goes about its ritual. Horace, by contrast, brings his poem full circle
by returning to the chorus in his final stanza, which, in its penultimate
line, looks once again to Phoebus and Diana, as had the poem's initial
verse.

Examining specifically the figure of Diana, we find that Horace's notices follow the order of their Catullan presentation. We have seen how
the *Carmen*'s first line refers to 34.10, to Diana as goddess of the wilder-
ness. Horace next turns, as does Catullus, to her role as presider over
parturition. The resonance is clear enough (13–16):

> rite maturos aperire partus
> lenis, Ilithyia, tuere matres,
> sive tu Lucina probas vocari
>   seu Genitalis.

> Ilithyia, gracious at fittingly bringing forth offspring in due season,
> protect our mothers, whether you wish to be called Lucina or Genitalis.

Horace now absorbs what Catullus directs specifically at Diana into more
general statement. Catullus's lines 19–20, for instance, dealing with Diana as a fertility goddess, are transformed into Horace's lines 29–30,
where Tellus receives the prayer:

> fertilis frugum pecorisque Tellus
> spicea donet Cererem corona.

> May Earth, teeming with crops and cattle, offer Ceres a wreath of
> corn.

Finally, if we attend to 34.22–24 in particular, Horace, appropriating Catullus's move from agricultural to human time, addresses the company of gods (47–48):

> Romulae genti date remque prolemque
>   et decus omne.

> Grant to the race of Romulus both resources and offspring and every distinction.[3]

Once more we are in the realm of history, contemplating the span from Romulus to Rome's present and asking a blessing on its future.

The reflection of Catullus's *sospites*, the first word in his final line (34.24), in *sospite* at *C.s.* 40, likewise initiating the last line of a stanza (37–40), lends the force of Catullus's final quatrains to another set of characters not present in his poem. The addressees are Apollo and Diana, who in the course of the sentence are amalgamated into a larger compendium of gods (*di*, 45 and 46):

> Roma si vestrum est opus Iliaeque
> litus Etruscum tenuere turmae,
> iussa pars mutare lares et urbem
>   sospite cursu.

> If Rome be your monument and if Ilian bands held the Etruscan shore, a remnant ordered to change their homes and city in a course unscathed.

The *cursus* of Diana's annual feracious progress that we find in Catullus (17), and the prayer that she defend the race of Romulus, are combined by Horace as he glances at the moment in pre-Romulean Rome when Aeneas and his followers make their way west from Troy. It is not unfitting that the attributes given to Diana, as fertility goddess and as protectress of Rome, both of which Horace has already mentioned, each time with gestures to Catullus, be also shared with Aeneas, and that Catullus's words, here, too, lend further force to Horace's evocation. The Trojan hero's journey is safe and saving, as he moves from the destruction of one city to the founding of another, preserving the past for the future. The compliment to Aeneas, and vicariously to Augustus, is clear.

Horace was intrigued by the act of writing the *Carmen saeculare* and mentions it twice elsewhere, again using language that he had first found in Catullus.[4] It is not unexpected, then, to the student of the entire corpus of Horace's writing, that the first allusion to Catullus 34 in the initial collection of odes is not in a hymn per se, but in a poem about the performance of a hymn, C. 1.21. As with the *Carmen saeculare*, Apollo joins his sister as co-recipient of this unusual hymn-in-progress:

Dianam tenerae dicite virgines,
intonsum pueri dicite Cynthium,
    Latonamque supremo
        dilectam penitus Iovi.

vos laetam fluviis et nemorum coma,   5
quaecumque aut gelido prominet Algido
    nigris aut Erymanthi
        silvis aut viridis Gragi,

vos Tempe totidem tollite laudibus
natalemque, mares, Delon Apollinis   10
    insignemque pharetra
        fraternaque umerum lyra.

hic bellum lacrimosum, hic miseram famem
pestemque a populo et principe Caesare in
    Persas atque Britannos   15
        vestra motus aget prece.

Sing of Diana, tender virgins, sing, boys, of unshorn Apollo, and of Latona, deeply beloved by almighty Jupiter. [Sing her, girls,] who delights in streams and in the sylvan foliage, (5) which stands out either on chill Algidus or on the dark forests of Erymanthus or of green Gragus. You, young men, glorify with equal praise Tempe and Delos, birthplace of Apollo, (10) and his shoulder, brilliant with its quiver and his brother's lyre. Moved by your prayer, he will drive tearful war, will drive sad hunger and disease from the people and from Caesar, their prince, onto the Persians and the Britons. (15)

At the start, with the naming of the goddess in the ode's initial word, the presence of Catullus is strongly felt. The words *o Latonia . . . Iovis*, demarcating 34.5–6, become *Latona . . . Iovi*, which bound C. 1.21.3–4. Catullus's third stanza, with its extraordinary assonance and a pattern of rhyme worthy of the future Christian hymn, permeates Horace's second quatrain,[5] and, although *montium* is replaced by the detailed specificity of *Algido, Erymanthi*, and *Gragi*, there is a residue of Catullus's emphatic rhyming in the near anagram, abetted by etymological play, of *gelido . . . Algido* and in the balances of *silvis* with *nigris* and of *Erymanthi* with *Gragi*.

At this point Diana leaves the poem, but *Delon* serves as a reminder of *Deliam . . . olivam*, and the last stanza, where we are assured that Apollo will give ear to the boys' prayer, could be seen as an elaboration of Catullus's final lines. Again Horace offers greater detail and specificity, but it is not so far from "keeping safe the race of Romulus with good resource" to the negative request to ward off war, disease, and hunger from Caesar, the new Romulus, and his people.

Parallels, however, also highlight differences, as so often the case when we watch Horace reuse and revamp Catullus. These start with the notion of authorial framing: in Horace we are dealing not with a hymn, but with a teacher rehearsing his chorus for a hymn's performance. The chorus's "we," and the repetitions that announce its make-up, are replaced by the "you" of the speaker's commands, with reiteration now given over to the chorus-master's imperative (*dicite . . . dicite*, 1–2). *Latona* may remind us of *Latonia*, but Horace has in fact brought a new character into his poem, the mother of Apollo and Diana, who had a statue beside those of her twin offspring inside the temple of Apollo on the Palatine that Augustus had dedicated in 28 BCE.[6] Horace's expansive imagination, moreover, takes us, in stanza 2, from the Alban Hills to Arcadia to Lycia and, in stanza 4, from Rome to the Parthians in the east and the Britons in the north.

One final difference: the negative element that enters the poem at its conclusion brings to the fore a further contrast with Catullus. The earlier poet ends with a prayer for Rome's well-being. Horace builds up a list of what might go wrong at Rome only to announce, with assurance, that Apollo will ward off any evil. The fact that he will do so, because moved by the singers' prayer, puts a particularly Horatian stress, absent from Catullus, on the power of song. This is implicit not only in the chorus's act of presentation, but also in what they sing, the product of Horace's genius with the incitement of Catullus in the background.

In tracing the history of Catullan influence on Horace, we also find that there are groups of odes where we note the presence of one or more works by the earlier poet throughout the sequence. An instance is Horace's gestures to Catullus 34 in *C.* 3.21–23.[7] The references vary, just as the poems themselves are distinct from one another. But the result gives a satisfying, if passing, sense of unity in the midst of the coruscating diversity that characterizes Horace's *Carmina*.

The first in the series, *C.* 3.21, is in fact not a hymn but a brilliant parody of the hymnic form where a wine jug (*pia testa*, 4) replaces a god or goddess as the object of praise and prayer:

O nata mecum consule Manlio,
seu tu querellas sive geris iocos

seu rixam et insanos amores
  seu facilem, pia testa, somnum,

quocumque lectum nomine Massicum   5
servas, moveri digna bono die
  descende, Corvino iubente
    promere languidiora vina.

non ille, quamquam Socraticis madet
sermonibus, te neglegit horridus: 10
  narratur et prisci Catonis
    saepe mero caluisse virtus.

tu lene tormentum ingenio admoves
plerumque duro, tu sapientium
  curas et arcanum iocoso   15
    consilium retegis Lyaeo,

tu spem reducis mentibus anxiis
viresque et addis cornua pauperi
  post te neque iratos trementi
    regum apices, neque militum arma.   20

te Liber et si laeta aderit Venus
segnesque nodum solvere Gratiae
  vivaeque producent lucernae,
    dum rediens fugat astra Phoebus.

O holy jug, born with me when Manlius was consul, whether you are fomenting groans or giggles, whether a brawl or loves' madness, or easy sleep, for whatever purpose you are harboring your choice Massic, (5) worthy to be poured on an apposite day, make your descent, since Corvinus orders us to broach a gentler vintage. Although steeped in the dialogues of Socrates, he will not shun you out of sternness. (10) Even ancient Cato's principles were said to have often felt wine's warmth. You apply gentle torture to the dull of wit. You reveal the concerns of the wise and their abstruse ruminations (15) through the play of Lyaeus. You restore hope and strength to troubled minds, you add horns to the poor man who, in your wake, shudders at neither the angry crowns of kings nor soldiers' weaponry. (20) Liber and Venus, if her happiness will be at hand, and the Graces, slow to break their bond, and living lamps will parade you in, until the return of Phoebus routs the stars.

During the course of the poem we learn of the wine's birth and its powers, whether to bring relaxation to Messalla Corvinus in a philosophical mode or to Cato's intractable uprightness, whether to help explain the teachings of the inscrutable, to bring hope to the anxious or courage to the poor. The speaker prays for the jug's epiphany, that it "descend" (*descende*, 7), in this case not from heaven but from the wine-storage area, to make its appearance accompanied by an entourage consisting of Bacchus, Venus, and the Graces.[8] She will stay with her devotees the night through, so ends the poem, until Phoebus returns to put the stars to flight. Prayer and celebration become coterminous as the speaker announces the future fulfillment of both.

We learn from the ode's initial line that there is a special relationship between poet and jug. They are coevals and presumably have grown to maturity together.[9] And wine, to Horace, regularly verges on being a metonymy for poetry. We remember, for instance, the wine his seemingly autobiographical speaker offers Maecenas in *C.* 3.29 as well as *C.* 1.20, where his "cheap Sabine," instead of the present poem's "choice Massic" (5), is preserved in a "Greek jug" (*Graeca . . . testa*, 2). In both instances, the vintage comes close to standing for the poet's thoughts and the jug for their astonishing, inherited verse framework that his mentor can absorb. Like the parallelism between invocation and *convivium*, the productive qualities of wine and the inspired, witty poetry that tells of them merge together.

The repetition of *quocumque . . . nomine* from Catullus 34.21–22 at *C.* 3.21.5 shows that the earlier poet was part of Horace's own inspiration. Yet already here the odist adds his own stamp. The phrase in Catullus refers to names that the poet has given Diana and serves to relieve the petitioner of guilt if he has failed to supplicate the goddess by a title that she might have preferred. For Horace, *quocumque nomine* looks to the account or purpose for which the jug preserves its contents. After all, a wine jar, pious as it might be, cannot claim the lofty nomenclature of Juno Lucina, Trivia, or Luna, however creative its contents may prove to be in the future, for those from Cato to Messalla Corvinus, or from the wise to the timid.

This said, Catullus is much with us. The two poems are the same in length, and the fourth and fifth stanzas of each begin with *tu*, as their poets follow the regular procedure of ritual prayer. Above all, the element of parody of the standard hymn, which runs through *C.* 3.21, carries with it a compliment to its model. Horace, on one level, may again be spoofing Catullus's seriousness in poem 34, but in the process he also discreetly acknowledges his predecessor's power to inspire, to offer vintage poetry for Horace to play with and to re-form into his own fresh creation.

The second ode of the trio, C. 3.22, resonates still more closely with Catullus 34:[10]

> Montium custos nemorumque, virgo.
> quae laborantis utero puellas
> ter vocata audis adimisque leto,
>   diva triformis,
>
> imminens villae tua pinus esto,   5
> quam per exactos ego laetus annos
> verris obliquom meditantis ictum
>   sanguine donem.

Guardian of mountains and of groves, virgin, you who, thrice called upon, heeds girls laboring in childbirth and, three-formed goddess, rescues them from death, let the pine that looms over my country dwelling be yours, (5) so that joyfully after each year has run its course I might offer it the blood of a boar pondering its sidelong thrust.

The opening stanza compresses into a virtual précis what Catullus covers in 34.9–16. *Domina* changes to *custos*, as if to eliminate any hint of sexuality associated with the virgin goddess, but the essence of Catullus remains, with Diana again the presider over childbirth, called upon three times for the positive magic such a gesture might insure, but also appropriately, for a divinity with its three forms associated with heaven, earth, and the underworld. The reader, therefore, because of this rich allusiveness, expects that the same themes that Catullus voices in his final stanzas will suffer a similar transformation in the ode.

Once more, however, as in the case of C. 3.21, our expectations are reoriented. We turn from Catullus's public prayer to private dedication in Horace, from a presumably urban setting to a country villa and the pine that overshadows it. We have left the poetry of prayer for speech as thank offering, one that will happen year after year (*per exactos annos*, C. 3.22.5). There is a residue here of Catullus's hymn when the chorus implores Diana's help for the husbandman, as she "measures her yearly course" (*metiens iter annuum*, 34.18). But now we are dealing not with farmers in general but with the persona of a particular individual possessing a Sabine villa who happens also to be a poetic genius.

Likewise, the poem itself suddenly becomes personalized: gone is the chorus of virginal youngsters, replaced by a strongly expressed *ego* who commands that the pine be dedicated to the goddess, a gift affirmed by animal sacrifice, in particular with the blood of a boar. Once more a comparison with C. 1.20 may reveal some aspects of the speaker's meaning.

There, too, an emphatic *ego ipse* (2) offers Maecenas Sabine wine that he has bottled himself in a Greek jug, which is to say poetry of his own manufacture, with its particular past and present. In *C.* 3.22, blood replaces wine as the speaker's presentation, but here, too, the lexical choice suggests that the presentation is in part a surrogate for what poets can in fact offer, in this case the language of praise. The years are *exactos*, brought to exacting fulfillment the way good verses should be, the boar is meditative, like his creator, and his "thrust" is paralleled elsewhere in Horace by the beat of the poet's thumb, in *C.* 4.6, as he teaches the *Carmen saeculare* to its choir.[11] And here again, with great immediacy, his Catullan past is a spur to Horace's own verse-making.

The final ode in this trio, *C.* 3.23, likewise has a religious theme that connects it with its predecessors. It begins:

> Caelo supinas si tuleris manus
> nascente Luna, rustica Phidyle,
>   si ture placaris et horna
>   fruge Lares avidaque porca,
>
> nec pestilentem sentiet Africum   5
> fecunda vitis nec sterilem seges
>   robiginem aut dulces alumni
>   pomifero grave tempus anno.

If you have lifted up your hands to heaven at the coming of the moon, rustic Phidyle, if you have placated your Lares with incense and the year's produce and a greedy pig, then your fruitful vine will not feel the disease-ridden wind from Africa, (5) nor your crops the mildew that brings sterility, nor your sweet nurslings the sickly season when the year brings apples.

We turn now from parody of a hymn, and from a poem as dedicatory offering to a goddess, to an ode where the speaker advises "rustic Phidyle" on the proper procedures for sacrifice if she wishes her little farm to avoid disease during the season when it most threatens.[12] She needs, the poem continues, no grand sacrifice, of bull or lamb, to win the gods' protective favor. In her case, rosemary and myrtle, to crown her household divinities, and an offering of meal and salt are sufficient to maintain their loyalty.

Details also link the two adjacent odes. We move from wild boar (*verris, C.* 3.22.7) to tame pig (*porca, C.* 3.23.4) as victim, joined later by the meal and salt that replace any more luxurious gift. The course of years over which the speaker will sacrifice to Diana (*exactos annos,*

C. 3.22.6), merges into the annual produce (*horna fruge*, 3–4) and autumnal season (*pomifero anno*, 8) in C. 3.23. The villa we see in C. 3.22 becomes the vines, crops, and animals of Phidyle's farm as well as the interior of her rural dwelling with its Lares (4) and Penates (19) that introduce and conclude the poem.[13] Catullus, too, helps us make the transition. Mention of *Luna* coopts Diana, in her role as celestial sign, into Phidyle's life. *Luna*, we recall, is cited at line 16 of Catullus's poem, which goes on to address the goddess as someone who (19–20)

> rustica agricolae bonis
> tecta frugibus exples.

Catullus's "rustic dwellings" are absorbed into the special domain of *rustica Phidyle*, while the generalized produce (*frugibus*) of the earlier poet's hymn, as Diana makes her annual progress (*iter annuum*) through the heavens, becomes the particular yield (*fruge*) of Phidyle's yearly efforts (*horna, anno*).

The language of Catullus's unique hymn, though doubtless written for public, choral performance, nevertheless permeates this variegated Horatian trio of poems on sacred subjects. It helped to stimulate the later poet's imagination to compose a parody of the hymnic form in C. 3.21; to write C. 3.22, a lyric version of a dedicatory poem that would ordinarily have been written as epigram; and, finally, to compose C. 3.23, with its advice on the content and procedure of sacrifice. Catullus's hymn helped beget each of Horace's poetic rituals on ritual.

One final variation by Horace on the pattern of hymn deserves discussion here, the beautiful apostrophe to the Bandusian fountain (C. 3.13):

> O fons Bandusiae, splendidior vitro,
> dulci digne mero non sine floribus,
>   cras donaberis haedo,
>   cui frons turgida cornibus
>
> primis et venerem et proelia destinat—   5
> frustra, nam gelidos inficiet tibi
>   rubro sanguine rivos
>   lascivi suboles gregis.
>
> te flagrantis atrox hora Caniculae
> nescit tangere, tu frigus amabile   10
>   fessis vomere tauris
>   praebes et pecori vago.

fies nobilium tu quoque fontium
me dicente cavis inpositam ilicem
   saxis, unde loquaces   15
      lymphae desiliunt tuae.

O spring of Bandusia, more gleaming than glass, worthy of sweet wine
and flowers, tomorrow you will be offered a billy goat whose brow,
swelling with nascent horns, designates it for both love and battles
(5)—in vain, for the offspring of the lusty flock will stain your chill
waters with red blood. The dark hour of the burning Dog Star knows
not how to touch you, you furnish loving chill to oxen, (10) tired from
the plowshare, and to the wandering flock. You will also become one
of the famous fountains as I tell of the ilex tree placed over your
hollow rocks, whence your talkative waters leap down. (15)

In one of his most memorable odes, Horace both invents and, by literal
fiat, ennobles a source of inspiration that is remarkably like himself. The
symbiosis, with one protagonist telling of the other's loquacity, is en-
hanced, first, by *variatio* that Horace again practices on hymnic structure,
and second, by rich figuration. The sacrificed boar in C. 3.22—also, as
we have seen, a poem in part concerned with the making of poetry—is
replaced by a young goat, ready for passion's battles. Its oblation to the
glistening spring occasions a series of near-oxymora where red blood
merges with bright waters to enrich a setting that is at once loving and
cold. Our fountain accepts the sacrifice of a kid primed for amatory violence, and yet both virginally wards off the Dog Star's heated advances
and furnishes refreshment to cattle and flock.

    Catullus is present here, too, but it is not his hymn that now was sug-
gestive to Horace. His first direct appearance is in the phrase *vomere
tauris* (11), which the Augustan poet found at 64.40 (*vomere taurus*,
also at line ending). We meet him again in the next line: the phrase
pecori vago looks back to *vaga pecora* at 63.13 (the phrases again appear at the conclusion of their respective verses). Finally, in Catullus 68
we have an abundance of lexical parallels that are scarcely coincidental:
dicam, dicite, and *loquatur* from 45–46, *lympha* and *prosilit* from 54–58
(where *perlucens* reappears as *splendidior vitro* and *lapide* as *saxis*), and
flagrans, frustra, sanguine from 73–78.[14]

    These references all have in common that they are from Catullus's so-
called long poems, clustered in the middle of his corpus. Moreover, all
deal, either directly or implicitly, with sexuality and marriage, whether
perverse or gone awry. The first echo follows shortly upon Attis's emascu-
lation, where he stains "the earth's soil with fresh blood" (*recente terrae
sola sanguine*, 63.7). The result is an aberrant liaison between feminized

male and Cybele, the omnivorous Great Mother. The second forms part of the lead-in to the wedding of Peleus and Thetis, a union that brought forth Achilles, during whose time at Troy, in the words of the prophecy of the Fates, "the Phrygian fields will be sodden with Trojan blood" (*Phrygii Teucro manabunt sanguine <campi>*, 344) and whose exploits anticipate a later moment of decadence when "the hands of brothers have flowed with their brothers' blood" (*perfudere manus fraterno sanguine fratres*, 399). Finally, poem 68, as we have seen, is built around the difficulties in the adulterous relationship of the poet and Lesbia visualized against the background of the rape of Helen by Paris and its resultant war. Concomitant with the latter events, but also used in simile to qualify the intimacy of Catullus and his girl, is the wedding of Laodamia and Protesilaus, the first Greek warrior to be killed at Troy, whose ill-fated marriage had not been blessed by the blood sacrifice demanded by the gods.

Horace's discreet allusivity first reminds us of the suitability of blood-offering when the context is appropriate. But animal sacrifice here serves two purposes. It honors the fountain by enlivening it with the adolescent goat's energy. It also eliminates sexuality from the fountain's sphere and anticipates the inability of "burning" Canicula to "touch" its flow. The virginal waters, which Horace's song exalts, take their place with the great fountains of Greece, as homes for the Muses and sources for poets. Though Horace apostrophizes an unknown fountain associated with the inspiration for his masterful sequence of odes, he, too, nevertheless has his own sources, and one of them is the poetry of Catullus, whose energy he incorporates and accommodates to his own genius.

Another genre deserving of further attention in our survey is the epithalamium. We have already touched on the connections between Catullus's first wedding hymn, 61, and C. 1.36 and C. 3.27, a link that specifically reinforces the latter poem's theme of marriage.[15] Let us look now at an ode where the association is even more prominent, C. 2.8:

> Ulla si iuris tibi peierati
> poena, Barine, nocuisset umquam
> dente si nigro fieres vel uno
>   turpior ungui,
>
> crederem: sed tu simul obligasti   5
> perfidum votis caput, enitescis
> pulchrior multo iuvenumque prodis
>   publica cura.

expedit matris cineres opertos
fallere et toto taciturna noctis   10
signa cum caelo gelidaque divos
    morte carentis.

ridet hoc, inquam, Venus ipsa, rident
simplices Nymphae ferus et Cupido
semper ardentis acuens sagittas   15
    cote cruenta.

adde quod pubes tibi crescit omnis,
servitus crescit nova nec priores
inpiae tectum dominae relinquunt
    saepe minati.   20

te suis matres metuunt iuvencis,
te senes parci miseraeque nuper
virgines nuptae, tua ne retardet
    aura maritos.

If any punishment for a perjured vow had ever done you harm, if
you became uglier by a blackened tooth or single nail, I would
believe you. But as soon as you have bound your treacherous head
with promises, (5) you gleam much more beautifully and come forth
as the universal concern of the youth. It helps you to swear falsely by
the buried ashes of your mother, by the silent stars of night (10)
along with the whole heavens, and by the gods who lack the cold of
death.

    Venus herself, I say, laughs at this, the artless Nymphs and vicious
Cupid, always whetting his burning arrows on bloody stone. (15)
Besides, all the young are growing up yours, your new band of slaves
is growing, and earlier ones do not leave the dwelling of their impious
mistress, though they have often threatened. (20) You, mothers fear
for their offspring, you, sparing fathers and wretched brides, recently
virgins, lest your breeze slow their husbands' course.

The clearest, often-noted, parallel to Catullus lies between the ode's final
stanza and 61.51–55. The addressee is Hymen, god of marriage:

te suis tremulus parens
invocat, tibi virgines
zonula soluunt sinus,

> te timens cupida novos
>   captat aure maritus.

You a father, atremble with age, calls on for his children, for you
virgins free their garments from their girdle, for you the fearful new
husband listens with eager ear.

Both structure and vocabulary call attention to the similarities.[16] The
anaphora of *te* and the tricolon are paralleled in Horace. Both virgins
and husbands make appearances, and *tremulus parens* is replaced by
senes parci. But now it is the mothers, fathers, and young brides who are
fearful for the husband, not the young husband himself, who in Horace
is soon to be the prey of Barine. The masterful change from Catullus's
concluding *aure maritus* to Horace's final *aura maritos* cements the
point. In the epithalamium, the bridegroom is eager to hear sounds of
Hymen's arrival because it announces the beginning of the ceremony. In
Horace, the groom's ear becomes Barine's "aura," her destructive emanation ready to lure him away from his husbandly duties.

Horace had already played on the ambiguity of *aura* as breeze or seductive aura in *C.* 1.5 when dealing with Pyrrha, who attracts men to their
destruction on the sea of love (*aurae*, *C.* 1.5.11).[17] But there is another
link between the two odes. Pyrrha's allure is metaphorically characterized
by her golden quality (*aurea*, 9, in clear anticipation of its assonantal
anagram two lines later) and her gleam. *Miseri, quibus / intemptata nites*:
"Pitiable creatures for whom you gleam without having been put to the
test" (12–13), says the enlightened speaker. *Nites* anticipates *enitescis*,
used of Barine at line 6, before we learn the full extent of her ruinous
aura. This is the only use of *eniteo* in either simple or inchoative form in
Horace, while Catullus's is at 61.21, where it is employed to describe the
bride Iunia (*enitens*). Once again, parody of the epithalamium form and
emulation of Catullus combine in Horace's portrayal of Barine as the an-
titype of a true bride, one who in fact is bent on destroying marriage by
enticing husbands away from their mates.

Finally we have the verb *prodis* at *C.* 2.8.6. Catullus 61 offers five uses
of *prodo* in a ritual repetition, in the second-person singular, when the
chorus asks for the appearance of the lovely bride: *prodeas nova nupta*,
"Come forth, new bride."[18] Horace's witty variation on this is *prodis
publica cura*. There is no need for the hortatory subjunctive here. Barine
has already come forth, both literally and figuratively, at work not only
seducing husbands from wives but playing the perverse bride as well. In
sum, as in the case of *C.* 3.21 in relation to the Catullan hymn, Horace
offers a dexterous, witty travesty of a form exemplified in high seriousness by his predecessor, but it is a parody that has its own satiric message.

As often in Horace's bows to Catullus, the major allusion is supplemented by a secondary example that supports the first. Here it is to be found in the phrase *taciturna noctis / signa* (C. 2.8.10–11). Horace is thinking of the comparison that Catullus makes (7.7–8) of the number of kissings of Lesbia—that would be enough, or more than enough, for him—to

> sidera multa, cum tacet nox,
> furtivos hominum vident amores.

> the many stars, when night is silent, that look upon men's stolen loves.

Furtivos is a key word in making the connection between the two poems. The context as a whole speaks to the evanescence of human activity when seen against the backdrop of the eternal heavenly bodies. But *furtivos* gives the analogy an autobiographical twist by also suggesting the surreptitious nature of Catullus's adulterous affair with Lesbia. The immortal heavenly bodies see into the illicit doings of men to which other humans should not be privy.[19] Horace, in his borrowing, thus takes the clandestine and makes it public. Barine can swear by the stars at night that she will be faithful, which is to say that, though a courtesan, she will adopt the habits of a bride. The poem shows that, far from this being the case, she will in fact lead her life as an adulteress, making newly married husbands unfaithful while keeping old liaisons going as well. If Catullus's own relationship with Lesbia mocks the customariness of marriage, Horace takes matters one step further, at least vis-à-vis the narrative moment of Catullus 7, by making Barine a *publica cura*, someone for whom everyone cares and against whom everyone should be on guard.

Finally, in our survey of the influence of Catullus's epithalamia on Horace, let us turn to C. 3.26:

> Vixi puellis nuper idoneus
> et militavi non sine gloria:
>   nunc arma defunctumque bello
>   barbiton hic paries habebit,

> laevom marinae qui Veneris latus   5
> custodit: hic, hic ponite lucida
>   funalia et vectis et arcus
>   oppositis foribus minacis.

> o quae beatam diva tenes Cyprum et
> Memphin carentem Sithonia nive,   10

regina, sublimi flagello
   tange Chloen semel arrogantem.

I have lived until recently congenial with girls and soldiered not
without renown. Now this wall, which guards the left side of Venus of
the sea, (5) will claim my weapons and my lyre, done with war. Here,
here put in place the glimmering torches and the levers and the bows
that threaten blocked doors.

   O queen, who possesses wealthy Cyprus and Memphis, lacking the
snows of Thrace, (10) touch haughty Chloe once with your lofty lash.

This charming ode forms a careful, chiastic balance with C. 1.5 at the
beginning of the collection. If Neptune's temple wall there receives his
dripping garments, as offering from someone the god has saved from
love's treacherous seas, here Venus's shrine will accept the speaker's
weaponry as final thanksgiving for a lover's life well fought. The context
suggests that, in regard to the speaker's liaison with Chloe, however,
matters have not fared so well. Hence, as a final prayer to his patroness,
he asks that Venus touch the unresponsive girl with one of her own
weapons, a whip. The goddess is to make her feel the same hurt that she
has given Horace's protagonist. If in the past she has failed to react to
him, let her in turn now sense the pangs of unrequited love.[20]

   In his powerful ending, Horace is thinking back to a moment in Catullus's second epithalamium, poem 62. There the chorus of boys is responding to their female counterpart's comparison of a girl, while she is *intacta*
(untouched and therefore virginal, 45), to a protected flower, cherished by
all. To them, by contrast, while she remains *intacta* (56), she is (49–52)

ut vidua in nudo vitis quae nascitur arvo,
numquam se extollit, numquam mitem educat uvam,
sed tenerum prono deflectens pondere corpus
iam iam contingit summum radice flagellum.

like an unwedded vine that grows up in a bare field, it never raises
itself up, never produces a mild grape, but, bending down its tender
body with weight thrust forward, it now, even now, touches its
topmost tendril with its root.

Catullus calls attention to his final phrase by inverting what the reader
expects, namely that the vine would be said to touch its root by the tip of
its tendril. This in turn brings out the play on the verb *contingit*, compounded from *cum* and *tango*. The only "touching" that will occur to
the vine in her barren location, sequestered from contact with the living,

be they farmers, bullocks, or the marrying elm (54–55), is solipsistic, with self touching only self.

Horace, in appropriating Catullus's powerful expression, simplifies *contingit* into *tange* and alters *summum* to *sublimi*. Most striking, however, is the change of meaning in *flagellum* from the whip-like shoot of a vine to the lash of Venus. We hear elsewhere of the word *verber* standing for Venus's whip, for instance at Tibullus 1.8.6, where *verbera* are among the instruments that Venus employs to educate her suffering slave of love.[21] Since Horace's use here is the only instance of *flagellum* with such a meaning, its appearance suggests that he is directly assimilating Catullus to his own special purposes.

The lesson to Chloe would seem to be double. Perhaps now, in response to the speaker's prayer, she will learn from Venus to suffer in love as well as to inflict suffering. But the reference to Catullus's epithalamium may contain a still deeper message. Arrogance is cousin to self-absorption, and self-absorption leads to solitude, which is to say, in this context, to an unattached life. Horace may not be suggesting that marriage lies in Chloe's future but that, as a form of compromise with Catullus, at least a potential liaison will come her way that she wants but that will never be fully hers, unless she forgoes the pride that Horace gives her as the poem's final word.[22]

Finally, let us turn to two love poems. Here comparison between the two poets arises initially not from complementary lexical uses that lead us to further considerations but from questions of overall structure. The first is Catullus 45:

Acmen Septimius suos amores
tenens in gremio "mea" inquit "Acme,
ni te perdite amo atque amare porro
omnes sum assidue paratus annos,
quantum qui pote plurimum perire,   5
solus in Libya Indiaque tosta
caesio veniam obvius leoni."
hoc ut dixit, Amor sinistra ut ante
dextra sternuit approbationem.
    at Acme leviter caput reflectens   10
et dulcis pueri ebrios ocellos
illo purpureo ore suaviata,
"sic," inquit "mea vita Septimille,
huic uni domino usque serviamus,
ut multo mihi maior acriorque   15
ignis mollibus ardet in medullis."

hoc ut dixit, Amor sinistra ut ante
dextra sternuit approbationem.
  nunc ab auspicio bono profecti
mutuis animis amant amantur.   20
unam Septimius misellus Acmen
mavult quam Syrias Britanniasque:
uno in Septimio fidelis Acme
facit delicias libidinesque.
quis ullos homines beatiores   25
vidit, quis Venerem auspicatiorem?

Septimius, holding his love Acme in his lap, says, "My Acme, unless I
love you overwhelmingly and am further prepared to love you
unceasingly for all time, as madly as any man can be in love, (5) may I,
alone in Libya or sunburned India, meet face-to-face a grey-eyed lion."
When he said this, Love, though before on the left, sneezed approval
on the right.

  But Acme, lightly bending her head (10) and kissing with her purple
lips the drunken eyes of the sweet boy, says, "So let us continuously
serve this one master, my little Septimius, my life, as surely as a much
greater and fiercer fire (15) burns my soft marrow." When she said
this, Love, though before on the left, sneezed approval on the right.

  Now, having set out from a good auspice, they love and are loved
with mutual response. (20) Lovesick Septimius prefers Acme to places
like Syria and Britain, in Septimius alone faithful Acme takes her pleasure and delight. Who has seen any happier creatures, (25) who has
seen a more auspicious love?

Our usual Catullus, who so regularly seems to speak to his addressees,
and to us, of his immediate feelings, is here replaced by someone who
makes a point of arranging the story of two lovers with whom he has no
apparent personal interest except to tell their tale.[23] In a twenty-six-line
poem, the suitors' voices are directly heard for only ten lines, less even
than half the work's length. The rest is made up, first, of third-person
narrative that describes the setting for each lover. These segments, the
initial lines devoted to Septimius and the subsequent ones to Acme, are
followed by two exactly repeated verses noting Amor's approval of their
posture and words. The poem concludes with an eight-line commentary
by the narrator on the situation of the two lovers and ends with a seemingly rhetorical question: Who has ever seen happier people or a more
propitious love?

  When the lovers do speak, the heightened tone of their words catches
our attention. Septimius pleads the depth of his emotion: he is prepared

to meet a glaring African lion if his sentiments aren't true. Acme plights her troth to love's mastery, since she senses passion's burning more greatly and acutely than ever before. Their story, as the narrator tells it at the end, helps justify such hyperbole. Septimius, now, prefers Acme to places like Syria and Britain. (Had he, in the past, abandoned her for repeated travel elsewhere, the presumption being that he had favored the exigencies of his career over his amatory interest at home?) Acme finds sexual satisfaction only in Septimius. (Had she not done so previously, however, on the several occasions that the plural *libidines*, and perhaps also the comparative adjectives of line 15, may suggest?[24])

The intercalary lines, which the narrator tells us were spoken by Amor, also hint that the emotional situation of the lovers was different in the past from what it is now or, if we accept a presumption of the final lines, will be in the future. When Love had sneezed before on the left, their amatory developments, in all probability, had not been proceeding smoothly. Love's repeated, positive auspice, combined with the emphasis of the narrator's final word, which itself echoes *auspicio bono* (10), presumes that their intimacy is now off on the right track with better prospects for happiness than existed once upon a time.

But the fact that Catullus dispenses so pointedly with his usual immediacy may allow us to read the potential irony of the concluding interrogative back into the poem itself. What if there in fact might be happier people and a more auspicious amour, and what if the poem as a totality adumbrates the possibility? The creator's need for control of his material, especially in comparison to the openness that we expect from Catullus, is one argument in favor of irony. We have, for instance, the perfect balance between the opening segments devoted to the lovers (nine lines each), then the finely crafted, eight-line chiasmus at the end, with *auspicio* reiterated in *auspicatiorem*, and each lover given a carefully aligned duet of verses in between, the first commencing with *unam* (21), the second with *uno* (23). Then there are the repeated, intercalary lines, which lend further weight to the poem's stress on order and equilibrium.

On the surface, then, we have the prospect of happy intimacy, supported by the lovers' protestations of affection and fidelity—what we might expect from Catullus, especially if the two protagonists had spoken directly to each other, and if their words had been understood as such by a reader drawn without mediation into their implications. But the constant intervention by the narrator in his presentation gives us reason to add another dimension to an interpretation of the poem based on their words alone or on the narrator's perception of them. The parallelisms, the repetitions, especially in the litany of the intercalary lines, and even the narratorial framing, all suggest a need on the author's part to regulate his material, to give it a highly disciplined form. It is as if the narrator had to exercise the magic of his own charm, especially by means of the poem's incantatory repetitions, to make the story work. Mutuality of words stands to create mutuality of affection in the characters of which they tell.

Perfect as the newly reestablished bond between Acme and Septimius may seem, there is a tension between the poet's orderings and his creatures' passionate hyperboles, as if the only way that such a paragon among Catullan relationships could continue to endure were by being steadied and fixed through authorial disposition. The finale, with its many parallelisms (*amant, amantur, beatiores, auspicatiorem,* along with *unam, uno*), is a bit too neat, too obtrusively crafted, as if Catullus had deliberately adopted a clinical detachment or, better, as if the logic in his own arrangements was both requisite and quixotic at the same time.

It is requisite, if we trust the poem as an ideal vision of love effectuated at last. It is quixotic, if we realize how fallible such a patterning is elsewhere in Catullus. Such a gamut of intonation allows the reader to choose between, or to amalgamate, humor and sorrow depending on whether he views the poet as either serious about or amused over his protagonists' impetuosities. One final reaction is that of irony toward them and toward the possibility of their, or any, happy union. We need only take note of the regularly negative change from past to present in Catullus's descriptions of love's denouement, especially in his depiction of his affair with Lesbia, to realize both the vulnerability of his lovers in poem 45 and the need for him to use his rhetorical powers to hold them together.

Horace's "imitation" is C. 3.9:

"Donec gratus eram tibi
   nec quisquam potior bracchia candidae
cervici iuvenis dabat,
   Persarum vigui rege beatior."

"donec non alia magis   5
   arsisti neque erat Lydia post Chloen,
multi Lydia nominis
   Romana vigui clarior Ilia."

"me nunc Thressa Chloe regit,
   dulcis docta modos et citharae sciens,   10
pro qua non metuam mori,
   si parcent animae fata superstiti."

"me torret face mutua
    Thurini Calais filius Ornyti,
pro quo bis patiar mori,   15
    si parcent puero fata superstiti."

"quid si prisca redit Venus
    diductosque iugo cogit aeneo,
si flava excutitur Chloe
    reiectaeque patet ianua Lydiae?"   20

"quamquam sidere pulcrior
    ille est, tu levior cortice et inprobo
iracundior Hadria,
    tecum vivere amem, tecum obeam lubens."

"As long as I was pleasing to you and (as long as) no youth, more preferred, put his arms around your white neck, I flourished more blissful than the kings of Persia."

"As long as you did not burn more for another (5) and (as long as) Lydia was not second to Chloe, I, Lydia of great repute, flourished more famous than Roman Ilia."

"Now Thracian Chloe, learned in sweet songs and skilled on the lyre, (10) rules me, for whom I will not fear to die, if the fates allow her, my soul, to survive."

"Calais, son of Ornytus of Thurium, burns me with a flame he shares, for whom I will twice suffer death, (15) if the fates allow my boy to survive."

"What if our old love returns and compels us, driven apart, under a brazen yoke, if blonde Chloe is expelled and the door is opened for rejected Lydia?" (20)

"Although he is more beautiful than a star, you more fickle than cork and more temperamental than the unruly Adriatic, with you I would love to live, with you I would gladly die."

Horace fancied Catullus's Acme, addicted to love's fires and pleasures, as the ancestress for his Lydia. He also clearly draws on the interaction of infidelity and faithfulness seen against a subtle background of temporal evolution. But the differences between the two poems are as telling as their similarities. For all its suggestions of a past in his lovers' lives and ambiguous hints of a future (will it repeat the past, or not?), Catullus's poem deals essentially with the present, with a pivotal "now" in the romance of his protagonists. Horace devotes equal attention to past, present, and time to come, with no illusions about love's permanence except what issues from the mouths of his characters.

Above all, and in dramatic contrast to Catullus, Horace has no setting in which to place his characters' words. There is no narrative frame or apparent attempt at authorial control of his subjects. Horace's repetitions and careful balances (*donec . . . donec, me . . . me*), as well as the sudden, powerful imbalance of the final stanzas, clearly modeled on those of Catullus, are generated by the lovers themselves, who speak more of differentiation than commonality in the middle stanzas, where they are closest lexically and farthest apart emotionally. Their inner life seems ours to behold as they are allowed at least the appearance of freedom to cap each other, in a verbal dance of lovemaking. They create antiphonally their own exchange, with its conclusion and climax in the question and answer that bring them finally back together. Lydia's ultimate verse confirms this unity by the reflection of its repeated *tecum* in the opening line's *tibi*.

If we make a direct comparison, we find the ordinarily direct, impassioned Catullus imagining other lovers' avowals of fidelity and encapsulating them, as if only thus could a unique situation be preserved. Antithetically, Horace, by nature more contemplative, more concerned than Catullus with grander problems of man and his destiny, allows his duo to seem to have free rein to resolve their fate. Each poet, however, is also much himself. Horace, by allowing Lydia and friend apparent independence from a shaping voice, bluntly reveals the cyclic vagaries of emotion between two people in the rhetorical counterpoint they employ. Catullus, tracing the ardent outbursts of his lovers and touching gently on their past, takes refuge in the role of authorial matchmaker, but in so doing betrays as well his own deep involvement by imposing a pattern of disciplined enclosure not of their manufacture.

Immediate Catullus, so fond of determined self-questioning, could be seen here as the contriver, more aloof Horace as the realist, urging that process in human relationships is both reasonable and predictable. Catullus, playing the third party external to their situation, yokes Acme and Septimius by his own ceremony of words. As excited raconteur, he intones the reflections and iterations that conjoin. Horace, the more remote craftsman and tolerant as always of man's caprices, allows his subjects, with the help of Venus, to enmesh themselves in their own verbal toils. They establish, dissolve, and recreate linguistic unities of their own making, most markedly in the last two stanzas, where the male takes Catullus's artful correlations to himself and the female exerts her response both for and against them.

Catullus verges on the extreme, either in the attempt to capture the ideal present or in the implicit cynicism that lies behind knowledge of its propensity for failure. At the end of his poem, we question his tone, as if it bordered on self-parody. With Horace, more relaxed, more cosmopolitan, and less personally tortured (such, at least, is his persona) in matters of the heart, aware that a poet's power need not always be direct, the human condition, here at least, can evolve gently of itself while the seemingly distant poet works with kindly irony from within the dialogue, avoiding any need for a probing presence.

This is the Horace who can tell us, at the conclusion of C. 1.6, that, whether he is free of love (*vacuus*) or burning in its flames, he is always *levis*, at ease with himself, not ever given to deep commitments that might turn hurtful. It is not without its irony that this is the same adjective, used in the comparative form, that Lydia adopts to describe the lover, whose return she would gladly accept, at the end of C. 3.9. It is suitable also, however, for a poet who can so cleverly create the impression of authorial non-involvement while at the same time making what could be considered his most studied obeisance to the other supreme master of Latin personal poetry.

In this final comparison between our poets, we have two amoebean exchanges between lovers that form also an example of reciprocity between poets. It is as if (and we have seen other, parallel instances of this pattern) Horace was inspired to respond to Catullus's final, seemingly rhetorical, question with a lyric of his own. Support is lent to this possibility by the fact that Horace nearly ends his sparkling poem with an interrogation of his own. We face an irony: at the moment in the plot of Horace's poem where reconciliation between the two protagonists appears suddenly possible, both the languages of the lovers and the rhetoric of their presentation seem most disparate. But, just as Horace answers Catullus's query with a poem in reply, so, within his own masterful effort, a question ends the penultimate stanza, while response brings closure both to the dialogue within his own poem and to the interchange between poets that it so brilliantly documents.

There is surprisingly little lexical overlap between poems otherwise so complementary, but one word stands out, *mutuus*. It is employed by Catullus's narrator in the poem's epilogue to describe the feelings that are now apparently shared by his protagonists (*mutuis animis amant amantur*, 45.20), a line in which the asyndeton confirms the lovers' newfound, or newly restored, closeness. Horace ironizes against his model by giving the adjective to Lydia not on the occasion of her potential reconciliation with her lover, which brings the poem to a conclusion, but in the poem's central, present time, to describe the liaison with her amour of the moment (*me torret face mutua / Thurini Calais filius Ornyti*, C. 3.9.13–14). Perhaps Horace is saying to Catullus that true mutuality, even, or especially, one imposed by a narrator, is never to be expected in amatory matters, and that its movement from moment to moment, from affair to affair, suggests more the permanence of infidelity, or of amatory flexibility, than the endurance of any singular union.[25] Thus one word used in common suggests how Horace differentiates himself from Catullus while at the same time coopting, and commenting upon, aspects of his predecessor's genius. Such barter defines, on some unplumbable level, the sincerest form of poetic mutuality.

Conclusion

By way of synopsis, let us consider some patterns that emerge from tracing Horace's acceptance of Catullus into his imaginative world. To generalize broadly, these modes of reception fit under two sets of rubrics. The first might be labeled the psychological or emotional sphere. A major area of this book's enterprise has been to observe the response of Horace to questions of both theme and tone that he found in his predecessor. A second category might be entitled the stylistics of allusiveness. This heading looks to the means of the Augustan poet's response to Catullus rather than to the matter that he exploited.

As we explored this further area of concern, we have been observing in particular the rhetorical designs by which Horace reveals the influential presence of the earlier poet, as distinct from the Catullan subjects that drew his attention and elicited his varied reactions. Both domains are often intermeshed, to be sure, in the acts of creation and criticism, and are in some instances inseparable. But the division, however theoretical, will help lead us to a few summary remarks on the results of our inquiry. These, in turn, may serve as suggestions for further study of a topic by its nature boundless.

If we attend first to Horace's emotional attitude to Catullus, we have found sustained confirmation of the later writer's regular suppression, or amelioration, of Catullan eroticism. The Augustan poet will often make use of the art of poetry, of poetry-crafting, as a way of controlling and mastering the fervor of feeling that he found in his earlier colleague. Where Catullan emotionality is forward and immediate, Horace's is more distant and restrained. The later poet is measured and circumspect, whereas his predecessor tends to be directly impassioned. Catullus's persona battens on the publicity of his feelings, on relishing the revelation of his individuality. Horace's slides smoothly, and readily, from particular to general, from the personal to the universal.

If we turn to poetic figuration, we have found that Catullus delights in forms of metonymy, whereas Horace works his magic as much through aspects of metaphor and allegory. Let me offer as examples two spring poems of each master. In Catullus 46, the poet makes a swift transition, from the arrival of the new season to its effects on first the mind, then the feet, of the excited speaker. This movement in turn leads to thoughts of journeying and of return home—all in the compass of eleven lines. When Horace writes of spring's advent in C. 1.4, he, too, thinks of feet, but it is to make a distinction between the lightness of primaveral dances and the inexorability with which death's heavy, impartial foot pounds on the door of rich and poor alike. The speaker's "I" enters in only as part of an assemblage that shares in a destiny common to all mankind. Catullus, it could be said, works through self-extensions, Horace by means of revaluations that easily adopt aspects of the symbolic.

When we think back on Catullus's *phaselus*, it is the novelistic adventures of the boat that engage us as it tells of carrying its master from east to west through a motley geographical, meteorological, and emotional itinerary. In Horace's hands, the history of a boat, if we think of C. 1.3 and the *navis* that is taking Virgil to Greece, progresses quickly from literal to figurative, from the particular bark, to which the speaker's poet-friend is entrusted, to an emblem for all seafaring and its hazards, from its inception until the present. This in turn provokes a largely visionary meditation on the pitfalls of human ambition and on the folly of acting under the influence of hubris, especially when it is flaunted against the gods, conduct for which the first mariner stood as paradigm.

When we focus specifically on the subject of eroticism, we encounter a similar pattern. If we concentrate on the first seven poems of the Catullan corpus, we find that two deal with the pet sparrow of the speaker's beloved, a creature with which he would also like to play (and, it is implied, would also gladly become). Two others center on a swirl of kisses strong enough to extract lovers, at least momentarily, away from time's magnetic grip, and poem 6 introduces an intuitive narrator who imagines in detail the confidential lives of two inamorati on the verge of being immortalized in and through his verse. In all instances, we readers are entranced by a world of immediacies and contiguities, of the palpable and the concrete.

By contrast, Horace's first amatory ode (C. 1.5), the brilliant apostrophe to Pyrrha, shifts effortlessly from tangible to intangible, from actual people in an actual setting into what the characters signify. The female protagonist, as her names adumbrates, is alluring for the blonde beauty of her hair (*flavam*), and, in the eyes of her entranced lover, for her golden character (*aurea*). But she soon is changed, through the poem's transcending music, into a beacon fire whose flames lure unsuspecting devotees to their doom, shipwrecked in love's treacherous waters. Here, too, then, in this comparison of poets, we find Catullus the more directly experiential, while Horace, by contrast, readily flows from particular to general, from an apparently authentic vignette of life in progress toward what such realism symbolizes.

If we turn to the stylistics of Horace's allusions to Catullus, again certain schemata emerge. We have seen, for instance, that within several of Horace's odes, one clear reference to Catullus is often supplemented, and supported, by one or more others. C. 1.32 is a particularly interesting example of this phenomenon because the compounded, yet indirect, suggestions of the poet's Roman literary past come in an ode that forthrightly names Alcaeus, one of Horace's most salient models in the poetry of archaic Greece. C. 1.22 offers a particularized variation on this characteristic because it incorporates bows to the two poems of Catullus written in the meter that bears Sappho's name, the same meter that Horace utilizes for his brilliant meditation on the sacrosanctity of poets and poetry.

Subject matter also plays as important a role as meter in helping formulate such connections. Sometimes several poems of Catullus that are linked thematically appear in a single Horatian ode (I think particularly of those concerned with travel). On other occasions, Horace's genius will merge diverse topics of his predecessor into a powerful, idiosyncratic amalgam. C. 4.7 is a case in point. The ode makes reference to two ostensibly diverse works of Catullus, poem 5, on the countless kisses the speaker requires of Lesbia, and poem 46, with its dynamic précis of the effect of spring on mind and body. Both of the earlier poems deal with versions of temporality: the first urges us to live to the full the frenzy of the moment because mortality's dark night will soon bring one continuous slumber; the second reminds us of the invigorating effect of seasonal change and of the increased activity that follows in its wake. Horace's rich melancholy builds on both, in the first instance to emphasize the loss of individuality that death brings, in the second to affirm that spring is part of a seasonal round with its own regimen of triumph and loss. But whereas nature's continuity, whatever its vicissitudes, is assured, the cycle of a human existence occurs only once, and death forms its inevitable conclusion.

Another propensity on Horace's part is to take a theme that appears in several guises in Catullus and reorganize it over a series of interconnected poems. Odes 15–17 of the later writer's first book, for example, draw on a diverse array of gestures toward Catullus in a trio of odes that look at the figure of Helen from different points of view. We have also traced a complementary phenomenon, where Horace takes a single poem of Catullus and scatters allusions to it throughout a group of odes. Such indications, while they both adopt and transfigure what Horace found in his predecessor, also serve as a unifying factor within the Horatian corpus. Odes 21–23 of the third book of *Carmina* form a case in point, as they draw on Catullus's unique venture into hymn to help animate a variety of contexts.

Finally, I would like to call attention to two further points. The first is the continued, constant presence of Catullus in the fourth book of odes. The ten-year gulf that separated the publication of the initial gatherings of lyrics in 23 BCE from the last collection saw no diminution of the effect of the Republican poet on his Augustan heir. If anything, it is deepened. C. 4.7, as we have seen, is a distinguished example, but it is scarcely accidental that in C. 4.12, Horace's valedictory to Virgil, the heritage of unnamed Catullus plays a decisive thematic and structuring role.

Second, we should take due note of Horace's pervasive sense of humor. The self-distance that allows Horace to laugh at himself, "a plump, glistening pig from the drove of Epicurus" (*Epi.* 1.4.15–16), as he styles himself to his fellow poet Albius Tibullus, also helps him embrace a long view of high seriousness, whether his own or that of Catullus. This ability to laugh, both at himself and at his predecessor's intensities, takes several forms. It can be seen in terms of genre, where, for instance, Catullus's hymn or epithalamia are subjected to Horatian parody, or in terms of subject matter. Both are brilliantly combined in C. 3.27, where the figure of Europe suffers macabre marriage to Jupiter as bull, while at the same time her story serves to deflate the hyperbolic emotionality of the Ariadne that Catullus creates in his poem 64, and to subject it to comic inversion.

But even here we are left, in the end, with the sense that, however discreetly, the later bard is paying the homage of emulation to the earlier. This judgment in turn allows us to reiterate our sense of the Augustan poet's compliment to his intellectual forbear, as we pursue the endless task of reading Catullus through his eyes, and of marveling at the genius of both.

Notes

INTRODUCTION

1. Throughout this volume, the translations are my own.
2. The pattern is set at the start of Book 1 with C. 1.9, 1.14, and 1.18.
3. Cf. *Epi.* 1.19.23.
4. *Institutio oratoria* 10.1.96. At 10.1.94, Horace is selected as the outstanding practitioner of satire for the concision and clarity of his language. Compare also the famous judgment that Petronius puts into the mouth of Eumolpus when he speaks of Horace's *curiosa felicitas*, his painstaking appropriateness of expression (*Satyrica* 118.5).
5. For general evaluations of lyric and lyricism, see in particular W. R. Johnson 1982; the chapters on ancient lyric by Jonathan Culler in his yet-unpublished essay on lyric theory will be of great value to all students of Catullus and Horace as well as of lyric poetry in general.
6. Horace's failure to name Catullus may not at first seem unusual. In the two books of his *Satires*, for instance, Lucretius is never mentioned, though he is clearly a major influence. My point rests on the question of genre. As far as his first publications are concerned, Horace is writing satiric poetry, Lucretius didactic. But in the *Carmina*, where Alcaeus is invoked by name twice and Sappho once (and where each is alluded to obliquely on several other occasions), we might expect at least a direct, if passing, reference to the "lyric" Catullus.
7. For a more detailed discussion of the parallels, see Putnam 1986, 40–41.

CHAPTER 1: TIME AND PLACE

1. We should note Horace's only mention of Remus at *Epodes* 7.19, where it is also juxtaposed to *nepotibus* (20). Horace gives Remus the adjective *immerentis*, but the Horatian context likewise deals with moral decline that for the Augustan poet stems from a fratricide that anticipates the continuity of civil war in late Republican Rome.
2. As commentary on this and other parallel situations, we should remember the observation of Commager (1962, 145): "Catullus . . . often adjures himself by name in order to see himself, psychologically as well as grammatically, as a third person."
3. For the meaning and sexual connotations of *glubo*, see Penella 1976; Arkins 1979; Jocelyn 1979; as well as Adams 1982, 74 and 169.
4. For 1.25, see in particular Lee 1975, 36.
5. At line 20 I follow the universal reading of the manuscripts, *Hebro*. Here, and elsewhere on occasional matters of orthography and punctuation, I differ from the text I follow throughout the book (F. Klingner, ed., *Q. Horati Flacci*

Opera [Leipzig, 1959]). At line 20, Klingner, following the 1501 Aldine edition of Horace's works, emends *Hebro* to *Euro*.

6. Cf. the uses of *domus* at 68.68 and 156, and the discussion by Elder (1951). The text of Catullus followed is the Oxford Classical Text of R. Mynors (Oxford, 1959).

7. *De rerum natura* 4.1177.

8. Lydia is also *levis* because she will become dry and therefore light as a leaf in winter. She can afford to take no love seriously because none will then come her way.

9. Horace's only use of the word *moechus* in his lyric corpus is at *C.* 1.25.9. It occurs, used of male adventurers, in Catullus also at 11.17 and 37.16, the latter a poem that has much in common with 58. The setting is outdoors, in the center of Rome, at a *taberna* in the Forum. We are nine columns from the temple of Castor and Pollux, watching Lesbia sitting there, once "beloved as much as no one will be loved" (*amata tantum quantum amabitur nulla*, 12). Her affections are now bestowed ubiquitously, on men "of rank and fortune" (*boni beatique*, 14), as well as on "all petty sorts and back-street adulterers" (*omnes pusilli et semitarii moechi*, 16). The nonce word *semitarii* has some of the same resonance as *angiportis* in 58, defining those who, whether male or female, ply their trade in the by-ways.

10. Horace's gerundives in *C.* 2.14 all appear at the beginnings of lines; *dormienda* concludes its line in Catullus (6).

11. For the etymology of Faunus from *faveo*, see ServiusD on Virgil *Georgics* 1.10, and *Dictionnaire étymologique de la langue latine*, ed. A. Ernout and A. Meillet (Paris, 1959), s.v. Faunus.

12. At line 8 I read *urit* instead of the equally strong *visit*.

13. We find *nunc* at lines 9, 11, and 20, *iam* at 3, 5, and 16, with all except the first serving as the initial word of a verse. For further discussion of Catullus 5, see also Chapter 4.

14. Besides the several mentions of Catullus 46 in the present chapter, see discussion in Chapter 4.

15. Horace may have drawn his mention of Favonius from Catullus 64.282, which tells of the flowers that the "fertile breeze of warm Favonius begets" (*aura parit . . . tepidi fecunda Favoni*).

16. Cf. Catullus 3.12, of the underworld "whence they say no one returns" (*unde negant redire quemquam*).

17. The noun *campi* is also repeated at line endings at 46.4 and *C.* 4.7.1. Poem 46.5 concludes with *aestuosae*, *C.* 4.7.9 with *aestas*.

18. The repetition of *sollicitam* (16) in *sollicitus* (26) connects the troubled brow of the rich, who could and should find useful a stay in a poor man's dwelling, with Maecenas himself, for whom the substitution of country for city, poor for rich, a poet's appropriate philosophizing for troubles of state, is in order, according to the speaker's suggestion.

19. I differ from the text of Klingner by extending the quotation from *vixi* through to the end of line 48.

20. The adjective *impotentia* (18), which I translated as "wild," can also mean something like "powerless." However raging the waters might be, they offer no danger to the *phaselus* and its passenger.

21. The powerful personification of the boat is abetted by the denomination of its passenger as *erus* (19). The boat is slave, its passenger, master. Much the same distinction holds true of the relation between Sirmio and its *erus* (31.12) in a poem, as we will see, closely linked to 4.

22. *Bithunos campos* (31.5–6) and *Phrygii campi* (46.4) are self-reflective; *lacum* (4.24) is further explained by *Lydiae lacus undae* (31.13).

23. For this suggestion, see Putnam 1962.

24. For a different approach to Catullus 4, which views it as a study in stylistics, see Davis 2002.

25. See Chapter 4.

26. See, e.g., J. Pucci 1992. See also Chapter 4.

27. On the punctuation of both text and translation here, see Quinn 1980, 152 (on *C.* 1.14.9–15).

28. On the echoes of Catullus here, see Mendell 1938, 148.

29. Quintilian *Institutio oratoria* 8.6.44.

30. Fr. 208 Campbell. Some scholars, among them Kiessling and Heinze (1955, 71), find little in common between Horace's words and the Alcaeus fragment. Fraenkel (1957, 155) resorts to litotes, seeing Horace here as "not independent of the Lesbian poet."

31. See Mendell 1935, 298–99; Lee 1975, 36; and, in particular, Zumwalt 1977.

32. We should note also that the form *cave* (*C.* 1.14.16) appears only once elsewhere in the *Carmina* (*C.* 3.7.24). Two of Catullus's three uses occur at 50.18 and 19 (the other is to be found at 61.145) in a warning to Calvus not to scorn the speaker's affection.

33. Before we leave the influence of Catullus 4 on Horace, it is worth noting that the only use of *phaselus* (*-os*) in Horace is at *C.* 3.2.29, where the subject is again an allegorical journey. In his moral progress through life, "Horace" will not "unmoor his barque" (*solvat phaselon*) with anyone who makes public the rites of Ceres.

In the previous lines he states that he will not allow the same person "under his roof" (*sub isdem / . . . trabibus*, 27–28). The metonymy is striking. The same figuration is used by Catullus for the *phaselus* (4.3) and has already been adopted by Horace at *C.* 1.1.13 for a boat.

34. On *C.* 1.22, see Commager 1995, 131–36; Zumwalt 1975; Olstein 1984; G. Davis 1987, 1991, 67–69; Lowrie 1997, 189–94; Hubbard 2000, passim.

For detailed treatments of Sappho and Catullus in the background of Horace's ode, see McCormick 1973; Ancona 2002.

35. At *Epi.* 1.10.1, Fuscus is styled *urbis amatorem*. Horace therefore may be wittily asking him, in his mind, to leave Rome and to follow the speaker in his own spiritual journey from the Sabine territory to points remote. Horace is also playing with the name Fuscus, he of the dark skin (see Lee 1975, 39). The reader is helped by the name of the slave *fuscus Hydaspes* at *Sat.* 2.8.14. Even though Fuscus is attached to Rome, Horace separates his name by only four lines from the Hydaspes, at *C.* 1.22.4–8. Perhaps the poem's addressee should think of himself, as well as his poet friend, as having a connection with India. On Fuscus, see further Harrison 1992, as well as R. Nisbet 1959.

36. On poem 51, see further discussion in Chapters 2 and 3.

37. The whole poem is no. 31 in *Poetarum Lesbiorum Fragmenta*, ed. E. Lobel and D. Page (Oxford, 1955). See also D. Page, *Sappho and Alcaeus* (Oxford, 1965), 19–33.

38. The influence of Catullus 11 on other odes of Horace deserves separate treatment. Foremost among them are *C.* 2.6 (and through it *C.* 2.7), *C.* 2.17, and, perhaps most richly, *C.* 3.4, where the poet's invulnerability also features prominently among his credentials for lecturing Caesar. See note 40 below.

39. The striking use of *integer* as the poem's opening word may also be meant to remind the reader of the preceding ode, as the speaker prepares a chorus to hymn Diana and Apollo. The *tenerae virgines* and *pueri* who fulfill this duty (*C.* 1.21.1–2) are in turn a reminder of the *puellae et pueri integri* (34.2) who actually sing Catullus's hymn to Diana.

40. Horace makes several other bows to Catullus 11, especially when the theme of travel is paramount. *Aestuat unda* at *C.* 2.6.4, for instance, is a clear allusion to the phrase *tunditur unda* in the same verse of Catullus 11 (see Mendell 1935, 297 n. 3). But perhaps the most interesting, extensive reference back on Horace's part comes in his longest ode, *C.* 3.4. There the speaker begins by displaying the credentials that allow him license to offer counsel to Caesar—the core of the poem. He was miraculously free from harm even as a child. Since then the Muses have guaranteed his sacrosanctity, saving him, among other hazards, from death at sea (here *Sicula Palinurus unda*, 28, are the words that recall *tunditur unda*). Whatever treacherous journey he might undertake, the Muses will see him safely through (29–36):

> utcumque mecum vos eritis, libens
> insanientem navita Bosphorum   30
>   temptabo et urentis harenas
>   litoris Assyrii viator,
>
> visam Britannos hospitibus feros
> et laetum equino sanguine Concanum,
>   visam pharetratos Gelonos   35
>   et Scythicum inviolatus amnem.

Whenever you will be with me, as a sailor I will gladly make trial of the raging Bosphorus (30) and, as a traveler by land, the burning sands of the Assyrian shore, scatheless I will view the Britons, fierce to their guests, and the Concanus who delights in the blood of horses, I will view the quivered Geloni (35) and Scythia's river.

Here the parallels are particularly intense. Catullus's *temptare* (14) is altered to *temptabo* (31), his *visens* (10) to *visam* (33, 35); the *Britanni* are a common presence, while Catullus's *sagittiferos Parthos* (the adjective is apparently his coinage) become *pharetratos Gelonos*. The earlier poet's quintuple use of *sive* or *seu* to begin lines from 2 to 9 is mimicked by Horace's anaphora of *visam* and *et* at the start of lines 33–36. Finally, one Caesar, in Catullus's line 10, leads to another at the start of Horace's subsequent stanza.

In the symbolic world with which Horace replaces Catullus's palpable geography, the literal journey that "Catullus" contemplates in the company of Furius and Aurelius mutates into the imagined itinerary that Horace envisions in the company of the Muses, a journey that proves his invulnerability through prowess of mind. And the vivid words that Catullus's speaker commands his comrades to convey to Lesbia become Horace's own discreet moralizing to Octavianus Caesar on the restrained uses of power. As so often, Catullan immediacy suffers metamorphosis into Horatian spirituality but serves as its impetus as well.

41. Among the lexical parallels here between the two poems (and poets) is the verb *vagor*. It is used by Catullus but once (46.7) and by Horace only twice in the *Carmina*, at C. 1.22.11 and C. 3.14.19.

42. Alcaeus 338 Campbell.

43. Note also that *puellae* appears in the first line, and *digitum* in the third, of Catullus's poem, while the same space separates *puellae* from *digito* in C. 1.9.22–24. Horace's use of *repetantur* (20) may find its source in Catullus's *appetenti* (3). Likewise, Catullus's *malum* is at least sonically echoed in *male*, Horace's penultimate word.

44. The manuscripts show no division in the thirteen lines, but there has been no uniformity among critics about the final three lines, with some opting for the manuscripts' continuum, others positing them as part of poem 2 but with the omission of one or more lines, and a third group seeing them as a fragment of a different poem. Reasons for and against unity are given by virtually all commentators. See especially Fordyce 1961; Quinn 1970; and Thomson 1997, ad loc.

45. Catullus's *spectat* has no counterpart in Sappho's original.

46. For the connection between the two poems, see, among others, Quinn 1970 (on Catullus 9.9); Nisbet and Hubbard 1970, on C. 1.36.6; West 1995, 176–79; and the more extended comparison of Syndikus 1972, 325–28.

47. Horace deftly compresses Catullus's *os oculosque* (9.9) into *oscula* (C. 1.36.6).

48. The aloof tone and lack of apostrophe stand out, especially in a poem nominally welcoming back a friend from abroad. Excitement on the part of the speaker and apostrophe to the poem's addressee are both present in a parallel ode, C. 2.7, on "Horace's" pleasure at the return of (an unknown) Pompeius, but there the influence of Catullus is more adumbrated than direct.

49. The connection is pointed out, among others, by Fordyce (1961, on 61.34) and West (1995, 180–81). We should also compare the parallel simile at 61.102–6.

50. It is noteworthy that Horace may have gained inspiration for his phrase *Cressa . . . pulcra dies nota* (10) from Catullus's description of a day on which Lesbia favors him (*lapide illa dies candidiore notat*, 68.148), apparently the first appearance of the image. The context happens also to concern an adulterous union where marriage is apparently out of the question.

51. For *alloquerer* (4) and the importance of dialogue to Catullus, see poem 38 and its double use of *allocutio* (5, 7).

52. Cf. Horace's use of the same language in a similar context at C. 4.2.20.

CHAPTER 2: SPEECH AND SILENCE

1. In Chapter 3 I examine in detail how Catullus's anaphora of the word *otium* here is drawn upon by Horace at the opening of C. 2.16, by way of seeking the difference between each poet's treatment of the noun's meaning. The interconnection will prove to be one of the most visible examples of Horace's emulation of the earlier poet and of how we read Catullus through him.

2. On the idea of mortality implicit in the phrase *lumina nocte*, cf. Virgil's imitation at *Aeneid* 10.746.

3. We should note, however, the use of *vacuam* at C. 1.5.10, where the adjective implies a freedom from emotional involvement that also suggests sexual availability.

4. At line 13 I read *gaudete*, with G and R, instead of *gaudente*, the emendation of Bergk adopted by Mynors.

5. Horace's only use of the form *salve* occurs at C. 1.32.15.

6. For further discussion of Catullus 31, see Chapter 1.

7. This same section of Catullus 68 was also a prime influence on Horace as he wrote C. 3.13. Forms of *lympha* (68.54, 3.13.16), of *rivus* (68.58, 3.13.7) and of *dulcis* (68.61, 3.13.2, each at the beginning of a line) appear in each poem. *Prosilit* (68.58) becomes *desiliunt* (3.13.16). *Perlucens* (68.57) finds its counterpart in *splendidior vitro* (3.13.1) and *viatori lasso in sudore* (68.61) in *fessis vomere tauris* (3.13.11), while the phrase *cum gravi . . . agros* is reflected in *atrox hora Caniculae* (3.13.9). For a detailed discussion of the ode, see Chapter 5.

8. Horace may also glean the phrase *Musas Veneremque* from Catullus 68.10 (*muneraque et Musarum hinc petis et Veneris*, "and you seek from me the gifts of the Muses and of Venus"), where the conjunction probably serves as a hendiadys for love poetry.

Horace mentions Alcaeus by name on four other occasions in his poetry (C. 2.13.27 and 4.9.7, *Epi.* 1.19.29 and 2.2.99), and alludes pointedly to him on several other occasions, usually when the poetry of Lesbos is mentioned.

9. In this context, Horace's use of *laborum* (14) looks, among other possibilities, ambiguously at the efforts of poetry-making and the trials of love. Cf. the use of *labore* at Catullus 50.14 (as well as at 31.9 and 11, mentioned above). Certainly the last stanza, while dealing with an abstraction, also abstracts us, but never completely, from the physical exactitude of the previous stanza's rhetorical journey from Bacchus to Lycus's hair and eyes. Apostrophe to the lyre draws us away from a concentration on passion, but Horace's mention of *labores* leaves us wondering whether the lyre's *lenimen* effects the same outcome for him.

10. See discussion in Chapter 1.

11. It is not happenstance that the subsequent ode in the Horatian corpus, C. 1.33, is a spiritual dialogue between poets, in this case between Horace and his addressee, probably the elegist Albius Tibullus. Horace pits lyric, at least his

version of lyric, which here offers the detached view of *Horatius vacuus* on amatory affairs and their innate inconstancy, against the obduracy of Albius's mournful song.

12. LP/Campbell fr. 342.

13. For details, see Nisbet and Hubbard 1970, 227–28 (introduction to commentary on C. 1.18).

14. See Martin 2002, passim.

15. On the erotic connotations of the noun *labor*, see R. Pichon, *Index Verborum Amatorium* (Hildesheim, 1966), 180.

16. We think, for instance, of the famous bore of *Sat.* 1.9 who shares Horace's walk along the Via Sacra and of whom we learn much, but never his name.

17. See Nisbet and Hubbard 1970, on C. 1.27.17, for the connection, as well as the elaboration of Wray 2001, 153–56. Fitzgerald (1995, 54) notes how the theme of revealing and hiding connects Catullus 6 with its more famous neighbors, 5 and 7.

18. The elimination of any announcement on Horace's part of the power of his poetry to immortalize is also complementary to its understatement or nonstatement.

19. On the complex structure of this jewel of a poem, see Putnam 1969b.

20. See also discussion of poem 76 in Chapter 1.

21. *Historia naturalis* 14.63.

22. See Nisbet and Hubbard 1970, 312–13 (on C. 1.27.5).

23. For Catullus's last line (*hic merus est Thyonianus*), see Isidore's definition of *merus* (*Origines* 20.3.3): *dicimus cum vinum purum significamus; nam merum dicimus quidquid purum atque sincerum est* ("We speak of *merus* when we refer to unmixed wine, for we call *merus* whatever is pure and unadulterated"). See also Chapter 4, note 5.

Thyonianus is a nonce word. The closest that Horace comes to it is the rare metronymic *Thyoneus* (C. 1.17.23), of Bacchus the "Seether," son of Semele, blasted by Zeus's fire. This suggests a moment when wine-drinking might get out of hand, something that will not happen when Tyndaris visits the speaker.

24. Cf. the use of *deduci* at C. 1.37.31, of Caesar's (failed) attempt to lead Cleopatra in his triumphal procession after the battle of Actium and the fall of Alexandria.

25. Catullus's use of *perenne* in juxtaposition to *plus uno saeclo* may pose a paradox that in fact also allies him with Horace. At *De rerum natura* 1.118, Catullus's contemporary, Lucretius, applies the adjective to the foliage that forms Ennius's poetic crown. Catullus's humorous self-deprecation and self-limitation in fact harbor hints of the eternal survival that Lucretius bestows on Ennius, and Horace on himself.

26. For this interpretation of Catullus 1, see Rauk 1996–97, especially 324–25. The same tonal ambiguity permeates Catullus's poem to Cicero, 49.

27. On *Epi.* 1.19, see also Chapter 3, as well as Dilke 1973; Macleod 1977; Reckford 2002.

28. In an epistle dealing with the tempering of Archilochean diatribe, it is appropriate that the allusion to Catullus 69 center on a poem that combines both epigram and invective. Though 69 is not the first of Catullus's poems written in

elegiac couplets, it initiates the segment of his corpus devoted primarily to short epigram.

The satiric tone of the same poem had already been mitigated by Horace at *Epi.* 1.6.1, where the opening *nil admirari*, with its counsel of philosophical restraint, echoes Catullus's initial *noli admirari*, part of a more pragmatic admonition.

29. See Oliensis 1995, for an excellent analysis of *Epi.* 1.20.

Chapter 3: Helen

1. See especially Santirocco 1986, 49–52, for a discussion of salient points of unity among these odes.

2. See Lowrie 1997, 128–35, for a detailed discussion of C. 1.15 in its poetic setting.

3. *Phaedrus* 243a.

4. For an examination of Horace's use of the palinode, see Cairns 1978. The *testimonia* for Stesichorus's Helen palinodes are collected in Campbell 1991, 92–97. See also Davies 1982.

5. The representation of heat and rain at C. 1.16.11–12 anticipates C. 1.17.3–4, and the mention of Liber at C. 1.16.7, in a context that stresses Bacchus's negative force, looks ahead to the appearance of *Semeleius Thyoneus*, which can best be translated as "wild son of Semele who makes people wild," at C. 1.17.22–23.

There are also connections between poems 15 and 17. For example, the form *vitabis* appears at the beginning of line 18 of each poem.

6. The punning relation between Pan's Mt. Lycaeus (C. 1.17.2) and the *lupos* (9) that cannot threaten Horace's animals may suggest a further link with C. 1.15. There, at 29–30, Paris, pursued by Diomedes, is compared to a deer who has sighted a wolf (*lupum*), which stands out in its context for replacing the lion in Horace's Homeric model (*Iliad* 3.23). Adulterers are menaced in C. 1.15; in C. 1.17, lovers are danger-free.

If C. 1.16 is, secondarily, a *recusatio* of the preceding poem, which associates Helen with the Trojan War, C. 1.17 makes more direct amends by lyricizing Helen and making her song complementary to the odic singer's own.

7. Cf. Quintilian's judgment (*Institutio oratoria* 10.1.62): Stesichorus "sings of the greatest wars and the most famous leaders and on the lyre shoulders the burdens of epic song" (*maxima bella et clarissimos canentem duces et epici carminis onera lyra sustinentem*).

8. For the repetition, see Wills 1996, 232–33 and n. 24.

9. The first line of C. 1.16 may serve as a link between *pastor* Paris of C. 1.15 and "Horace" as implicit goatherd in C. 1.17. The rare use of an adjective in both positive and comparative forms in a single line may remind us of the conclusion of Daphnis's epitaph at Virgil *Eclogues* 5.44: *formosi pecoris custos, formosior ipse* ("[I], guardian of a beautiful flock, more beautiful myself"). A possible allusion to Virgilian pastoral not only forges a bond between present and

preceding poems, it also adds a touch of humor, which lightens the tone of C. 1.16 and connects it with the several aspects of wit in C. 1.17.

The line is also remarkably close to Plautus *Asinaria* 614 (quoted by Nisbet and Hubbard 1970, ad loc.): *oh melle dulci dulcior tu es* ("Oh you are sweeter than sweet honey"). Not only are the rhythms similar, but there is the parallelism between *oh* and *o*, *melle* and *matre*, *dulci* and *pulcra*. If Plautus was on Horace's mind, then a comic element is also mixed in with iambic become lyric, to further lighten the tone.

10. *Ars poetica* 79.

11. On *Epi.* 1.19, see also discussion in Chapter 2.

12. For a detailed examination of poem 36 as a whole, see Wray 2001, 75–80. The connection between poem 36 and C. 1.16 is noted by Santirocco (1986, 195 n. 26).

13. The anthropomorphism by which the *iambi* are described makes them palpable, quasi-comic self-extensions of this speaker of iambs. I follow the manuscript tradition in reading *vestra* at line 4.

14. There is also a form of *facio* in the middle line of each final triad (*proficere*, 42.23; *fias*, C. 1.16.27).

15. The words *pudica* and *proba* appear together, in reversed order, in a fragment of Afranius (116R) quoted by commentators: *proba et pudica quod sum consulo et parco mihi* ("Because I am upright and chaste, I take care of and watch out for myself "). But the order of the adjectives and the second-person apostrophe that they have in common make it clear that direct reference from epode 17 to Catullus 42 is meant (though cf. the demurral of Mankin [1995, ad loc.]).

For further discussion of the connection between the two poems, see Hahn 1939; Fraenkel 1957, 64–65; Lindo 1969; Oliensis 1991; Porter 1995.

16. On the interpretation of the phrase, see Barchiesi 2001, 158.

This is the only occasion where Horace uses a form of *perambulo* in the future. Catullus's unique usage in the future opens line 9 of poem 29, written, as is epode 17, in pure iambic trimeters. The poet is lampooning Caesar's notorious henchman Mamurra: *perambulabit omnium cubilia* ("He will make his way through the couches of all"). Horace may write *astra sidus aureum* in a pretense of complimenting Canidia, but the Roman reader would expect, and hear, *omnium cubilia*, with all its implications.

17. For a detailed discussion of the possible meanings of the name, see Mankin 1995, on *Epodes* 17.42–44, and app. 2, 299–301. The connection between *Canidia* and *canis* is made, among others, by Oliensis (1991) and Gowers (1993, 188–89).

18. Shame is a major component of Helen's story. See Austin 1894, passim, and for further details, commentators on *Iliad* 3.180; Heubeck, West, and Hainsworth 1988 on *Odyssey* 4.145 (quoting J. Redfield on the dog as symbol of adultery); West 1978 on Hesiod *Works and Days* 67. For a general study, see Lilja 1976, esp. 21–22. On *pudor*, see Kaster 1997.

19. On the conclusion of Catullus 51, see also Chapter 2.

20. The fact that Catullus's own relationship with Lesbia—a relationship that poem 68 develops in some detail—was adulterous is worth noting in this context.

21. Catullus 63 has also entered Horace's thoughts when dealing with the feminization of Paris. The only occasion in which Catullus uses a form of the root *anhel-* is in connection with the emasculated Attis at 63.31 (*anhelans*). Horace's unique usage is at the same line number in *C.* 1.15 where the noun *anhelitus* describes the breathing of "soft" (*mollis*) Paris. As the poem's first line reminds us, Paris is shepherding on Mt. Ida when he makes his famous judgment, and Ida is the location for Attis's adventure (63.30, 52, and 70). For *mollis* and *mollitia* in Horace, see commentators on *Epodes* 14.1, e.g., Mankin (1995) and Watson (2003).

22. See Chapter 2.

23. On the name Grosphus, see Nisbet and Hubbard 1978, on *C.* 2.16.17 (*iaculamur*).

24. We are reminded of the javelins and arrows of which the sacrosanct poet-lover has no need in *C.* 1.22.2–3. See above, Chapter 1.

25. Grosphus is addressed in the final lines of *C.* 2.16 as *tibi, te, tibi, te*; the speaker as *mihi, mihi*.

26. Cf. 63.13 (*Dindymenae dominae*) and 91 (*domina Dindymi*).

27. Cf. 63.19, where we hear of Attis's *teneris digitis*, and 88, where he is directly called *tenerum*. (I accept the masculine adjective of the manuscript tradition rather than Lachmann's emendation to *teneram*. This is the last moment where Attis can be conceived of as both *tener* and masculine before being herded back into Cybele's service forever.) Horace's only mention of Dindymene is at *C.* 1.16.5.

Chapter 4: Virgil

1. Cf. Catullus 61.164, of a new husband waiting for his bride. On *C.* 2.11, see also Chapter 2.

2. See Lewis and Short, *A New Latin Dictionary* (New York, 1879), s.v. IA.

3. For the connection between *C.* 4.12 and Catullus 13, see, among others, Rutgers van der Loeff 1936, 112–13; Ferguson 1956, 11–12; Syndikus 1973, 402; Quinn 1980, 320; Clay 2002, 135–36.

4. See Maltby 1991, s.v. *mereo*.

5. See Maltby 1991, s.v. *merum*, quoting Isidore (*Origines* 20.3.3). For the full quotation, see Chapter 2, note 23.

6. See above, Chapter 1, note 8.

7. The origin of the simile lies with Homer (*Odyssey* 19.518–23), where the nightingale is the mother of Itylus. Since Catullus describes the singer as Daulias, he is most likely referring to Procne, wife of Tereus, who came from Daulis in Phocis. In Ovid's telling of the tale (*Metamorphoses* 6.424–674), Procne, mother of Itys, becomes a swallow, her sister, Philomela, the nightingale. I am presuming that Catullus is referring to Procne as a nightingale because of the intensity of her song, with perhaps a nod to Sappho 136LP: "The messenger of spring, the lovely-voiced nightingale." Horace, however, seems to equate Procne with the swallow, a bird much more associated with spring than the nightingale (see Thompson 1936, 319, and, for *C.* 4.12 in particular, Putnam 1986, 201 and 204). Virgil *Georgics* 4.511–15 is also in Horace's mind.

8. On this point and on C. 4.12 as a whole, see Clay 2002.

9. The most recent critique of C. 1.24 is by Thibodeau (2003).

10. For a study, in a numismatic context, of the language of economics at C. 1.3.5–8, where the vocabulary expands on C. 1.24.11, see Buttrey 1972, 47–48.

11. For other examples of Horace's dependence on Catullus 68, see above, this chapter, as well as Chapters 2 and 3.

12. See also Chapter 1.

13. *Epistles* 5.3.6.

14. C. 1.3.16, e.g., looks back at lines 18–21 of Catullus 4, and the use of *incolumem* at C. 1.3.7 may allude to Catullus's only use of the adjective, at 9.6, in a poem that tells of receiving back a beloved friend from a journey abroad. Here and in the discussion that follows, I take Horace's tone as fully serious. But perhaps its very vigor, largely foreign to the sympathetic "Horace" that attracts readers, is meant to suggest that humor lies not far beneath the surface of the speaker's seemingly dark stance. It is not hard to imagine Virgil chuckling over, rather than shuddering at, his friend's apparent gloom.

15. See Chapter 1.

16. Both phrases occur at line endings. These are the only uses in each poet of *fines* as bounds standing for the territory they embrace. Several of the parallels noted here are listed by Mendell (1935).

17. The use of the same verb (*imbuo*) at 64.11 not only brings the poem full circle but also implicitly connects the voyage of the *Argo* with humanity's moral decline.

18. I follow Horace's apparent spelling of his heroine's name.

19. Horace's only two uses of the noun *macies* are at C. 1.3.30 and 3.27.53.

20. Poem 64: *querellis* (130), *conquerar* (164), *questibus* (170); C. 3.27.66: *querenti*. See Mendell 1935.

21. Poem 64.132–33, and cf. 117 and 180; C. 3.27.34–35, 49, 57.

22. *Praeda*: 64.153; C. 3.27.55. Catullus's use of *dilaceranda* at 64.152 is unique (he never uses *lacero*); two out of Horace's three uses of *lacero* are at 3.27.46 and 71.

23. See Lowrie 1997, 310. The description of Europe takes up a full line; Ariadne's ends 64.197. See also 64.54, 94, 405, and cf. 124 (*furentem*) and 254 (*furebant*).

24. For instance, the perfidy that Horace allots to Venus at C. 3.27.66 is a constant theme for Ariadne (see 64.132–33, 174, and cf. 322).

25. We might note the following further parallels: Catullus's only use of a form of *invictus* is at 64.204, and Horace's, in his lyric corpus, is at C. 3.27.73. Catullus employs *expallesco* (in the phrase *expalluit auri*) only at 64.100, and never *pallesco*; Horace has a form of *pallesco* (in the phrase *palluit audax*) in his lyric work only here, and never uses *expallesco*. Forms of the verb *carpo* appear at 64.310 (of the Fates working their wool) and at C. 3.27.64, where Europe imagines the possibility of woolworking in a servile future.

26. On ancient etymologies of *oscen* connecting it with bird song and *cano*, see Maltby 1991, s.v. *oscen*.

27. C. 1.3.5 and C. 3.27.26 (and cf. C. 1.24.11). The phrase *niveum latus* (25–26) is a witty reference to *Eclogues* 6.53, where Virgil uses the words to

describe the bull of whom Pasiphaë, wife of Minos and therefore daughter-in-law of Europe, became enamored. Ovid adopts the same language in his telling of the story at *Metamorphoses* 2.865.

28. Williams (1969, 139, on C. 3.27.53–56) speaks of the poet as "gently mocking his heroine." Horace may also be burlesquing Attis's address, in his final moment of sobriety, to his fatherland at Catullus 63.50–73. Its initial verses—*patria o mei creatrix, patria o mea genetrix, / ego quam miser relinquens* ("O fatherland my creator, o fatherland by begetter, whom I now leave in my misery")—may also lie behind Europe's opening words: *pater—o relictum filiae nomen* ("Father—o name of daughter I left behind").

29. The emphasis on flowers at C. 3.27.29 and 43–44 is standard in epithalamia. Both passages may look back to Catullus. The phrase *in pratis studiosa florum* draws on Catullus's complex symbolism at 11.22–23, and *recentis carpere flores* resembles *carptus defloruit* (62.43), by which, in Catullus's second epithalamium, the chorus of virgins describes the bride as an unloved, plucked flower.

CHAPTER 5: GENRES AND A DIALOGUE

1. We note, as did ancient etymologists, the association of *Lucina* and *Luna*, names that frame the fourth stanza, with words for light.

The meter of the poem is also closely parallel to that of Catullus's first epithalamium, 61, with a number of glyconic lines followed by a pherecratean. It, too, starts as a hymn, to the god of marriage.

2. For a detailed examination of the *Carmen saeculare*, see Putnam 2000, 51–95.

3. Romulus is mentioned at 34.22 and C.s. 47. It is not a coincidence that both lines are also hypermetric.

4. We have mention of the *Carmen* at C. 4.6.29–44 (directly) and at *Epi.* 2.1.132–38 (indirectly).

5. *Silvarum* is repeated in *silvis*, and *virentium* finds its associate in *viridis*; *amnium* becomes *fluviis*, and *nemorum* is also paralleled in *silvarum*.

6. See Pliny *Historia naturalis* 36.24.

7. On the relationship of C. 3.22 and Catullus 34, see Henderson 1995, 106–13.

8. With *descende*, cf. the use of the same imperative to begin C. 3.4, a prayer to the muse Calliope to sing the poet's song, which also happens to be Horace's longest ode.

9. Has Horace over time become akin to the *languidiora vina* ("mellower wine," 8) that the jug is harboring?

10. See Santirocco 1986, 136–38, for connections between C. 3.21 and 3.22.

11. With *exactos*, compare the use of *exigo* at C. 3.30.1; for *ictum*, see C. 4.6.36, where Diana is the subject.

12. For a more detailed discussion of C. 3.23, see Putnam 2002.

13. Horace's only use of the adjective *pestilens* is at C. 3.23.5, and Catullus's at 26.5. On both occasions, wind, or a wind, is involved. Catullus mentions a

villa only in poems 26 and 44. Here, then, a second Catullus poem may be among Horace's poetic antecedents as well.

14. For further details, see above, Chapter 2, note 7.

15. For C. 1.36, see Chapter 1, and for C. 3.27, Chapter 4.

16. See Nisbet and Hubbard 1978 ad loc., referring to Ensor 1902–3, 108–9.

17. On C. 1.5, see also Chapter 1.

18. The phrase appears first at 91 and is repeated at 92, 96, 106, and 113. Note also that Catullus's bride is called *pulchrior* at 61.84 as is Barine at C. 2.8.7.

19. On thieves protected by the darkness of night, cf. Catullus 62.34: *nocte latent fures* ("thieves lie hidden at night").

20. For this reading of the poem, see Jones 1971.

21. See also [Tibullus] 3.4.66.

22. Horace may in fact be wishing the fate of Catullus's unwedded vine upon Chloe, whereby the only eroticism allowed her is self-generated.

23. I have dealt in detail with Catullus 45 and C. 3.9 in Putnam 1977, several paragraphs of which are revised and incorporated here. See also Nielsen 1977.

24. Does she in fact now love him even more than he loves her? See Kroll 1929, 84 (on 45.13).

25. Such a reading, typical of Horatian *levitas*, is abetted by the poem's comic elements. The picture of Chloe, literally and figuratively thrown out of the house, has its counterpart in the vision of Septimius face-to-face with a grey-eyed lion.

Bibliography

Adams, J. 1982. *The Latin Sexual Vocabulary*. Baltimore.

Adler, E. 1981. *Catullan Self-Revelation*. New York.

Ancona, R. 1994. *Time and the Erotic in Horace's Odes*. Durham, N.C.

———. 2002. "The Untouched Self: Sapphic and Catullan Muses in Horace, *Odes* I.22." In *Cultivating the Muse: Struggles for Power and Inspiration in Classical Literature*, ed. E. Spentzou and D. Fowler, 161–87. Oxford.

Anderson, W. S., ed. 1999. *Why Horace? A Collection of Interpretations*. Wauconda, Ill.

Arkins, B. 1979. "*Glubit* in Catullus 58.5." *LCM* 4.5:85–86.

Armstrong, M. 1992. "*Hebro/Euro*: Two Notes on Hor. *Carm.* 1.25.20." *Philologus* 136:313–15.

Austin, N. 1994. *Helen of Troy and Her Shameless Phantom*. Ithaca, N.Y.

Barchiesi, A. 2000. "Rituals in Ink: Horace on the Greek Lyric Tradition." In *Matrices of Genre: Authors, Canons and Society*, ed. M. Depew and D. Obbink, 167–82. Cambridge.

———. 2001. "Horace and Iambos: The Poet as Literary Historian." In *Iambic Ideas: Essays on a Poetic Tradition from Archaic Greece to the Late Roman Empire*, ed. A. Cavarzere et al., 141–64. Lanham, Md.

Biondi, G. G. 1992. "Catullo 'eolico' in Orazio lirico." In *Atti del convegno nazionale di studi su Orazio*, published by the Associazione Italiana di Cultura Classica, 179–90. Turin.

Burgess, D. 1986. "Catullus c. 50: The Exchange of Poetry." *AJPh* 107:576–86.

Buscaroli, C. 1937. *Perfidum ridens Venus: L'Ode III 27 di Orazio*. Bologna.

Buttrey, T. 1972. "Halved Coins, the Augustan Reform, and Horace, *Odes* I.3." *AJA* 76:31–48

Cairns, F. 1978. "The Genre Palinode and Three Horatian Examples." *AC* 47:547–52.

Campbell, D. A., ed. 1982. *Greek Lyric*. Vol. 1. Cambridge.

———, ed. 1991. *Greek Lyric*. Vol. 3. Cambridge.

Clack, J. 1976. "*Otium tibi molestum est*: Catullus 50 and 51." *Classical Bulletin* 52:50–53.

Clay, J. 2002. "Sweet Folly: Horace, *Odes* 4.12 and the Evocation of Virgil." *Horace and Greek Lyric Poetry, Rethymnon Classical Studies* no. 1:129–40.

Commager, S. 1957. "The Function of Wine in Horace's Odes." *TAPhA* 88:68–70.

———. 1962. *The Odes of Horace: A Critical Study*. New Haven. Reprinted Bloomington, 1967; Norman, Okla., 1995.

Conte, G. B. 1994. *Latin Literature: A History*. Trans. and ed. J. B. Solodow, D. Fowler, and G. W. Most. Baltimore. Originally published as *Letteratura Latina* (Florence, 1987).

Crowther, N. B. 1978. "Horace, Catullus, and Alexandrianism." *Mnemosyne* 31:33–44.

Davies, M. 1982. "Derivative and Proverbial Testimonia Concerning Stesichorus' Palinode." *QUCC* 12:7–16.

Davis, G. 1987. "*Carmina/Iambi*: The Literary-Generic Dimension of Horace's *Integer vitae* (C. 1, 22)." *QUCC* 27:67–78.

———. 1991. *Polyhymnia: The Rhetoric of Horatian Lyric Discourse*. Berkeley.

———. 2002. "*Ait phaselus*: The Caricature of Stylistic Genre *(genus dicendi)* in Catullus *Carm.* 4." *MD* 48:111–43.

Dilke, O.A.W. 1973. "Horace and the Verse Letter." In *Horace*, ed. C.D.N. Costa, 94–112. London.

Edmunds, L. 2001. *Intertextuality and the Reading of Roman Poetry*. Baltimore.

Elder, J. P. 1951. "Notes on Some Conscious and Subconscious Elements in the Poetry of Catullus." *HSPh* 60:101–36.

Ensor, E. 1902–3. "Notes on the Odes of Horace." *Hermathena* 28/12: 105–10.

Feeney, D. 1993. "Horace and the Greek Lyric Poets." In *Horace 2000: A Celebration*, ed. N. Rudd, 41–63. Ann Arbor.

Ferguson, J. 1956. "Catullus and Horace." *AJPh* 77:1–18.

Finamore, J. 1974. "Catullus 50 and 51: Friendship, Love and *Otium*." *CW* 78:11–19.

Fitzgerald, W. 1988. "Power and Impotence in Horace's Epodes." *Ramus* 17:176–91.

———. 1989. "Horace, Pleasure and the Text." *Arethusa* 22:81–104.

———. 1992. "Catullus and the Reader: The Erotics of Poetry." *Arethusa* 25:419–43.

———. 1995. *Catullan Provocations: Lyric Poetry and the Drama of Position*. Berkeley.

———. 2000. *Slavery and the Roman Literary Imagination*. Cambridge.

Fordyce, C. J., ed. 1961. *Catullus: A Commentary*. Oxford.

Fraenkel, E. 1957. *Horace*. Oxford.

Frank, T. 1928. *Catullus and Horace*. New York.

Fredricksmeyer, E. 1970. "Observations on Catullus 5." *AJPh* 91:431–45.

Freudenburg, K. 1995. "Canidia at the Feast of Nasidienus (Hor. *S.* 2.8.95)." *TAPhA* 125:207–19.

———. 2001. *Satires of Rome: Threatening Poses from Lucilius to Juvenal*. Cambridge.

Gagliardi, D. 1971. *Orazio e la tradizione neoterica*. Naples.

———. 1986. "Orazio e Catullo (riscontri verbali e coincidenze d'ispirazione)." In *Studi su Orazio*, 115–42. Palermo.

Gilbert, P. 1937. "Catulle et Horace." *Latomus* 1:88–93.

Gowers, E. 1993. *The Loaded Table: Representations of Food in Roman Literature*. Oxford.

Hahn, E. A. 1939. "Epodes 5 and 17, Carmina 1. 16 and 1. 17." *TAPhA* 70:213–20.

Harrison, S. J. 1992. "Fuscus the Stoic: Horace's *Odes* I.22 and *Epistle* I.10." *CQ* 42:543–47.

Henderson, J. 1995. "Horace, *Odes* 3.22 and the Life of Meaning." *Ramus* 24:103–51. Reprinted in *Writing Down Rome: Satire, Comedy, and Other Offences in Latin Poetry* (Oxford, 1999), 114–44.

Heubeck, A., S. West, and J. B. Hainsworth, eds. 1988. *A Commentary on Homer's* Odyssey. Vol. 1. Oxford.

Hinds, S. 1998. *Allusion and Intertext: Dynamics of Appropriation in Roman Poetry*. Cambridge.

Hubbard, T. K. 2000. "Horace and Catullus: The Case of the Suppressed Precursor in *Odes* 1.22 and 1.32." *CW* 94:25–37.

Janan, M. 1994. *"When the Lamp Is Shattered": Desire and Narrative in Catullus*. Carbondale, Ill.

Jocelyn, H. D. 1979. "Catullus 58 and Ausonius, Ep. 71." *LCM* 4.5:87–91.

Johnson, W. R. 1982. *The Idea of Lyric: Lyric Modes in Ancient and Modern Poetry*. Berkeley.

Jones, C. P. 1971. *"Tange Chloen semel arrogantem." HSPh* 75:81–83.

Kaster, R. 1997. "The Shame of the Romans." *TAPhA* 127:1–19.

Kiessling, A., and R. Heinze, eds. 1955. *Q. Horatius Flaccus: Oden und Epoden*. Berlin.

Kroll, W., ed. 1929. *C. Valerius Catullus*. Leipzig.

Krostenko, B. 2001. *Cicero, Catullus, and the Language of Social Performance*. Chicago.

Lee, M. O. 1969. *Word, Sound and Image in the Odes of Horace*. Ann Arbor.

———. 1975. "Catullus in the Odes of Horace." *Ramus* 4:33–48.

Lilja, S. 1976. *Dogs in Ancient Greek Poetry. Commentationes Humanarum Litterarum* 56. Helsinki.

Lindo, L. I. 1969. "Horace's Seventeenth Epode." *CPh* 64:176–77.

Lowrie, M. 1997. *Horace's Narrative Odes*. Oxford.

Lyne, R.O.A.M. 1980. *The Latin Love Poets: From Catullus to Horace*. Oxford.

———. 1995. *Horace: Behind the Public Poetry*. New Haven.

Macleod, C. W. 1977. "The Poet, the Critic and the Moralist: Horace, *Epistles* 1.19." *CQ* 27:359–76. Reprinted in Macleod, *Collected Essays* (Oxford, 262–79).

Maltby, R. 1991. *A Lexicon of Ancient Latin Etymologies*. Arca no. 25. Leeds.

Mankin, D., ed. 1995. *Horace: Epodes*. Cambridge.

Martin, R. 2002. "Horace in Real Time: *Odes* 1.27 and Its Congeners." *Horace and Greek Lyric Poetry, Rethymnon Classical Studies* no. 1:103–18.

McCormick, J. 1973. "Horace's *Integer Vitae*." *CW* 67:28–33.

McDermott, E. A. 1981. "Greek and Roman Elements in Horace's Lyric Program." *ANRW* II.31.3:1640–72. Berlin.

Mendell, C. W. 1935. "Catullan Echoes in the Odes of Horace." *CPh* 30:289–301.

———. 1938. "Horace i. 14." *CPh* 33:145–56.

Miller, P. A. 1994. *Lyric Texts and Lyric Consciousness: The Birth of a Genre from Archaic Greece to Augustan Rome*. London.

Nappa, C. 2001. *Aspects of Catullus' Social Fiction. Studien zur klassischen Philologie* no. 125. Frankfurt.

Nielsen, R. 1977. "Catullus 45 and Horace *Odes* 3.9: The Glass House." *Ramus* 6:132–38.

Nisbet, R.G.M. 1959. "Notes on Horace, Epistles 1." *CQ* 9:73–76. Reprinted in Nisbet 1995, 1–5.

———. 1995. *Collected Papers on Latin Literature*. Ed. S. J. Harrison. Oxford.

———. 2002. "A Wine-Jar for Messalla: *Carmina* 3.21." In *Traditions and Contexts in the Poetry of Horace*, ed. T. Woodman and D. Feeney, 80–92. Cambridge.

Nisbet, R.G.M., and M. Hubbard, eds. 1970. *A Commentary on Horace: Odes: Book I*. Oxford.

———. 1978. *A Commentary on Horace: Odes: Book II*. Oxford.

Oliensis, E. 1991. "Canidia, Canicula, and the *Decorum* of Horace's *Epodes*." *Arethusa* 24:107–35.

———. 1995. "Life after Publication: Horace, *Epistles* 1.20." *Arethusa* 28:209–24.

———. 1998. *Horace and the Rhetoric of Authority*. Cambridge.

Olstein, K. 1984. "Horace's *integritas* and the Geography of *carm*. 1.22." *GB* 11:113–20.

Pascal, C. 1915. "Orazio e Catullo." *Athenaeum* 3:262–68.

Pasquali, G. 1920. *Orazio lirico*. Florence. Reprinted 1966.

Pearcy, L. T. 1994. "The Personification of the Text and Augustan Poetics." *CW* 87:457–64.

Pedrick, V. 1993. "The Abusive Address and the Audience in Catullan Poems." *Helios* 20:173–96.

Penella, R. 1976. "A Note on *(de)glubere*." *Hermes* 104:118–20.

Pöschl, V. 1970. *Horazische Lyrik: Interpretationen*. Heidelberg. Rev. ed. 1991.

Porter, D. 1987. *Horace's Poetic Journey: A Reading of Odes 1–3*. Princeton.

———. 1995. "*Quo, Quo Scelesti Ruitis*: The Downward Momentum of Horace's Epodes." *ICS* 20:107–30.

Pucci, J. 1992. "Horace and Virgilian Mimesis: A Re-Reading of *Odes* 1.3." *CW* 85:659–73.

Pucci, P. 1961. "Il carmine 50 di Catullo." *Maia* 13:249–56.

Putnam, M.C.J. 1962. "Catullus' Journey (*Carm*. 4)." *CPh* 57:10–19. Reprinted in Putnam 1982, 3–12.

———. 1969a. "Horace *c*. 1.20." *CJ* 64:153–57. Reprinted in Putnam 1982, 102–106.

———. 1969b. "On Catullus 27." *Latomus* 28:850–57. Reprinted in Putnam 1982, 37–44.

———. 1977. "Horace Odes 3.9: The Dialectics of Desire." In *Ancient and Modern: Essays in Honor of Gerald F. Else*, ed. J. H. D'Arms and J. W. Eadie, 139–57. Ann Arbor. Reprinted in Putnam 1982, 107–25, and in Anderson 1999, 180–94.

———. 1982. *Essays on Latin Lyric, Elegy, and Epic*. Princeton.

———. 1986. *Artifices of Eternity: Horace's Fourth Book of Odes*. Ithaca, N.Y. Reprinted 1996.

———. 1992. "The Languages of Horace Odes 1. 24." *CJ* 88:123–35.

———. 1994. "Structure and Design in Horace Odes 1. 17." *CW* 87:357–75.

———. 2000. *Horace's* Carmen Saeculare: *Ritual Magic and the Poet's Art*. New Haven.

———. 2002. "Horace c. 3.23: Ritual and Art." In *Rome and Her Monuments: Essays on the City and Literature of Rome in Honor of Katherine A. Geffcken*, ed. S. K. Dickison and J. P. Hallett, 521–43. Wauconda, Ill.

Quinn, K., ed. 1970. *Catullus: The Poems.* New York.

———, ed. 1980. *Horace: The Odes.* London.

Rand, E. K. 1906. "Catullus and the Augustans." *HSPh* 17:15–30.

Rauk, J. 1996–97. "Time and History in Catullus 1." *CW* 90:319–32.

Reckford, K. 1969. *Horace.* New York.

———. 2002. "*Pueri ludentes*: Some Aspects of Play and Seriousness in Horace's *Epistles.*" *TAPhA* 132:1–19.

Reitzenstein, R. 1922. "Philologische Kleinigkeiten 5. Zu Horaz und Catull." *Hermes* 57:357–65.

Richmond, J. 1970. "Horace's 'Mottoes' and Catullus 51." *RhM* 113:197–204.

Rutgers van der Loeff, A. 1936. "Quid Horatio cum Catullo?" *Mnemosyne* ser. 3, no. 4:109–13.

Santirocco, M. 1986. *Unity and Design in Horace's Odes.* Chapel Hill, N.C.

Scott, W. 1969. "Catullus and Calvus (Cat. 50)." *CPh* 64:169–73.

Segal, C. 1968. "Catullus 5 and 7." *AJPh* 89:284–301.

———. 1969. "Horace, Odes 2.6 (*Septimi, Gadis aditure mecum*): Poetic Landscape and Poetic Imagination." *Philologus* 113:235–53.

———. 1970. "Catullan *Otiosi*: The Lover and the Poet." *G&R* 17:25–31.

———. 1989. "*Otium* and *Eros*: Catullus, Sappho and Euripides' Hippolytus." *Latomus* 48:817–22.

Selden, D. 1992. "*Ceveat Lector*: Catullus and the Rhetoric of Performance." In *Innovations of Antiquity*, ed. R. Hexter and D. Selden, 461–512. New York.

Simpson, F. P., ed. 1879. *Select Poems of Catullus.* London.

Skinner, M. 1981. *Catullus' Passer: The Arrangement of the Book of Polymetric Poems.* New York.

Syndikus, H. P. 1972. *Die Lyrik des Horaz: Eine Interpretation der Oden.* Vol. 1. *Impulse der Forschung* no. 6. Darmstadt.

———. 1973. *Die Lyrik des Horaz: Eine Interpretation der Oden.* Vol. 2. *Impulse der Forschung* no. 7. Darmstadt.

Thibodeau, P. 2003. "Can Vergil Cry? Epicureanism in Horace Odes 1.24." *CJ* 98:243–56.

Thompson, D. 1936. *A Glossary of Greek Birds.* London.

Thomson, D. F. S., ed. 1997. *Catullus.* Toronto.

Traglia, A. 1981. "Catullo e i poeti nuovi visti da Orazio." In *Letterature comparate, problemi e metodo: Studi in onore di Ettore Paratore*, vol. 2, 467–86. Bologna.

Traina, A. 1975. "Orazio e Catullo." In *Poeti Latini (e Neolatini): Note e saggi filologici*, 253–75. Bologna.

Ullman, B. L. 1915. "Horace, Catullus and Tigellius." *CPh* 10:270–96.

Watson, L. C., ed. 2003. *A Commentary on Horace's* Epodes. Oxford.

West, D. 1995. *Horace: Odes I: Carpe Diem.* Oxford.

———. 1998. *Horace: Odes II: Vatis Amici.* Oxford.

———. 2002. *Horace: Odes III: Dulce Periculum.* Oxford.

West, M. L., ed. 1978. *Hesiod: Works and Days.* Oxford.

Williams, G. 1969. *The Third Book of Horace's Odes*. Oxford.

Wills, J. 1996. *Repetition in Latin Poetry: Figures of Allusion*. Oxford.

Woodman, T. 1966. "Some Implications of *otium* in Catullus 51.13–16." *Lato-mus* 25:217–26.

———. 1979. "*Exegi monumentum* (Horace, *Odes* 3,30)." In *Quality and Plea-sure in Latin Poetry*, ed. D. West and T. Woodman, 115–28. Cambridge.

———. 2002. "*Biformis Vates*: The *Odes*, Catullus and Greek Lyric." In *Tradi-tions and Contexts in the Poetry of Horace*, ed. T. Woodman and D. Feeney, 53–64. Cambridge.

Wray, D. 2001. *Catullus and the Poetics of Roman Manhood*. Cambridge.

Zumwalt, N. K. 1975. "Horace, C. I.22: Poetic and Political Integrity." *TAPhA* 105:417–30.

———. 1977. "Horace's *navis* of Love Poetry." *CW* 71:249–54.

Index of Poems Cited

General Index

Achilles: 73–75, 88, 109–10, 128
Acme: 133–38
Actium: 10, 151n24
Aegean: 26, 32
Aegeus: 110
Aeneas: 19–21, 30, 109, 111, 119
Afranius: 153n15
Agrippa: 51, 76
Alcaeus: 1–2, 5–6, 32, 39–40, 53–55, 69, 83, 93, 143, 145n6, 147n30, 149n42, 150n8, 151n12
alleyway: See *angiportum*
Allius: 53
Anacreon: 75, 79–80, 92
anaphora: 19, 26, 87, 90–91, 98, 130, 148n40, 150n1
angiportum (alleyway): 5–6, 11–14, 146n9
Apollo: 50, 54, 68, 76–77; and Diana, 110, 118–23, 148n39
Archilochus: 69, 80, 151n28
Archytas: 16
Argonauts: 109–11, 114, 155n17
Ariadne: 109–10, 112–14, 144, 155nn23–24
Atalanta: 39–40
Athenaeus: 55
Attis: 92, 127, 154n21, 154n27, 156n28
Augustus: 10, 67, 76, 107–8, 118–21, 148n38, 148–49n40, 151n24
Aurelius: 35–36, 149n40

Bacchus: 50, 53, 58–59, 63, 66, 76–77, 94–96, 115, 122–23, 150n9 151n23, 152n5
Bacchylides: 75, 80, 92
Bandusian spring: 35, 126–28
Barine: 128–31, 157n18
Bithynia: 6–7, 18, 22, 26, 28, 38, 147n22
boat: *See* ship

Caecilius: 91–92
Caelius: 11
Caesar, Julius: 10, 35–36, 81, 149n40, 153n16
Calais: 137–39

Callimachus: 1
Calvus, Licinius: 1, 48–49, 54, 147n32; death of wife Quintilia, 104–106
Canicula (Dog Star): 78–79, 126–28, 150n7
Canidia: 85–86, 153nn16–17
Carmen saeculare: 118–19, 125, 156nn2–4
Castor, and Pollux: 25, 27–29, 53, 85; temple of, 146n9
Cato: 122–23
Catullus, brother of: 6, 44–46, 99–101
Censorinus: 44–46
Chloe: in C. 3.26, 132–33, 157n22; in C. 3.9, 136–37, 157n25
Cicero: 151n26
Cinna: 82
Circe: 32, 75, 78–79
consolatio: 101
convivium: 23–25, 51, 56–66, 93–98, 123
Corvinus, Messalla: 122–23
Cybele: 128, 154n27
Cyclades: 31–32
Cyrus: 75, 78–79, 91–92

Daedalus: 108–9
Damalis: 42–44
Diana: 20–22, 110, 123–26, 156n11; as subject of hymn, 4, 8, 116–21, 148n39
Dindymene: 76–77, 92, 154n27
Diomedes: 75, 152n6
Dog Star: See *Canicula*
Donatus, Tiberius Claudius: 97

ekphrasis: 109
Ennius: 1, 46, 151n25
epic: 30, 51, 75, 79, 81–83, 89, 92, 109–11, 114, 152n7
epicedium: 101, 105
epigram: 126, 151–52n28
epithalamium (wedding song): 3, 5, 7–8, 43–44, 114–15, 116, 128–33, 144, 156n29, 156n1. *See also* hymn
epyllion: 109
Europe: 111–15, 144, 155n18, 155n23, 155n25, 156nn27–28